The Way
of Strategy

Also available from ASQC Quality Press

Management by Policy: How Companies Focus Their Total Quality Efforts to Achieve Competitive Advantage
Brendan Collins and Ernest Huge

Managing the Process, the People, and Yourself
Joseph G. Werner

Quality Function Deployment: Liking a Company with Its Customers
Ronald G. Day

A Quality Transformation Success Story from StorageTek
A. Donald Stratton

Breakthrough Quality Improvements for Leaders Who Want Results
Robert F. Wickman and Robert S. Doyle

Excellence Is a Habit: How to Avoid Quality Burnout
Thomas J. Barry

The ASQC Total Quality Management Series

> *TQM: Leadership for the Quality Transformation*
> Richard S. Johnson

> *TQM: Management Processes for Quality Operations*
> Richard S. Johnson

> *TQM: The Mechanics of Quality Processes*
> Richard S. Johnson and Lawrence E. Kazense

> *TQM: Quality Training Practices*
> Richard S. Johnson

To request a complimentary catalog of publications, call 800-248-1946

The Way
of Strategy

William A. Levinson

ASQC Quality Press
Milwaukee, Wisconsin

The Way of Strategy
William A. Levinson

Library of Congress Cataloging-in-Publication Data
Levinson, William A.
    The way of strategy / William A. Levinson.
      p. cm.
    Includes bibliographical references and index.
    ISBN 0-87389-227-5 (alk. paper)
    1. Strategic planning. 2. Industrial management 3. Competition.
  4. Strategy. I. Title.
  HD30.28.L492 1994
  658.4'012—dc20   94-6143
                                                      CIP

© 1994 by ASQC

Acknowledgments
Cleary, Thomas, (translator). From *Mastering the Art of War,* by Zhuge Liang and Liu Ji. © 1989 by Thomas Cleary. Reprinted by arrangement with Shambhala Publications, Inc., 300 Massachusetts Ave., Boston, MA 02115.
Hayes, Robert H., Steven C. Wheelwright, and Kim B. Clark. *Dynamic Manufacturing: Creating the Learning Organization.* Copyright © 1988 by The Free Press, a Division of Macmillan, Inc. Reprinted with the permission of the publisher.
Kipling, Rudyard. "Road Song of the Bander-Log," from *Rudyard Kipling Complete Verse.* © 1940 by Elsie Kipling Bambridge, Doubleday, New York. Used with permission.

10 9 8 7 6 5 4 3 2 1

ISBN 0-87389-227-5

Acquisitions Editor: Susan Westergard
Project Editor: Jeanne W. Bohn
Production Editor: Annette Wall
Marketing Administrator: Mark Olson
Set in Berkeley by Montgomery Media, Inc.
Cover design by Montgomery Media, Inc.
Printed and bound by BookCrafters, Inc.

ASQC Mission: To facilitate continuous improvement and increase customer satisfaction by identifying, communicating, and promoting the use of quality principles, concepts, and technologies; and thereby be recognized throughout the world as the leading authority on, and champion for, quality.

For a free copy of the ASQC Quality Press Publications Catalog, including ASQC membership information, call 800-248-1946.

Printed in the United States of America

 Printed on acid-free recycled paper

ASQC
Quality Press
611 East Wisconsin Avenue
Milwaukee, Wisconsin 53202

To my father, Herbert H. Levinson

To all teachers, past and present

Bhishma:	"String your bow, Brahmana!"
Drona:	"And what on the bowstring? The hurricane winds, the snow and the sleet, the shattering rain, the hot fire—the illusions of war that burn and drown?"
Bhishma:	"This only: with Kripa, teach the Kuru princes, and your own son with them, what each may learn. And to the best of them reveal what weapons you wish."

—*Mahabharata* [William Buck trans.]

Contents

Preface

This project began in 1982, although I didn't know it.

I was at Cornell University, studying chemical engineering. I was also taking Shito-Ryu karate, and had some interest in Japan. There were news articles about Japanese success secrets. Like everyone else (or so it seemed), I had read James Clavell's *Shōgun*. This encouraged me to buy Miyamoto Musashi's *A Book of Five Rings*. The cover touted it as, "Japan's Answer to the Harvard MBA." *Time* magazine's endorsement said, "On Wall Street, when Musashi talks, people listen."

I read the book, but couldn't see how it related to business management. There were a lot of martial arts concepts. Some of them looked adaptable to karate. They definitely applied to kendō (Japanese fencing). How could these techniques apply to business?

Several years later, I enrolled in Union College's night school program in Poughkeepsie, New York. There were two required courses in organizational behavior and psychology. I wasn't looking forward to them. Like most engineers, I was very comfortable with numbers and calculations. Human behavior doesn't follow nice scientific laws. My apprehension, however, was probably an advantage. I had to take the courses as I found them. I couldn't rely on applying previous skills to them. (Much later, I remembered that the Japanese refer to this attitude as "beginner's mind.") I approached these courses without any preconceptions or prejudices. These courses turned out to be among the most valuable I have ever taken.

The professor, Dr. Robert B. Miller, made his students go beyond memorizing the course principles. We had to apply them to real-life case studies. We had to think, "How does what I'm learning in this course apply to my job and other business situations?"

The second course covered the four problem-solving styles. People perceive information by sensing and intuition. They analyze it by thinking and feeling. Individuals prefer one of four sets: sensing-thinking (typical of engineers and accountants), sensing-feeling, intuitive-thinking, and intuitive-feeling. People "rise to their levels of incompetence" (Peter Principle) because the requirements change during a career. Sensing-feeling is helpful in direct management or supervisory roles; however, upper management requires the intuitive-thinking style.

As I read this material, I remembered a line from *A Book of Five Rings:* "Polish the twofold spirit heart and mind, and sharpen the twofold gaze perception and sight."

Was Miyamoto Musashi ahead of Dr. Laurence Peter (and Myers-Briggs) by 300 years? Had Musashi described other basic principles of management and leadership? I went back and read Musashi's book very carefully. This time, it made sense. This led to an article in *Chemical Engineering's* "You & Your Job" feature (Levinson 1987).

Some time later, I saw James Clavell's translation of *The Art of War.* I didn't buy it because $9.95 seemed expensive for an 82-page hardback. A brief glance showed it to contain esoteric Chinese aphorisms. There were some items on fighting with ancient weapons—not very applicable to anything today. (How many other thousands of people have made the same mistake?) Fortunately, I got a second chance.

I was reading Yoshikawa Eiji's biographical novel, *Musashi.* The Japanese made this 970-page book into a three-part movie. Mifune Toshiro plays Musashi. He went on to co-star as Yoshi Toranaga in the TV series version of *Shōgun. Shōgun* ends with Yoshi Toranaga (Tokugawa Ieyasu) marching off to the Battle of Sekigahara. There, he defeats Ishido (Ishida Mitsunari) to win mastery over Japan.

Musashi begins with Takezō (later Miyamoto Musashi) and a companion on the losing side at Sekigahara. As a youth, Takezō was something of a juvenile delinquent. The Zen monk Sōhō Takuan reformed him by locking him in a library for three years. One book, which Takezō read many times, was *The Art of War* (Yoshikawa, 1981, 96).

I quickly went back and bought *The Art of War.* It was a bargain at $9.95.

In his foreword, James Clavell (1983) wrote

I would have it written into law that all officers, particularly all generals, take a yearly oral and written examination on these thirteen chapters, the passing mark being 95 percent—any general failing to achieve a pass to be automatically and summarily dismissed without appeal, and all other officers to have automatic demotion. (p. 7)

Having read the book, I'd go further. I'd apply these requirements to all representatives, senators, and the president. This book would have changed history, if the right people had read it.

The second chapter would have told Lyndon Johnson exactly what he was doing wrong in Vietnam. Sun Tzu spent half the chapter warning his readers against fighting protracted wars. It cost the United States 57,000 lives to rediscover what Sun Tzu wrote 2500 years ago.

If Kaiser Wilhelm II had read *The Art of War,* Germany would have won the Battle of Verdun, and the First World War. General Falkenhayn's plan to destroy the French Army by attrition would have succeeded if the Kaiser hadn't interfered. If the British and French leaders had read it, they wouldn't have defended Verdun. Marshal Pétain wouldn't have had the chance to say, "They shall not pass!" But the Entente would have saved half a million men.

English, German, and French translations of *The Art of War* were available before 1914; however, westerners did not recognize the book's importance—with perhaps one important exception. The first Western translation was by a French Jesuit priest, Father J. J. M. Amiot, in 1772. The translation attracted a lot of attention in contemporary literary journals (Sun Tzu 1963). James Clavell cites a legend that Napoleon Bonaparte read the book. Clavell says Napoleon used many of Sun Tzu's principles to conquer most of Europe. He lost only when he didn't heed Sun Tzu's guidance (Clavell 1983).

In 1937, a Japanese writer published an essay on *The Art of War* in German. Samuel Griffith writes, "Happily for the Western Allies, neither Hitler nor members of the OKW or OKH appear to have seen this particular article." (Sun Tzu 1963, 183). If they had, the Nazis might easily have won the Second World War. Sun Tzu warned against the sovereign interfering with his generals. Hitler's interference with his generals cost at least 500,000 men at Stalingrad. Stalingrad was only one of many such incidents. Sun Tzu also suggested treating defeated enemies humanely. The general who does this can add them to his own forces. The Ukrainians hated the Russians. Stalin had killed seven million of them by planned starvation. If the Nazis hadn't persecuted the "racially inferior" Ukrainians, they would have helped Germany conquer Russia.

If Neville Chamberlain had read Niccolò Machiavelli's *The Prince,* however, Hitler's ambitions would have gone nowhere. Machiavelli warned that no one should ever submit to an evil to avoid a war. You never avoid the war by submitting. You merely defer it, to your disadvantage. In hindsight, we agree that Chamberlain shouldn't have let Germany take the Sudetenland. Machiavelli foresaw situations like this, and gave us ample warning.

This is when I decided it was worthwhile to develop a book on the Way of strategy.

My management control professor, Dr. Lawrence Carr (now at Babson College in Wellesley, Massachusetts), introduced me to General Carl von Clausewitz's *On War*. Clausewitz specifically recognized the similarity between business and war. He also recognized the Peter Principle—perhaps a century before Laurence Peter's birth.

Musashi, Clausewitz, Sun Tzu, Niccolò Machiavelli, and other writers have vital lessons for modern business, political, and military leaders. This book presents the key ones. If the right people pay attention, this book will have been of some service to our nation.

Note: The Japanese and Chinese place the family name first, and the personal name second. For example, Sun is the family name of Sun Tzu. Tzu is his personal name. The first three Tokugawa Shōguns were Tokugawa Ieyasu, Tokugawa Hidetada, and Tokugawa Iemitsu. This book uses this convention for Japanese and Chinese names.

Introduction

*Among those who control the world and protect the state
there's no one who doesn't employ swordsmanship in his mind*
—Yagyu Muneyoshi (1529–1606),
sword instructor to Tokugawa Ieyasu

*Of course, you are familiar with General Sun Tzu's Art of War—you
know, the classic Chinese work on military strategy? I assume any
warrior in your position would be intimately acquainted with such an
important book.*

—Yoshikawa Eiji, *Musashi*

> The Way of strategy is the art and science of *managing organizations*
> in *competitive situations.*

Something is wrong with American business. Automobile imports have
displaced thousands of autoworkers. The Japanese supply most of our
consumer electronics and optics. Manufacturing, or adding value to
physical products, has declined. Skilled manufacturing jobs are disappearing. Their replacements are low-skill service jobs. This phenomenon
has produced the euphemism *downward mobility.* In August 1993, we are
still in a recession. What happened? What can we do to effect a turnaround?

Many books promise new ideas and easy solutions. This book looks at some very old solutions. The answers have existed for thousands of years. Most of today's competitive improvements are rediscoveries of the ancient Way of strategy. *The Way of strategy is the art and science of managing organizations in competitive environments.*

People, Organizations, and Management Systems

> The overriding message of this book is that *people, organizations,* and *management systems* win wars and capture market share. People, organizations, and systems design and deliver quality products and services.

Physical technology alone does not win wars, and it cannot win in business. The Austrian victory at Lissa (1866) proved that iron men in wooden ships can beat wooden men in iron ships. The Italians had more ships and more modern guns. They had 12 ironclads to the Austro-Hungarians' seven. Rear Admiral Wilhelm von Tegetthoff correctly believed his sailors were better. He also knew the Italian admiral was indecisive. Tegetthoff accepted battle. Tegetthoff's flagship *Ferdinand Max* sank two Italian ironclads, one by ramming. The Italians fled, although they still outnumbered the Austrians (Preston 1981, 24–26). *If the difference in technology is not too disparate, a good organization will beat a mediocre one.* We do not, however, discount technology. Iron men in iron ships can beat anybody.

Quality Comes from People and Systems

> The Malcolm Baldrige National Quality Award and ISO 9000 criteria focus on organizations, people, and management systems. Eleven of Deming's 14 points address organizational culture, leadership, and people. Feigenbaum calls quality "a way of managing an organization."

The Way of strategy focuses on organizations, people, and systems. The Malcolm Baldrige National Quality Award and ISO 9000 standards focus on systems. The ISO 9000 standard (ANSI/ASQC Standard Q90-1987) says, "Technical specifications may not in themselves guarantee that a customer's requirements will be consistently met, if there happen to be any deficiencies in the specifications or *in the organizational system to design and produce the product or service.* [author's emphasis]" The Baldrige criteria give points for leadership, management, and use of human resources. In 1990, a quarter of the points were exclusively for leadership and use of human resources. Statistical techniques have a place, but are not paramount. "The Baldrige guidelines use the word *statistics* only once. . . . This reflects the American TQC [total quality control] point of view, contrary to the Japanese, that the use of specific statistical techniques is a tactical rather than strategic issue" (Dooley et al. 1990, 13). Here are the 1993 Baldrige criteria.

Area	Points
Leadership	95
Information and analysis	75
Strategic quality planning	60
Human resource development and management	150
Management of process quality	140
Quality and operational results	180
Customer focus and satisfaction	300

Dooley et al. cite Armand Feigenbaum. "Quality is not a technical program, department, or awareness program . . . good management means continuous and relentless emphasis on quality *through personal leadership in mobilizing the knowledge, skills, and positive attitudes of everyone . . . quality is a way of managing an organization.* (author's emphasis) (p.1). Hradesky (1988) says productivity and quality improvement through statistical process control (SPC) is 10 percent statistics and 90 percent management.

When people think of W. Edwards Deming, they think of SPC. Only 4 of Deming's 14 points even involve statistics or engineering methods. The others emphasize the corporate culture, organizational structure, leadership, people (human resources), and policies. The following table shows the 14 points and their underlying themes (Tribus 1992, 31).

W. Edwards Deming's 14 Points

1.	Create constancy and continuity of purpose.	*Culture* *Leadership*
2.	Refuse to allow commonly accepted levels of delay for mistakes, defective material, and defective workmanship.	*Culture*
3.	Eliminate dependence on mass inspection. (Don't "inspect quality into the product." Build or design the quality in.)	*Technology* *Culture*
4.	Reduce the number of suppliers. (John Deere Co.:—SOQ NOP—Sell On Quality, Not On Price.)	*Technology* *Policy*
5.	Continually seek ways to improve the system.	*Culture*
6.	Institute modern methods of training using statistics.	*Technology*
7.	Focus supervision on helping people to do a better job. Provide the tools and techniques for people to have pride in workmanship.	*Leadership* *People*
8.	Drive out fear. Encourage two-way communication.	*Culture* *Leadership*
9.	Break down barriers between departments. Encourage problem solving through teamwork.	*Culture* *Structure*
10.	Avoid numerical goals, slogans, or posters for the workforce.	*Culture* *Leadership*
11.	Use statistical methods to drive continuing improvement of quality and productivity. Avoid standards that prescribe numerical quotas.	*Technology* *Policy*
12.	Remove barriers to pride in workmanship.	*Culture*

13. Institute a vigorous program of educa-   *Leadership*
    tion and training. Keep people abreast of   *People*
    new developments in materials, meth-
    ods, and technologies.

14. Clearly define management's permanent   *Culture*
    commitment to quality and productivity.   *Leadership*

People, organizations, and management systems produce quality products and services. They use technology and statistical methods. Tribus
(1992, 30) writes, "The CEO and all the managers understand that the
workers work *in* a system and that the job of a manager is to work *on* the
system, to improve it with their help."

   We will now consider our basic premise. Business, like war, is *a competition between organizations and systems.*

PREMISE: BUSINESS IS WAR

Business, war, and statecraft are *contests between organizations.* They
differ only in their weapons or *tools of competition.*

General Carl von Clausewitz (1780–1831) stated this critical concept 163
years ago. "Rather than comparing it [war] to art we could more accurately compare it to commerce, which is also a conflict of human interests
and activities; and it is still closer to politics, which in turn may be considered as a kind of commerce on a larger scale." (1976, Book 1, chap. 3).

   Long-time Green Bay Packers' coach Vince Lombardi recognized
this, too. "Running a football team is no different than running any other
kind of organization—an army, a political party, or a business. The principles are the same. The object is to win—to beat the other guy."

   Weapons need not be destructive devices. Long ago, the words for
weapons also meant tools. A weapon is any physical, mental, or organizational instrument of competition.

War drove the development of techniques for leadership, organization, and competition.

Nations and armies (organizations) have fought wars for thousands of years. War was the only competition between large organizations. Two hundred years ago, the typical business was a trade under the direction of a master craftsman. An entrepreneur might own a merchant ship. There was little need to manage or lead large organizations in business competition. Instead of developing new principles for business, we can apply war's long experience.

> This book will cite organizational and managerial characteristics that produced military victories. We need the same attributes for success in business.

This book cites some famous generals and some military victories. It does not, however, deeply examine the mechanical aspects of the victories. For example, we mention the naval maneuver of crossing the T. Few business managers care about winning battles with sailing ships. They can relate to the maneuver's dependence on a well-trained and disciplined crew. Frederick the Great was a tactical and strategic genius; however, attrition of his experienced veterans prevented him from realizing tactical masterpieces later in his career. Corporate Napoleons also need good people to achieve outstanding results.

TODAY'S CRISIS— DANGER AND OPPORTUNITY

> Today's business environment is dynamic, turbulent, and unstable. It presents opportunities for organic, flexible, adaptive, and innovative companies. It is perilous for rigid, mechanistic ones.

Tom Peters describes today's business environment in *Thriving on Chaos* (1987). Flexibility and the need to respond to dynamic competitive conditions are key themes. Peters writes, "Violent and accelerating change, now commonplace, will become the grist of the opportunistic winner's mill. The losers will view such confusion as a 'problem' to be 'dealt' with" (p. 14). Skillful competitors will ride the whirlwind of chaos, turbulence, and change. The same tempest will sweep the losers away.

The Chinese/Japanese characters for crisis are danger and opportunity.

Thriving on Chaos begins, "There are no excellent companies" (p.3). It continues, "In 1987, and for the foreseeable future, there is no such thing as a solid, or even substantial, lead over one's competitors. . . . Moreover, the 'champ to chump' cycles are growing ever shorter" (p. 3). Corporate leaders must pilot their organizations through this storm of chaos. We cannot say, "to safe harbor," for there is none. There is no finish line, only today's front-runner. There is no peace treaty, and no Armistice Day. There is only today's King of the Hill.

We will see that organic and adaptive organizations can thrive in this environment. Mechanistic bureaucracies cannot survive.

MEETING THE CHALLENGE— THE DAY OF THE WARRIOR

> A master of the art of war foresees and prevents problems. He or she cures diseases in their infancy.

Movies and television portray "warriors" like the muscular sword-swinging Conan the Barbarian, or gun-toting Rambo. As individual adventurers and heroes, Conan and Rambo are superb. As masters of the art of war, they fall far short of the ancient standards. The Chinese general and philosopher Sun Tzu (~500 B.C.E.) describes the characteristics of a real warrior.

"Therefore, when those experienced in war move they make no mistakes; when they act, their resources are limitless. . . . Anciently, the skillful warriors first made themselves invincible and awaited the enemy's

*Teiwaz, Rune of the Warrior. Tyr, or Tiwaz, was the
Germanic god of war. His name appears in Tiwesdaeg, or Tuesday.*

moment of vulnerability" (Sun Tzu 1963, chap. 4). Sun Tzu's warrior does not gain renown by killing a dozen enemies single-handedly. He does not seek victory through a flash of steel and a clash of blades. Nor does he earn fame by winning battle after battle. He may actually remain very obscure.

One version of *The Art of War* begins with an interview with a physician. This doctor is famous for curing seriously ill patients. He tells of his oldest brother, who detects and stops illnesses in their infancy. This brother's name never goes beyond the house. His second brother cures diseases in their early stages. This brother's name does not get out of the village. The third brother cures serious diseases, so he is famous throughout the land (Cleary 1989a). The famous doctor is the Conan or Rambo who fixes problems that come from lack of planning and foresight. The elder brother who forestalls the problems is a master of the art of war.

Does this apply to twentieth century business? Tom Peters (1987, 1) quotes Dr. Lee Rivers, director of corporate planning at Allied-Signal: "You can't get the CEO of a $5 billion company excited about a $100,000 market like ceramic scissor blades or razor blades. We shoot right from the start for the ceramic [auto] engine. We don't want to go through the learning process in smaller markets." The Japanese are making ceramic scissor and razor blades. They are selling ceramic-tip pens. They are gaining experience in making and selling ceramic products. One day the ceramic auto engine will arrive. Americans might even invent the technology; however, the Japanese will not meet American automakers on a level playing field. The Japanese will defeat opponents who have already lost.

The Timex success story is another example. Swiss watchmakers sold high-quality watches through jewelers. Instead of challenging the Swiss, Timex began to sell watches in drugstores. It took a while for the Swiss to even notice the competing products. By the time they did, Timex had entrenched itself in the market (Porter 1985, 533).

THE WAY OF THE WARRIOR

The Way of the warrior—Japan's *Bushidō* and India's *Kshatriya Dharma*—is the Way of leadership and management.

The *dharma*, duty, or right conduct of India's *Kshatriyas* required them to "protect their dependents, rule justly, speak the truth, and fight wars" (Buck 1973, xv). *Ksei*, the Indo-European root of Kshatriya, means *to rule*. The Kshatriya caste included the professional, governing, and military occupations. Japan had Bushidō, the Way of the warrior. The samurai's role was to "manage many subordinates dexterously, bear himself correctly, govern the country, and foster the people, thus preserving the ruler's discipline" (Musashi 1974, 49–50). Kshatriya Dharma and Bushidō are clearly the Way of the organizational leader.

The Way of the warrior lives on in the corporate cultures of many Japanese companies. The employees are the retainers, and the managers and owners are the lords. There is a code of mutual loyalty and duty between them. Such an organization has an inherent strength that makes it virtually invincible. We will examine the full impact of commitment and loyalty later.

Bushidō, the Way of the warrior.

武　士　道

FACING THE CRISIS

> Thunderclouds do not fear lightning. Hurricanes do not fear wind.
> To prosper in a turbulent, chaotic marketplace, become the storm.

Can bureaucrats and analysts meet today's crisis? Can their organizations ride the whirlwind of chaos? Can they even live in the turbulence of violent and accelerating change? Only those who know the Way of the warrior can meet this challenge.

Takeda Shingen (1521–1573) had a famous banner that carried the words, "Swift as the wind, silent as a forest, fierce as fire, immovable as a mountain." This is part of a passage from Sun Tzu's *Art of War* (1963, chap.7). Here is the full passage.

> *When campaigning, be swift as the wind;*
> *in leisurely march, majestic as a forest;*
> *in raiding and plundering, like fire;*
> *in standing, firm as the mountains.*
> *As unfathomable as the clouds, move like a thunderbolt*

This is the art of the general or business manager. Move rapidly to seize advantages. "Speed is the essence of war," according to Sun Tzu. Promote confidence, commitment, and trust between employees and leaders. Assure clear and open communications. Such an organization is calm and orderly, like a forest. "In good order they await a disorderly enemy; in serenity, a clamorous one" (Sun Tzu 1963, chap.7). Fire suggests positive energy. Niccolò Machiavelli called positive energy *virtù*. Tom Peters calls it "a bias for action." Principles and values are reliable and steady, like a mountain. Like Shakespeare's Julius Caesar, they are "constant as the northern star." They are Stephen Covey's (1991) organizational compass. The organization does not compromise on basic principles and beliefs. It does not skimp on product quality to meet a quota or to save money.

Thunderclouds swirl through the sky on changing winds. No one can predict their shape or course. "The ultimate in disposing one's troops is to be without ascertainable shape" (Sun Tzu 1963, chap. 6). The organization alters its campsites and marches by devious routes. Opponents cannot predict its intentions (chap. 10). Only an organization with discipline and

War banner of Takeda Shingen.

commitment can feign disorder (chap. 5). Such discipline and commitment do not come from rules and laws. They must come from adherence to immovable principles by all organizational members.

Thunderheads contain potential energy. "His potential is that of a fully drawn crossbow; his timing, the release of the trigger" (Sun Tzu 1963, chap. 5). "The fog must thicken and form a dark and menacing cloud out of which a bolt of lightning may strike at any time" (Clausewitz 1976, Book 6, chap. 26). An agile, flexible organization is like this—a whirling, but purposeful, thunderstorm.

The warrior adapts to changing circumstances, and does not use rigid strategies. Sun Tzu wrote that water adapts to its surroundings. In war, conditions are always changing. Water changes its shape and flow to match the conditions. The able commander wins by shaping his or her tactics to the enemy and the situation (Sun Tzu 1963, chap. 6). This does not mean letting the flow of events sweep us away. Instead, we become the river that rises in flood. We flow into distribution channels and market niches. Our products conform to the needs of the marketplace. Fluidity, adaptability, and flexibility are the keys to victory.

The warrior uses large and small weapons, or large and small forces. Tom Peters warns that large businesses cannot adapt quickly. Small companies are often more innovative and more responsive to customer needs. Sun Tzu wrote, "He who knows how to use both large and small forces will be victorious" (chap. 3). Musashi noted that a large group of men cannot change direction quickly; however, a single man can easily change his mind. The advantages of large and small units depend on the circumstances. A master of strategy recognizes these circumstances and acts accordingly.

ABOUT THIS BOOK

This book's goal is to reveal the heart and soul of the art of war. It searches for underlying concepts and primordial ideas. It looks back even to the dawn of history. It uncovers common threads that have run through many societies for centuries. It traces these threads back to their origins in human thought.

During the past hundred years, we have surrounded these ideas with scientific details. Business students devote years to studying these ideas and learning their many names. This is useful if students learn the underlying principles. It can be especially enlightening if students read classical and ancient books on the art of war. Even ancient myths and legends about gods and magic take on new, practical meanings. These myths and legends point to ideas and concepts that have ridden the human mind from antiquity to the present.

Simple Solutions, Not Easy Solutions

> The principles in this book are easy to understand. It takes effort to make them work. Anything worth doing takes effort.

The Way of strategy is easy to understand; however, it does not promise easy solutions. It is foolish to seek such solutions. There are no magic bullets or philosopher's stones. There are no one-minute recipes or instant success secrets. General von Clausewitz wrote, "Everything in war is very simple, but the simplest thing is difficult." Figure skaters, ballerinas, sword dancers, acrobats, or jugglers make their art look easy. We know how much talent and practice it takes to excel in these arts.

Peters and Waterman's *In Search of Excellence* describes corporate success stories. The excellent companies make success look easy; however, application of the basic concepts requires effort and commitment from management. Leaders must have the strength of character and firmness of mind to follow through with the plans. They must persevere despite thousands of diversions. (Clausewitz 1976, Book 3, chap. 1).

Even mere knowledge of the elemental principles of the Way of strategy is immensely valuable. Companies and nations have shown complete ignorance of these principles throughout history. The organizational and human bodies of the fallen litter millennia of history. Vietnam was just one example.

No Cookbook Recipes

> Recipes cannot replace thinking. Principles and concepts are valuable guides for independent thinkers.

This book is not a cookbook of recipes. There are no cookbook recipes in the Way of strategy. Miyamoto Musashi called his *A Book of Five Rings* "a spiritual guide for the man who wishes to learn the Way." Thousands of miles away and 200 years later, Carl von Clausewitz wrote, "Theory then becomes a guide to anyone who wants to learn about war from books." Theory is not a set of recipes to take to the battlefield (Clausewitz 1976, Book 2, chap. 2). We apply concepts and principles, not mechanistic formulas.

Sun Tzu warned that those who do not heed his guidance suffer defeat. Yet he added the following in the same paragraph. "While heeding the profit of my counsel, avail yourself also of any helpful circumstances over and beyond the ordinary rules and modify your plans accordingly" (Clavell 1983, chap. 1). Sun Tzu avoided mechanistic rules, and saw his book as a guide. We will use this approach.

THE KEYSTONE OF VICTORY

> The Way of strategy is the arbiter of survival or extinction in organizational competition. Right conduct, dharma, Tao, or Dō is the foundation of the Way of strategy. It is a vital part of leadership, management, and rulership. It is the keystone of flexible, dynamic, and entrepreneurial organizations.

Evolution of Words and Ideas

> The evolution of words shows the underlying concepts behind them.

We can use language to find underlying, primordial concepts or ideas. We can find elemental parts of the human psyche that have come down through millennia of history. Proto-Indo-European is the common ancestor of most Western and Southeast Asian languages. Linguists have reconstructed this language by studying its descendants.

Language reveals prehistoric concepts of God. According to the *American Heritage Dictionary of the Engligh Language, deity* comes from the Indo-European root *deiw*. It means, *shine, sky, heaven,* or *god*. *Pəter* is the ancestor of the Latin word *pater* or *father*. Then dyeu-pəter is the Sky-Father. This god is familiar as the Romans' *Jupiter,* or Greeks' *Zeus-pater*. Figure I.1 shows the evolution of some modern languages from Indo-European.

Figure I.1

Anthropological psychology through language evolution.

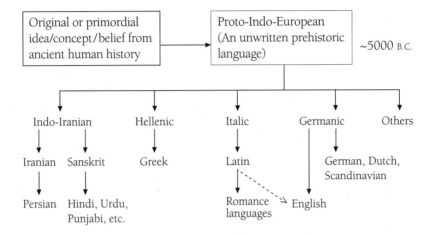

Leadership and Management

> The Indo-European root for *dharma* evolved into words for leadership and management.

Language also reveals primordial concepts of leadership and management. *Dharma* is Sanskrit for *right conduct,* or *the Way.* The corresponding Chinese word is *Tao,* or *Way.* Tao found its way to Japan as *Dō.* Bushidō is the Way of the warrior (*bu = war, shi = man, dō = way*). Here is a working definition of dharma: *Dharma is a set of duties and responsibilities that go with a station in life.* The station can be a profession or an organizational position. There are dharmas for physicians, lawyers, and engineers. There are dharmas for managers and leaders. Dharma is the right Way for the holder of a station to act.

According to the *American Heritage Dictionary of the English Language,* dharma means statute or law, "that which is established firmly." Its Indo-European root is *dher.* Dher means, "to hold firmly or support." Dher implies leadership or rulership in many languages. As *dhr-ono,* it became *thronos* (seat, throne, or support) in Greek. To the Persians, dher meant "to hold." It is part of the name of the Persian King Darius. In India, a *jemadar* is a lieutenant, or "holder of a body of men." A *sirdar* is "a person of rank in India, Pakistan, or Afghanistan." Ressaldar and havildar are Indian military ranks. Hindus even personify Dharma as the god of justice.

Stephen Covey's *Principle-Centered Leadership* (1991) comes across as a rediscovery of dharma. Covey discusses "natural law," and why management must follow it. He discusses "the law of the unenforceable." Covey says strong mores (customs, culture) make laws or mechanistic rules unnecessary. Weak mores make laws unenforceable. We will later see that dharma and organizational culture govern organic, adaptable organizations. The mechanistic organization that seeks stability through regulations cannot live in today's competitive environment.

Natural law is a Western philosophy that corresponds to dharma. "[Natural law] held that right is 'natural,' not a mere invention of men. . . . Right and law, in the ultimate sense, exist outside and above all peoples" (Palmer and Colton 1971, 317). John Locke (1632–1704) said that a government's authority rests on its conformance with natural law. If a government violates natural law (or dharma) by threatening the natural rights of its citizens, "the governed have a right to reconsider what they have done in creating the government" (Palmer and Colton 1971, 320). Locke's writings influenced the U.S. Declaration of Independence.

Chapter 2 discusses the Way of leadership. This is *Kshatriya Dharma*, the right conduct of the warrior or king. It is the Tao of the general. It is Bushidō, the Way of the warrior. Right conduct creates a firm bond between leaders and followers. This bond is commitment. It is a fortress of adamant we can find in the hearts of our followers.

The ancient Hindus said those who protect and honor dharma gain its protection. Dharma destroys those who violate it. Germanic mythology includes the same concept. Yggdrasill, the World Ash Tree, is the framework that supports and nourishes the universe. Wotan (or Odin), the ruler of the gods, cut a spear shaft from its branches. "Deep in the shaft he cut his runes, telling of truth to pacts" (Wagner 1972, act I, scene 2). The spear is the foundation of Wotan's power and authority. If Wotan ever broke his word, his spear would shatter and his power would end. Organizations that violate dharma and break commitment become easy prey for competitors. A section in chapter 3 discusses commitment in detail.

Hindus believe that obeying or violating dharma affects karma. Karma is the soul's record. Good karma leads to rebirth in a higher caste, or even freedom from rebirth. Bad karma causes rebirth in lower castes, or as animals or insects. We don't, however, need to argue theology to recognize the merit of dharma. We don't have to worry about being worms in our next lives. Income statements and balance sheets reflect our karma in this life. Successes or failures of other organizational ventures also reflect the leaders' karma. Dharma has practical organizational effects we can see and recognize.

Dharma is the same as Tao or Dō. It is the Way. Reading the right translation of Sun Tzu's *The Art of War* reveals this critical point. The Wing (1988) translation shows the Chinese characters opposite the English translation. With a Japanese dictionary of *kanji* (Chinese characters), one can make out some characters.* *Strategy* is *hei-dō*—the Way of the soldier.** The Wing translation begins, "Strategy is the great Work of the organization. In Situations of life or death, it is the Tao of survival or extinction" (chap. 1). This gives us the Way of strategy.

The translation proceeds, "The Art is a flexible System, wherein the View and its officials employ the Tao." The View is the "master or sovereign." It is "the mind, vision, or principle behind events." The Clavell and Griffith translations refer to Tao as "moral law" and "moral influence." These terms accurately describe the benefits of following Tao, Dō, or dharma; however, they do not convey the idea of a Way of leadership.

This introduction has focused on the vital concept of dharma, right conduct, or the Way. To learn and apply the Way of strategy, we must adopt the role of a *Bushi* or *Kshatriya*. Chapter 2 discusses this role in detail.

Chapter 1 will clarify another important idea. Like war, business is a competition between organizations.

---

* The Japanese use Chinese ideographs, or characters, in their writing. They also use *hiragana* and *katakana*, or syllabic letters.
** Musashi uses *heihō*, the Method of the Soldier.

1

Business, War, and Organizations

COMPARISONS

Carl von Clausewitz begins *On War* by asking the question, "What is war?" This chapter begins by defining the relationships between business and war. Clausewitz cites four characteristics of war. These are danger, exertion, intelligence (and uncertainty), and friction. They also apply to business operations. The environment, or theater of operations, also affects competitive activities.

Polarity and Competition

Business and war are competitions beween organizations.

War assumes polarity. "In a battle, each side aims at victory; that is a case of true polarity, since the victory of one side excludes the victory of the other" (Clausewitz 1976, Book 1, chap. 1). Polarity means a zero-sum game, or win-lose situation. War, competitive sports, elections, and litigation are zero-sum games.

1

Competition for market share in a mature market is a zero-sum game. In a mature or declining market, the market pie has stopped growing. The only way to get a bigger piece of pie is to take someone else's. What benefits A must harm B. This is polarity. The competitors are at war. Business, however, is not always a zero-sum game. There is often the opportunity to create a new pie. Introducing a product does not require an attack on someone else's market share. (It may make their product obsolete.) In a growth market, the pie gets bigger. At this stage, companies compete for the growing market. Although there is competition, there may be enough for everyone.

There is also the option of entering a market niche or segment that everyone else has overlooked. We will return to this principle in chapter 6.

Unlike war, business is not a destructive activity. We do not have to destroy our competitors' assets to succeed. Business, however, is a competitive activity. Like war, business is a *competition between two or more human organizations.*

Risk and Uncertainty

Like war, business is full of risk and uncertainty.

Decisions are easy under conditions of certainty. Mathematical approaches such as linear programming can usually find the one best answer to a deterministic problem.

Risk means a probabilistic situation. We do not know what the outcome will be, however, we know the likelihood of each possible outcome. Casino gambling is a probabilistic operation. We can compute the chances of winning at craps, roulette, and similar games. The odds always favor the house slightly. Even if individual gamblers win, the house makes money in the long run.

We can model probabilistic situations with decision trees, statistical distributions, and simulations. A weakness of the decision tree is that real situations rarely allow infinite trials. Sometimes, we must bet the farm (or the company) on one throw of the dice.

Probabilistic models yield expectation values. The expectation is the weighted average of an infinite number of trials; however, we often can't base a good decision on expectation alone. Business decisions rarely involve infinite trials. This is a drawback of the decision tree. Suppose we offer middle-class people the following bet. They must stake their life savings, house, and car against $10 million. If they get heads on a fair coin, they win. If they get tails, they lose. Suppose their assets are worth $300,000. The expected gain on this bet is half of ($10,000,000 − $300,000), or $4.85 million. The bet, however, risks complete disaster. Few people would take this chance. Now suppose they can throw the coin 10 times. Each time, they stake a tenth of their assets against $1 million. The expectation is still $4.85 million. The difference is that the chance of total disaster is now $\frac{1}{1024}$. This also is the chance of winning $10 million. Most people, however, would prefer the near certainty of winning $3 to $8 million over a 50:50 chance of getting $10 million or losing everything. In business, the latter is a you-bet-your-company proposition.

Uncertainty means we don't even know the chance of each possible outcome. We may not even know all the possible results. Military and market research intelligence are rarely perfect. "War is the realm of uncertainty; three quarters of the factors on which action in war is based are wrapped in a fog of greater or lesser uncertainty" (Clausewitz, 1976, Book 1, chap. 3). This is the "fog of war." We face the same problem in business.

Decision Making Under Uncertainty

> We must avoid both recklessness and excessive caution.

There are three textbook approaches to making decisions under uncertainty. Maximax selects the option that provides the maximum (highest payoff) possible outcome. It is a very optimistic decision criterion. Playing the lottery is a maximax decision. (The lottery is a probabilistic situation, not an uncertain one.) The chances against winning are astronomical. A decision tree would show an expected loss. Lottery tickets, however, are cheap, so the loss is small. This encourages people to buy tickets and hope for the jackpot. This is obviously not an intelligent or scientific decision process.

Maximax's opposite is maximin. Maximin maximizes the minimum (lowest gain) possible outcome. Noting that a loss is a negative gain, maximin selects the option that loses the least. It is a very pessimistic approach. Consider a patient who has one year to live. There is an operation that cures 90 percent of all patients; however, the other 10 percent die on the operating table. (This becomes a probabilistic situation if we know the patient's normal life expectancy.) Most people would choose the operation. Maximin would reject the operation, because dying in a year is better than dying now. Unfortunately, many corporate executives think this way. This dooms their organizations to eventual defeat.

Finally, the "equally likely" criterion assumes that all results are equally likely. For each option, we assign equal weights to the potential results. Then we can model the situation with a decision tree. In practice, a straight analytical approach is rarely adequate. Rigid maximax and maximin are clearly deficient. We will later see that we cannot make good decisions with mechanical methods. "But any method by which strategic plans are turned out ready-made, as if from some machine, must be totally rejected" (Clausewitz 1976, Book 2, chap. 4).

The section on danger and exertion warns against recklessness and excessive caution. Recklessness means exposing oneself to losses, without the chance for gain. Self-destruction does not require outstanding performance by adversaries. Excessive caution means giving opponents the chance to make decisive moves or gain advantages. Although we do nothing wrong, dynamic opponents exploit our inactivity.

Friction—Sand in the Machine

> Minor annoyances and inefficiencies can stop a war machine or an economic engine.

Arthur Wellesley, Duke of Wellington, was the famous victor of Waterloo. According to British military legend, a subaltern asked him if he had a single success secret to teach. Wellington replied, "[Relieve yourself] when you can."

The Iron Duke's off-color reply contains a lot of truth. Suppose a soldier or officer had to go to battle quickly, without even a couple of minutes to spare. A nagging, increasingly insistent distraction would be a serious disadvantage on the field. This distraction is one example of friction—a seemingly minor annoyance that can disrupt an operation. Viewers and readers of *The Right Stuff* can appreciate the potential of this particular annoyance. It could have stopped the first Mercury space mission. Alan Shepard probably followed Wellington's advice, however, there were several mission holds while he sat in the capsule. Shepard's space suit didn't have the necessary plumbing, since it was only a 15-minute flight. He finally received permission to "do it in the suit."

Friction exists in war, business, sports, and politics. "Friction, as we choose to call it, is the force that makes the apparently easy so difficult. . . . Countless minor incidents—the kind you can never really foresee—combine to lower the general level of performance, so that one always falls far short of the intended goal" (Clausewitz 1976, Book 1, chap. 7). In war, rain can delay a march or impede a cavalry charge. The classic tale "For Want of a Nail" by Benjamin Franklin is an example of friction.

> *A little neglect may breed great mischief; for want of a nail the shoe was lost; for want of a shoe the horse was lost; and for want of a horse the rider was lost.*

Tom Peters and Nancy Austin (1985) cite a modern example of friction. General Bill Creech inherited the Air Force's Tactical Air Command in 1978. The peacetime sortie rate had fallen 7.8 percent per year for 10 years. The sortie rate shows the readiness of the military unit. General Creech led a turnaround, despite a shrinking maintenance budget. The secret was good management that reduced friction. "Planes don't fly because, for example, the pickup truck transporting a critical part broke a U-joint in a long-unrepaired pothole while coming across the base" (p. 56). Peters and Austin emphasize the role of supply and maintenance people in making an operation run smoothly.

We may make a high-tech product with the most features in the market. We may have a six-sigma (or 12-sigma) process that assures perfect quality. Friction can undo all the benefits. Electronics manufacturers know what electrostatic discharge can do to parts that have already passed acceptance testing. Alternately, Peters and Austin quote the president of a high-tech company. "The most important 'marketer' in our company is the man or woman on the loading dock who decides not to drop the damned box into the back of the truck" (p. 56).

Friction is the accumulation of minor or trivial annoyances to the point where they cause major damage. In industry, shipments may be late or contain defective parts. Machines may break down. Key workers may get sick. Some manufacturing companies deal with friction by storing raw materials, subassemblies, and finished goods. Inventory decouples supply from production, and production from distribution (Heizer and Render 1991). Keeping large inventories, however, creates other problems. It ties up cash, and there are storage and handling costs. Bureaucratic procedures tie people's hands and prevent them from making anything happen. Excessive bureaucracy is do-it-(to)-yourself friction!

Tom Peters (1987) cites the impact of friction in industry. "The accumulation of little items, each too 'trivial' to trouble the boss with, is a prime cause of miss-the-market delays" (p. 323). Friction can stop a war machine or an economic engine. We must understand and expect it, and try to reduce its effects.

Danger and Exertion

> Excessive caution, or risk-averseness, leads to failure.

War involves physical danger. The participant can suffer death, wounds, or captivity. The organization can suffer defeat and loss of its equipment. In business, danger includes failure of the individual or organization. Casualties are dollars instead of blood. Employees stake their careers, and stockholders risk their money.

Managers, like generals, are often unwilling to take risks. Excessive caution never accomplishes great deeds. At the Battle of Copenhagen (1801), Sir Hyde Parker signaled Horatio Nelson to break off action. Parker's irresolution would have thrown away a decisive victory. Nelson put his telescope to his blind eye and said, "I have only one eye, I have a right to be blind sometimes . . . I really do not see the signal."

When his guards hesitated at Kolin in 1757, Frederick the Great berated them. *"Ihr Racker, wollt ihr ewig leben?"* or "Rascals, would you live forever?" In the *Mahabharata,* the warrior Karna speaks to Krishna. "When is there a day or night that death may not come? Or are there any who have become immortal by not fighting?" (Buck 1973, 245).

Recklessness is bad, but risk-averseness is often a prescription for certain defeat. General Patton said, "When you dig a foxhole, you dig your grave" (Williamson 1979, 60). The foxhole offered temporary safety, but it was a static position. The enemy would eventually find it and kill the occupants. Staying in the foxhole meant eventual death. Taking the risk offered chances of life and victory. IBM's introduction of the System/360 is an example.

Betting the Company—The IBM 360

> To succeed, and even survive, organizations must make calculated
> bets on new technology.

He either fears his fate too much
Or his deserts are small
That puts it not unto the touch
To win or lose it all.
                    —James Graham, Marquis of Montrose (1612–1650)

How did IBM dominate the mainframe computer market for two decades?
The story began in 1964, when IBM introduced the System/360.

Facing stiff competition from companies like Remington Rand, General
Electric, and Honeywell as the 1960s began, IBM's top management
risked almost everything, investing five billion dollars on a new line of
computers that would make all existing ones obsolete. "We call this pro-
ject, you-bet-your-company," one executive told Fortune *magazine.*

During 1966–1971, IBM's gross and net income doubled. General
Electric could not compete, and left the computer industry by 1970
(Strothman 1990, 34; see also Carroll 1993).

Betting the Royal Navy—HMS Dreadnought

> Refusing to gamble on new technology is itself a gamble. It is a bet
> that no one else will take the risk and win.

At the end of the nineteenth century, all major countries had ironclad battleships. The typical battleship had four heavy (10–12-inch) guns in two
turrets. Most also had medium (6–8-inch) guns. The Battle of Tsushima
(1905) showed these medium guns to be ineffective against battleships.
They could actually confuse the gunners by masking the splashes of the
larger shells. Admiral John Fisher (1841–1920) conceived the idea of an

all-big-gun battleship. HMS *Dreadnought* was a major risk. A failure would waste a huge amount of money. A success would make the Royal Navy obsolete. It would, however, give England an irresistible super-weapon. Fisher overcame the political opposition, and the shipyards finished *Dreadnought* in 1906. The ship could fire a broadside of eight 12-inch guns—twice as many as any other battleship. Its turbine engines gave it the unprecedented speed of 21 knots. Predreadnoughts with reciprocating piston engines could make only 18 knots.

Dreadnought, however, did not give England absolute mastery over the oceans. Americans like Theodore Roosevelt and William Sowden Sims, and Germans like Alfred von Tirpitz, had been thinking the same way. Congress approved two *Michigan*-class battleships in 1905. The first one took to the water in 1909. The Kiel shipyards completed SMS *Posen* in 1908. The French, Italians, Russians, Turks, and Austro-Hungarians had to play catch-up. None of these countries' battleship fleets did anything noteworthy during the First World War. They did suffer ignominious losses to mines, torpedoes, and accidental explosions.

There is an important lesson here. Had England *not* proceeded with *Dreadnought,* she would have lost her maritime supremacy to Germany and the United States. The same lesson applies to product lines. Companies that introduce revolutionary products dominate the market. They leave their less-imaginative and less-adventurous competitors behind. The latter become also-rans.

Exertion and Persistence

> Victory sometimes goes to the side with the most endurance.

Fighting at sun-down, fighting at dark,
Ten o'clock at night, the full moon well up, our leaks on the gain, and
    five feet of water reported . . .
Not a moment's cease,
The leaks gain fast on the pumps, the fire eats towards the powder
    magazine.
One of the pumps has been shot away, it is generally thought we are
    sinking . . .
Toward twelve there in the beams of the moon they surrender to us.
                    —Walt Whitman, "An Old-Time Sea Fight,"
                    Bonhomme Richard versus *Serapis* (1779)

Everyone remembers John Paul Jones' defiant words, "I have not yet begun to fight!" Everyone knows the Americans won the battle. Why do we hear nothing of *Bonhomme Richard*'s later exploits? This was a very unusual sea battle. The losing ship sank the victor. After the British struck their colors, the Americans realized they could not save their ship. They transferred to *Serapis,* and *Bonhomme Richard* went down. This story shows the value of exertion and persistence.

Exertion is part of war. The victor is often the side that continues to prosecute the war despite fatigue and exhaustion. Clausewitz wrote that marches can be as destructive as engagements. Soldiers desert, cannot keep up, or fall to sickness. Napoleon lost a third of his army this way while marching to Russia (Clausewitz 1976, Book 5). Retreat to the interior of the country is indirect resistance. It "destroys the enemy not so much by the sword as by his own exertions" (Book 6, chap. 25). Clausewitz says, "it takes a powerful mind to drive his army to the limit" (Book 1, chap. 5).

Exertion is also part of business. Productivity means "a sustained high level of work activity despite fatigue, distractions, frustrations, annoyances, and social influences" (Miller 1985–1986). Intrinsic motivation raises productivity. We will discuss intrinsic motivation later.

The Competitive Environment

> The environment strongly affects organizational competition.

Competitions and noncompetitive operations occur in an environment. In war, the competitive environment includes weather and terrain. Weather covers changing or dynamic aspects of the environment. Terrain is static. Today we may break these aspects down as follows:

Dynamic Aspects	**(Relatively) Static Aspects**
Physical technology	National languages
Currency exchange rates	National cultures, customs
Interest rates, cost of capital	Infrastructure (means of trans-
Customer needs and wants	porting goods)
Laws (environmental,	Education of the labor pool
trade, labor, and so on)	

Organizations must always pay attention to the competitive environment. Musashi said, "Examine the environment." Sun Tzu (1963, chap. 10) wrote, "And therefore I say: Know the enemy, know yourself; your victory will never be endangered. Know the ground, know the weather; your victory will then be total."

Xerox's benchmarking program comes from a desire to know the enemy (Garvin 1988). In other companies, the emphasis is on hiding problems from upper management. These organizations know neither the enemy nor themselves. Sun Tzu (1963, chap. 3) wrote this of such organizations. "If ignorant both of your enemy and yourself, you are certain in every battle to be in peril."

ORGANIZATIONS

> Tom Peters (1989) says organizations and people are the decisive cornerstones of success and failure. Recall the assertion in the introduction to this book. People, organizations, and systems win wars and market share. They use technology to do this, but technology alone is not decisive.

Like war, business is a competition for resources. Instead of land, businesses seek market share and customers. A market niche or segment need not be geographical. Nonetheless, it is the object of contention in business.

Competition

> Competing entities assess their surroundings and each other. They act according to their perceptions and get feedback from their actions.

How do organizations compete? Figure 1.1 shows two organizations in a competitive situation. There are several critical features.

1. Organizations use their senses to assess the environment and each other.
2. Organizations act on their perceptions.

3. Organizations receive and analyze feedback from their actions.
4. Culture, customs, attitudes, and values affect an organization's decision process.
5. The control system is an organization's brain and nervous system.
6. Each organization has a physical capability.

The organizations in Figure 1.1 could be any of the following. In some cases, especially in business, there can be more than two competitors.

1. Two boxers in a boxing ring. The environment is the ring and its rules. Each boxer's speed and strength is his physical capability. The boxers constantly assess each other's actions as they move about the ring. They also get feedback from each punch or block they throw.
2. Two football teams on a football field. The environment is the field, which may be wet or windy. The players need to assess the field conditions to succeed. Again, there is constant feedback that the players and coach must assess. Which plays are successful? Which aren't? What works well against this opponent?
3. Two armies on a battlefield or in a theater of operations.
4. Two or more business organizations in a market segment.
5. Two or more political parties in an election campaign. The environment includes voter sentiment and public opinion.

Figure 1.1

Competitive activity.

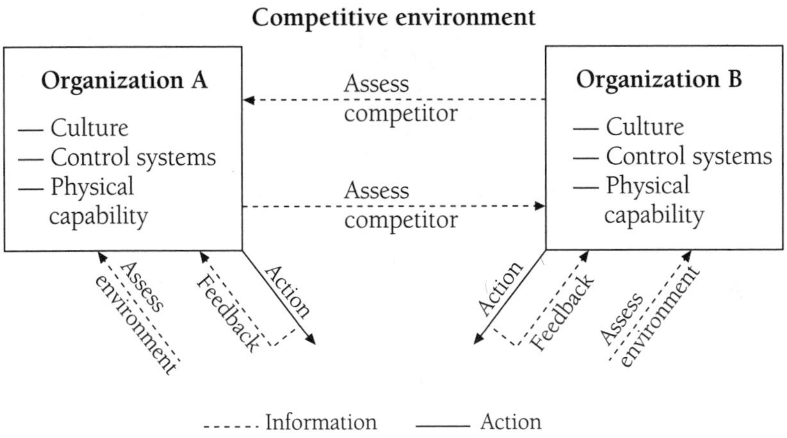

Competitive environment

------ Information   ——— Action

Sometimes there is only one competitor. This may happen when a business introduces a product or goes into an overlooked market segment. Some sports do not require a contestant to assess his or her opponents. In target shooting, javelin throwing, or pole vaulting, the actions of competitors do not affect a contestant's performance. Competitors' records may tell the contestant what he or she must do to win, however, the athlete is going to try for the best score or record anyway. Finally, the environment always affects personal or organizational performance.

The Living Competitive Environment

> Most of the business environment is alive and animate. Customers and suppliers have desires and needs.

In war, the environment is mostly inanimate. It includes terrain, weather, rivers, roads, and so on; however, part of the environment is alive. This includes the civilian population of the theater of operations. An army that treats the civilians well can recruit local guides and get other help. If the army mistreats the civilians, they will serve the enemy as partisans or spies. During the Thirty Years' War (1618–1648), many armies abused local populations. Looting and sacking were common. The peasants responded by killing or robbing soldiers. The Swedes under Gustavus Adolphus, however, were very strict about treatment of civilians. "The army could not afford to alienate those who supplied labour, guides, and intelligence of the enemy, as well as food and quarters" (Parker 1987, 200).

In business, most of the environment is alive. Rivers, mountains, and roads do not have desires or needs. Customers, suppliers, contractors, and distributors do. Like an organization, these are living entities. Customers hold the power of life and death over each competitor. Each customer may have its own battles to fight in another market. If so, it relies on its suppliers' products or services for survival. In international marketing, local customs and languages come into play. These are also part of the living competitive environment.

Organizations Are Living Entities

> An organization is a social system of human beings. It is an animate, living entity. To manage it, we must treat it as such.

Carl von Clausewitz (1976, Book 1, chap. 1) wrote, "War, however, is not the action of a living force on a lifeless mass . . . but always the collision of two living forces." A competitive organization is a living entity. It has a brain, nervous system, and body. The ground it stands on is its competitive environment. Opposing organizations stand on the same field. Each uses its strength and the advantages of the ground to win its goals.

The physicist Fritjof Capra (1992, 29) said, "I use the *living system*. A corporation is literally alive. It has its own rationality, its own mind, its own emotionality. And, of course, it has its own culture. So you cannot just dominate and control an organization like you can a machine, and you cannot just give instructions from the top." We will later discuss mechanistic organizations and their disadvantages. Their underlying assumption is that one can run an organization like a machine.

We can summarize this section with the following observations about organizations (Klein and Ritti 1984).

1. Organizations are systems. Their portions interact and affect each others' performances.
2. Organizations are open to their environments.
3. Organizations have goals and purposes.
4. Organizations are adaptive. (If they aren't, they don't survive.)
5. Organizations are subject to constraints. Constraints come from the environment and the organization itself.
6. Organizations need feedback.

ORGANIZATIONAL CULTURE

> Organizational culture is a set of shared values that affect organizational behavior. Organizational culture plays a critical role in productivity, quality, and competitiveness.

Organizational culture is "a system of shared values and beliefs that guide the behavior of organization members" (Schermerhorn, Hunt, and Osborn 1985, 372). Marvin Bower, managing director of McKinsey & Company, defined culture as "the way we do things around here" (Deal and Kennedy 1982, 4). Myths and legends are valuable as windows into organizational cultures.

Magic, Myths, and Legends: Windows into Human Thought

> Myths and legends reflect the attitudes, values, and beliefs of organizations. They show what the organization is like, or wants to become. Gods and heroes are role models. Stories and legends also are useful for shaping and changing organizational behavior.

We know that magic is superstition; however, its underlying psychological and anthropological basis is very real. Primitive people created myths and legends to explain what they could not understand. We know that angry gods do not strike mortals with lightning, however, lightning is real and can kill us. We know that evil spirits do not cause diseases, however, a shaman or medicine man can often cure diseases if the patient believes in evil spirits. The brain exerts real control over the body's immune system. Today we call this the psychosomatic or placebo effect (see Rubin 1993). If the patient believes the witch doctor is casting out the evil spirits, the patient may get better. Faith healing works the same way. Modern doctors take advantage of psychosomatic effects, too. Their patients believe in bacteria and white blood cells. Some doctors encourage the patients to picture their white cells as soldiers killing the bacteria. This mental imagery often helps the patients recover.

Similarly, a witch doctor can kill subjects who believe in voodoo. Evil spirits don't do the job. The victims' own minds kill them.

Gods and Heroes as Role Models

> Mythological gods were often role models for human occupations. They reflected the attitudes and values of trades and professions.

Myths and legends are useful (see Figure 1.2). They reflect the attitudes, values, and ideals of their societies. Primitive and ancient cultures created their gods in the cultures' own images. Their pantheons reflected what the society was, or wanted to become. Gods were often role models for human occupations. For example, Vulcan (Hephaestos) was the artisan of the Roman (Greek) gods. He embodied the professions of engineering and architecture. Apollo was the physician of the gods. He owned the

Figure 1.2

Value of legends, myths, and magic.

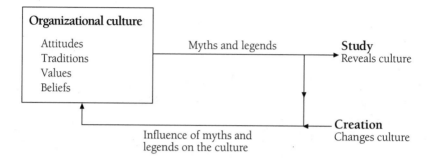

caduceus, or rod with two serpents entwining it. The caduceus symbolizes the medical profession today.

Role models can symbolize occupations. They also influence behavior. A boy may want to grow up to be a quarterback like Jim McMahon or Phil Simms. During the 1960s, boys idolized astronauts like John Glenn. (There were no woman astronauts then. Sally Ride became a role model for girls during the 1980s.) Some teenage girls "wannabee" like the singer Madonna. Organizations have their own heroes and role models.

Legends in Advertising

> People invent legends to get publicity.

People sometimes invent legends deliberately. William Laughead, an advertising agent for the Red River Lumber Company, invented the giant lumberjack Paul Bunyan. Joe Magarac is a giant Pittsburgh steelworker who squeezes molten iron into rails with his bare hands. The American Steel Corporation uses him to symbolize the role of steelmaking in modern society (Cavendish 1989).

Professional societies like the National Society of Professional Engineers want to improve the public image of technology. We suggest reintroducing Vulcan to symbolize the modern engineering profession. Engineering professional societies might show Vulcan in a modernized workshop. Instead of armor and chariots, Vulcan would make cars, computers, industrial robots, space shuttles, bridges, and all the other wonders of modern technology. The picture of a giant Roman god placing a bridge across a river would show the role of civil engineering in infrastructure.

Use of Legends to Influence Behavior

> People invent or use legends to influence behavior.

People may use or create legends to influence behavior. This application can be manipulative or benevolent. In George Orwell's *1984,* Winston Smith, the protagonist, works at Oceania's Ministry of Truth. He writes a story about a hero who gives his life for Oceania. The hero is a product of Smith's imagination. The Ministry of Truth uses such stories to control and manipulate the people.

Adolf Hitler used Teutonic Knights and Wagnerian operas to inspire militarism in Germany. The Nazis called themselves Aryans and adopted the Indo-European swastika. The Indo-European word *aryo* means "noble or ruler." Their swastika went counterclockwise. The Nazi swastika went clockwise. Some Aryans had blond hair and blue eyes, but others had dark skin. The Nazis found the latter fact inconvenient and ignored it.

Meanwhile, Benito Mussolini reminded Italians of the Roman Empire's glorious past. The Fascist salute was a revision of the ancient Roman salute. The Romans clenched their right hands over their hearts, and then opened their hands and extended their arms. (*Star Trek's* Romulans use the latter salute. Romulans are essentially Romans with spaceships.)

Mussolini was not the only ruler to use the legendary glory of the Roman Empire. The title *czar* comes from the Gothic word *kaisar,* which comes from *Caesar.* This is also the source of the title *kaiser.* Recently, Saddam Hussein made speeches about the glorious past of Babylon. Hussein compared himself with the Babylonian king and conqueror Nebuchadnezzar.

The Romans had their own legends. According to the *Aeneid,* the Trojan hero Aeneas founded the town of Lavinium near Rome. Two other heroes, Romulus and Remus, founded Rome itself. They were the sons of the war god Mars (Ares). Their evil uncle left them in the wilderness to die, but a female wolf adopted and raised them. The Romans used these legends of semidivine heroes to promote a militaristic culture. Real heroes like Horatius Cocles, who made a legendary stand with two companions against the Etruscans, promoted this culture. Finally, "Julius Caesar, a subtle propagandist, began to create his own legends" (Cavendish 1989,

168). The Romans even began deifying their late emperors. Then living emperors started believing their own propaganda. Caligula actually thought he was a god. His reign, though short, was fascinating. At least those who could watch from a safe distance thought so. His reign ended when he backed into a Praetorian Guard officer's sword.

Recently, cult leader Vernon Howell adopted the name, David Koresh. He named himself for the biblical king, David, and the Persian ruler, Cyrus. (*Koresh* is a derivative of *Cyrus.*) Again, we see the use of legends to influence behavior.

Mana and the Halo Effect (Perceptions of Power)

> Perceptions of power are often as effective as real power.

These examples show how people use myths and legends to gain *mana*. Mana is a supernatural force or divine power that resides in gods and sacred objects. When people associate themselves with legendary heroes, others perceive them as having *mana*. Image is often as important as substance. People follow the leader and do his or her bidding.

The *halo effect* is an organizational psychology concept similar to mana. Technical expertise is a source of informal authority in organizations and society. Some experts gain an aura of general competence. People assume they are experts on everything (Klein and Ritti 1984). For example, the Physicians for Social Responsibility advocate nuclear disarmament. Medical doctors know no more about strategic nuclear weapons than most people; however, people assume doctors are right because they are doctors. This is an example of the halo effect.

Use of Legends in Proselytization

> Christianity achieved worldwide growth by using local legends to convert the natives.

It is useful to study the organizational and cultural aspects of religions, which are organizations of people. We will examine Judeo-Christian and other religions from this position.

Early Christianity made very successful use of real and fictional heroes. Saints and martyrs became role models for Christians. Some saints were real people; however, "some Christian legends took over pagan figures and motifs. Saint Hippolytus was dragged to death by horses, as was his namesake, the son of the Greek hero Theseus" (Cavendish 1979, 214). The story of Saint George and the dragon was a revision of the legend of Perseus and Andromeda. Saint Brigid of Ireland may have originally been a pagan goddess. The story of Saints Barlaam and Joasaph may have been an adaptation of an Indian legend of the Buddha. The number of apostles, 12, equals the number of major Roman deities. Christmas falls suspiciously near the winter solstice, a major pagan holiday. Christmas decorations include elements of the Druid religion, such as a tree and mistletoe. Easter falls near the beginning of spring. Its theme of resurrection coincides with fertility symbols such as chicks, eggs, lambs, and rabbits. The Scandinavians, in turn, may have adapted the story of Jesus' crucifixion to their god Odin. Odin voluntarily hangs on the World Ash Tree to gain wisdom. His own sacred weapon, a spear, pierces him. He dies and rises again (Crossley-Holland 1980).

This analysis shows the outstanding success of a 1900-year-old mass marketing venture. Og Mandino's *The Greatest Salesman in the World* (1968) has the apostle Paul receive 10 ancient scrolls on salesmanship from the world's greatest merchant. Before receiving the scrolls, Paul's preaching had merely antagonized his audiences. Yet Paul later sold Christianity to the Roman world. In the book, Paul hears a voice. "Even the word of God must be sold to the people or they will hear it not. . . . Did I not speak in parables so that all might understand?" (p. 109). To Paul, this was a divine revelation. To us, it is a lesson in organizational behavior.

A parable is an allegorical story or symbolic narrative. Parables include legends, lore, fables, and myths. Aesop's Fables are parables. Parables can teach moral lessons or influence behavior.

As a Christian missionary in pagan times, how would one convert pagans? Would one attack the pagan religion and anger the prospective customers? Wouldn't it be better to superimpose Christianity on the pagan religion? Suppose the pagans had a spring fertility rite with themes of rebirth after the death of winter. Instead of displacing the pagan holiday, the missionary would superimpose the Christian one. There is a lesson here for those trying to change organizational cultures today.

Influence of Legends on Corporate Behavior

> Company legends influence corporate culture and behavior. Individuals can achieve heroic status.

Heroes and legends reflect an organization's attitudes, values, and beliefs. Thomas Edison and Charles Steinmetz are legendary heroes at General Electric (Deal and Kennedy 1982). Thomas Watson, Sr. enjoys similar status at IBM. J. Willard Marriott, Sr., is a larger-than-life figure at Marriott Hotels.

> *You think of Tom Watson, Sr., coming in after a hard day of selling pianos to farmers, and reporting to his headquarters in Painted Post, New York. And you think of what he became and why. You picture J. Willard Marriott, Sr., at that first food stand in Washington, D.C. And you see him now, at eighty-two, still worrying about a single lobby's cleanliness, although his food stand is a $2 billion enterprise. (Peters and Waterman 1982, 319)*

Some corporate heroes assume larger-than-life proportions. "These days, people like Watson and A. P. Giannini at Bank of America take on roles of mythic proportions that the real persons would have been hard-pressed to fill" (p. 75).

Tom Peters and Nancy Austin (1985) tell the following story. A Procter & Gamble manager saw an hourly employee bring in a bag of Jif peanut butter jars. The employee saw the jars in a store. The labels were uneven and sloppy. He did not want people to see poor-quality P&G products, or even labeling. He bought all the jars and trusted the company to pay him back. The company did. This story has probably spread through P&G and reinforces its commitment to excellence. The story also proves that frontline P&G employees have autonomy and pride in their company.

Another P&G story involves a sales manager who called a manufacturing manager in the middle of the night. "George, you've got a problem with a bar of soap down here." The sales manager insisted that the manufacturing manager come "down here." This meant a 300-mile trip in about five hours.

> *After you've finished your first three-hundred mile ride through the back hills of Tennessee at seventy miles an hour to look at one damned thirty-four-cent bar of soap, you understand that Procter & Gamble Company is very, very serious about product quality. (p. 327)*

Peters and Austin recount other stories. McDonald's founder Ray Kroc revoked a franchise after finding one fly on the premises. The fly didn't fit in with Quality, Service, Cleanliness, and Value. After this story circulated, every other McDonald's made a special effort to make sure there were no flies.

Stories do not even have to be true to be valuable.

> *[Alan] Wilkins concluded that some kinds of stories were powerful ways to motivate, teach and spread enthusiasm, loyalty, and commitment; others served an equally powerful purpose: to perpetuate cynicism, distrust, and disbelief. . . . The stories may not be factual, but that's wholly beside the point. What is valuable about them is that they reveal underlying beliefs or doubts people feel but are unwilling to confess to you directly. (pp. 328–329)*

Look at Figure 1.2 again. Stories help us understand and change an organization's culture.

Magic and sorcery are imaginary. Their underlying social and psychological aspects are very real

---

Magic is useful if we consider its underlying psychological and sociological aspects. Tarot cards have existed for more than 600 years. The value of these cards lies in their psychological implications. Each card has an assigned meaning. Their usefulness lies in the user's perception of their relation to his or her life. In this role, they are like Rorschach ink patterns. A skilled fortune-teller (reader) can relate the cards to the subject's life. This can stimulate introspection and reflection. This is especially true if the subject believes Tarot cards are magic. Thus, Tarot cards can predict or change the subject's future. It's not magic, however. It's psychology.

Some Tarot cards have meanings that are important to business organizations. We will see these later.

In summary, myths and legends serve the following purposes.

- They are role models for human behavior.
- They reflect the values of an organization.
- They influence cultures and behavior.

Importance of Culture

Organizational culture is a critical factor in success or failure. Culture drives behavior.

Organizational success may hinge on cultural change. Hradesky (1988) cites cultural change as a factor in productivity and quality improvement (PQI). PQI includes technical aspects like statistical process control (SPC) and design of experiments. Technology, however, cannot achieve results by itself. "In order for a company to successfully implement the PQI process, there must be a change in its culture that allows the improvements to be achieved and maintains the spirit and effort that led to the improvements" (p. 15). *Culture has a critical role in assuring product and service quality.*

ASD (Automatic Systems Development) Company's continuous quality improvement program recognized the need for cultural change. This meant a change in the "values and beliefs that influence day-to-day behavior and operations." ASD recognized that the quality culture had to pervade the organization. This required commitment from senior management. Upper management had to communicate this commitment throughout the organization (Courchaine and Williams 1992).

Cultural change is vital in implementing total quality management (TQM). Professor Eugene Melan (1992) asks, "How do you cause a permanent change in thinking and behavior?" Cultural change takes a long time in a big organization. Few companies have instilled the necessary changes. Professor Melan cites General Electric, British Airways, and Xerox as examples of success. Cultural change takes constancy of purpose and constant effort by management. Clausewitz (1976, Book 2, chap. 7) cites perseverance as a vital factor in achieving success. Management must persevere to overcome obstacles to cultural change. Among these are ingrained resistance and conflict with existing values (Melan 1992).

Culture is a critical factor in organizational success. A strong culture unifies an organization's members. A strong culture leads to predictable and reliable behavior by the members. "Without exception, the dominance and coherence of culture proved to be an essential quality of the excellent companies. . . . Everyone at Hewlett-Packard knows that he or she is supposed to be innovative. Everyone at Procter & Gamble knows that product quality is the sine qua non" (Peters and Waterman 1982, 75–76).

Culture as an Organization's True Name

A company's culture is its soul, or true name.

In magic, the name of a thing IS the thing. . . . The name contains in itself the essence of the animal's being, the quality which makes it what it is and not something else.

—Richard Cavendish, *Man, Myth, and Magic:
An Illustrated Encyclopedia of the Supernatural*

*Dragon: "You threaten me? With what?"
Wizard: "With your name, Yevaud."*

—Ursula LeGuin, *A Wizard of Earthsea*

This dragon obviously didn't go around introducing himself as "Yevaud." He would never reveal his real name! He had a common name, or nickname, for everyday use. In LeGuin's "The Rule of Names," he took human shape and went by "Mr. Underhill." In that story too, a wizard discovered his true name—but didn't live to regret it. It is interesting to note that LeGuin's father, Alfred Krueber, was an anthropologist.

Many primitive societies believed that each person had a secret or true name. If a magician discovered it, he or she gained power over the person (Cavendish 1970). This idea also appears in the story, "Rumplestiltskin." To defeat the gnome and save her firstborn child, the princess had to guess his name.

Even today, among the Yanomami Indians of Brazil, "Parents are forbidden to speak the birth names of living children, for fear others will have a power over them." This is according to Todd Lewin in his article "Tale of Horror Haunts Brazilian Tribe," published in the *Times Leader* of Wilkes-Barre, Pennsylvania on 19 September 1993.

In LeGuin's story, the hero said he was an even match for the dragon. Knowing the dragon's name made up for the latter's superior strength. If they fought, either could win. If our competitor is bigger and stronger, it is useful to have an edge like knowing its true name. Unfortunately, magic works only in fairy tales and legends. Or can it work in the real world? Consider the Wizard of Oz, the mundane showman who turned technology into magic. Everyone thought Oz was a wizard—until Toto slipped behind the curtain.

Psychology—the "Man Behind the Curtain"

The true name is a set of attitudes, values, beliefs, aspirations, and desires.

Sorcerers probably did use people's true names to control them. The name was not a simple word like *Yevaud*. It was probably the subject's attitudes, motivations, values, desires, hopes, and fears. These could even include the subject's belief in magic. Knowing a person's true name means knowing what makes him or her tick. If we know this, it is easier to manipulate the person. It also helps us predict his or her actions. Miyamoto Musashi hints at this in the chapter "To Become the Enemy." (Fire Book). This means mentally putting yourself in the other person's place. If the other person is an enemy, what are his or her fears? We can extend this to nonadversarial situations like marketing and sales.

Marketing consultant Robert Gropper (1992) cites Rapp and Collins' *The Great Marketing Turnaround*. Rapp and Collins (1990) urge readers to understand their prospective customers' or clients' attitudes and behavioral and psychological patterns. Learn your customer's name. This doesn't mean his or her use name, like Tom, Dick, or Mary. It means his or her true name.

This lesson about individual psychology applies to organizations. Organizations have attitudes, values and beliefs, too. They are the corporate culture.

Changing the Corporate Culture

> We create a better corporate culture by evoking the virtues of our employees.

The Wizard of Oz had no magical powers. Nonetheless, he successfully granted the wishes of Dorothy's companions. He gave the scarecrow a brain, the tin woodman a heart, and the cowardly lion courage. The audience knew Oz's physical gifts had no magical properties. Oz merely evoked virtues that were already in the characters. The characters always had these virtues, but did not believe they did. Oz's symbolic gifts gave the characters belief in their own virtues.

In *Man of La Mancha*, Don Quixote treats the barmaid Aldonza as a noble lady, Dulcinea. At first, she ridicules him. Nonetheless, he persists. We see a change in her character as the story proceeds. At the end, she declares, "I AM Dulcinea!"

Dale Carnegie (1977, 207) advised, "Give the dog a good name." This means attributing a desirable trait to a person even if he or she lacks it.

"Assume and state openly that the other party has the virtue you want him to develop." The person often tries to live up to your expectations. The trait becomes part of his or her psychological makeup. Carnegie cites the example of Warden Lawes who treated his prisoners at Sing Sing as honorable gentlemen. Many of the prisoners responded to this treatment. The same approach achieved "the startling transformation of a humble Belgian Cinderella" into a lady. The principle is: *Evoke the virtues in people.*

Psychological Transformation Through Role-Playing

> By acting out a role long enough, we become what we act.

People and groups can gain virtues by playing roles. In Kurosawa Akira's semihistorical drama *Kagemusha,* Takeda Nobukado finds a thief who resembles his brother Shingen. Nobukado spares the thief from execution and trains him to act as Shingen's double. The idea is to fool the clan's enemies. The thief learns to imitate Shingen's mannerisms and even his way of thinking. Shingen receives a mortal wound while besieging Noda Castle. Before dying, he orders his followers to conceal his death. Now the thief must play the role full time. By doing so, he *becomes* Takeda Shingen.

Nobukado speculates on what the end of the masquerade will do to the man's psyche. An accident reveals the thief as a double. The Takeda clan pays him for his services and releases him, however, he cannot free himself from the dead lord's identity. When he watches Shingen's funeral, he acts as if he were watching his own. He follows the Takeda Army to the disastrous battle of Nagashino. His reaction is as if Shingen's ghost were watching the end of his clan. The double finally runs onto the field to die with the Takeda warriors. His last act is to try to save the Takeda war banner.

The science fiction author Kurt Vonnegut Jr. writes the following about his short story "Mother Night." "We are what we pretend to be so we must be careful about what we pretend to be" (Klein and Ritti 1984, 175). This means that, by acting out a role long enough, we become what we act. We can use this to create positive organizational change. We can play Pygmalion to our subordinates and followers. If we treat hourly workers like valuable retainers, we will get valuable retainers. If we give them autonomy and training, we can evoke responsibility and initiative. The section on motivation will discuss the results Johnsonville Sausage achieved with hourly workers.

> We can use these principles to shape our organization's culture or true name.

We can create or change our organization's name. We can follow Dale Carnegie's advice to give our organization a good name. Myths, legends, and magic have roles to play here. Peters and Waterman (1982, 75) cite Bruno Bettelheim, author of *On the Uses of Enchantment*. "Bettelheim emphasizes the historically powerful role of fairy tales and myths in shaping meaning in our lives. . . . These stories, myths, and legends appear to be very important, *because they convey the organization's shared values, or culture.*" [author's emphasis]

Stewardship—A Feature of Top Performers

> Stewardship means the leaders exist for the benefit and well-being of the organization.

The prince is the first servant of his state.
—Frederick II of Prussia, Memoirs of the House of Brandenburg

Kagemusha also shows the vital concept of stewardship. There is a stark contrast between the behavior of Shingen's son Katsuyori and that of his generals. The generals see themselves as stewards or trustees of the Takeda clan. Takeda Nobukado and the generals Yamagata Masakage, Baba Nobuharu, and Naito Masatoyo always act for the welfare of the clan. Katsuyori's ego is his primary motivator. He has a chip on his shoulder because he lives in the shadow of his father's glory. He needs to show everyone that he is as good a general as his father. At Nagashino, Katsuyori is clearly not in control of himself. The three generals resign themselves to death. "We will meet again—with Shingen." (All three fell in the actual battle.) Nobukado survives, but his expression is of utmost horror. Katsuyori has thrown away everything Nobukado had dedicated his life to preserving. (Turnbull in *Battles of the Samurai* (1987) suggests that *Kagemusha* is unfair to Katsuyori. Nagashino was not exactly the one-sided massacre that the movie showed.)

We see the concept of stewardship in Caesar Augustus' lament after the Battle of Teutobergen Forest. "Quintilius Varus, give back my legions!" The legions were Augustus' resource. Varus was their steward. Augustus considered losing to German barbarians poor stewardship.

Here is stewardship in a modern context. "The CEO takes as the purpose of the company to remain in business forever, to provide meaningful employment for the people, useful goods and services for the public, and a fair return to the shareholders, *in that order of priority*" (Tribus 1992, 31).

Symbols

> Pictures are a powerful way to communicate ideas. Symbols are an important part of the corporate culture.

People and organizations have used symbols for centuries. Japanese warlords had *uma-jirushi* (horse insignia), or personal standards. Oda Nobunaga used a huge red umbrella, and Tokugawa Ieyasu had a golden fan. Toyotomi Hideyoshi added a golden gourd to his standard for each victory. People began calling it the thousand-gourd standard. This shows how an organizational myth can grow. Even the Napoleon of Japan could not have had time to fight a thousand battles. Nonetheless, Hideyoshi gained a reputation for invincibility. We have already discussed Takeda Shingen's banner with its quote from Sun Tzu's *The Art of War.* Samurai of the Ii clan wore red armor and earned the name Red Devils.

General Patton's ivory-handled revolvers were his personal symbol. He had captured them from a Mexican general during the Pershing expedition. Roman legions used an eagle, with the letters SPQR (Senate and People of Rome).

Sports teams name themselves for swift or dangerous animals, or warlike societies. Football teams are Bears (Chicago and Cornell species), Bengals, Lions (Detroit and Nittany varieties), Buffaloes, Broncos, Vikings, Redskins, and Trojans. Team banners display the symbol, and someone dresses as the mascot. The mascot symbolizes the team. Animals also can symbolize countries. There are the American eagle, British lion, and Russian bear.

Recently, IBM adopted Charlie Chaplin as a symbol. He is friendly and nonthreatening to people who see computers as intimidating. He is far more human than the blue and white IBM logo. Merrill-Lynch has its bull, and the Dreyfus Group has its lion. Scudder uses a ship pilot and calls its shareholder newsletter "At the Helm."

Personal standard of Takeda Shingen.

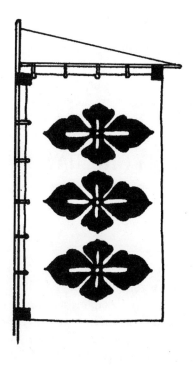

Should Procter & Gamble retire its man in the moon symbol? Some misguided people believe the symbol is satanic. They are pressuring P&G to stop using it. The symbol has nothing to do with Satanism or the occult. It started in the 1850s, when P&G made candles and soap. Many wharfhands were illiterate and needed a way to tell the boxes apart. They began making crosses on the candle boxes. Then they began vying with each other to create imaginative markings. One man made a star in a circle. Another made a cluster of stars. A quarter moon with a human profile soon joined the stars. Eventually, P&G began marking all its candle boxes with the moon and stars.

Later, P&G stopped using the symbol. When it did, a jobber rejected a shipment of P&G candles. The jobber thought the candles weren't genuine P&G products. The man in the moon had become a symbol of P&G quality (Deal and Kennedy 1982). P&G's retiring the moon and stars trademark would be like the United States' retiring Uncle Sam or the bald eagle.

Tom Peters (1987, 10) criticizes companies that discard their traditional symbols. "In rapid succession, U.S. Steel became USX, American Can became Primerica, and United Airlines became Allegis for a while. . . . The new names share a common trait—they're all more vague than their predecessors." Peters also says these companies lose their identities and sense of strategic purpose during mergers.

Our identity and sense of purpose define who we are. They tell us why we exist. Symbols help remind us of our identity.

PREDICTABILITY OF BEHAVIOR

> Organizational culture, norms, and customs are the best ways to assure predictable behavior. Rules cannot succeed by themselves.

All organizations seek predictability of action from their members (Klein and Ritti 1984). This is especially true in military organizations. In warfare and similar situations, discipline and predictability are vital to the safety of the group. Each person must rely on the other group members. Business and other civilian organizations also require predictability. People must know what behavior they can expect from others. Dharma, right conduct, or the Way is a source of predictability.

Rules and laws help make behavior predictable. The rule book is characteristic of mechanistic organizations. In these organizations, there is a rule to cover everything. Any organization must have some rules, however, we will later see that mechanistic organizations have trouble responding to dynamic competitive environments. Total reliance on rules and directives is not a good way to assure success.

Norms

> Norms and customs can support or undermine regulations.

Norms are "unwritten, perhaps unstated, mutual understandings as to what is appropriate behavior under given sets of conditions" (Klein and Ritti 1984, 64). Norms include the organizational culture. In a society or country, customs are norms. How do norms differ from rules and laws? Authority and official sanctions enforce laws, but not norms. Social pressure enforces conformance to norms. If the norms conflict with the laws, violation of a law may not result in social disapproval.

Norms' support of rules depends on the community's view of the prohibited or mandatory action. Prohibited actions can be *mala in se* or *mala prohibita*. Mala in se means inherently evil. Mala prohibita means they are illegal only because the rules say so (Anderson, Fox, and Twomey 1988). Social forces support and enforce rules against acts that are mala in se. They may not support rules against acts that are mala prohibita.

For example, the legal speed limit on New York superhighways is 55 mph. Exceeding the limit rarely brings social disapproval unless the driver also is drunk or reckless. In social discussions, most people will admit speeding. Many people see the 55 mph limit as a legal artifact and not a safety measure. The superhighway speed limits were once 65 mph. Their basis was the judgment of the engineers who designed the roads. Going 65 is mala prohibita—illegal because the rule says so. Americans have little respect for authority figures who use "because I say so" as a reason. People respond to such rules by looking for ways to get around them. The radar detector has been a classic response to the 55 mph speed limit. The use of the CB radio to report Smoky the Bear's position has been another.

Similarly, Prohibition failed because most people did not support it. It would have been impossible for speakeasies to flourish unless people looked the other way.

In countries like Japan, people are more amenable to authority. They may willingly obey rules with no more basis than "because I say so." This is not because the people don't think for themselves. It is because the society has an inherent respect for authority figures. In contrast, American culture respects nonconformance and individuality. The lone cowboy who makes his own rules is a hero of westerns. The western villain is not bad because he breaks rules. The good guy often breaks the rules. The villain is bad only because he hurts others. American culture even honors rebellion against authority. The Boston Tea Party is a famous example. In summary, norms vary widely among cultures.

In contrast with speeding, few people will admit drinking and driving. Many years ago, society tacitly accepted or winked at drunk driving. Today, society regards it as irresponsible. Society considers it mala in se, or at least inherently dangerous. People will often take a drunk's car keys, or otherwise discourage the drunk from driving. The same CB radio enthusiasts who give "Smoky" reports often report "Harvey Wallbanger" and "Willie Weaver." Some localities post the police telephone number on roads so that drivers with cellular phones can report drunks. This is an example of norms supporting the law or rule.

Norms and Corporate Performance

> Norms and culture strongly influence organizational performance.

Norms are not rules or policies. They do not even appear on paper. For example, IBM's manufacturing and research facilities do not have formal dress codes. At the East Fishkill site, everyone expects male managers and professionals to wear dress shirts and ties. Most do so, although there is no rule that makes it compulsory. At the Yorktown research site, even professional employees dress very casually. Blue jeans are within the norms.

If norms affected only dress, they wouldn't be very important; however, they also affect organizational behavior. Klein and Ritti (1984) cite blue-collar workers who limit output so the industrial engineers won't raise the work standards. A social norm can define "a fair day's work" (Miller 1985–1986).

In industry, the rule or standard may be 100 widgets per day. The norm among the workers may be 80 or 120, depending on their commitment to the organization. If the workers think beating the standard will bring a quota increase, they may hold back their full efforts. The group will censure rate busters. When there is mutual commitment between workers and the company, employees will vie to raise production. Social pressure will promote extra efforts. This is especially true in Japan. "If the other members of your group work hard and you don't, you will eventually be ostracized. And being excluded from the group is the most appalling thing any Japanese can imagine" (*Time-Life Library of Nations* 1985, 128).

Norms clearly affect organizational performance. The norms may support or obstruct the organization's goals. In government, business, and war, norms can work for or against us. We must consider norms in analyzing and changing organizational performance.

Roles

> A role is a norm that goes with a position or occupation. Roles and role pairs govern the behavior of the person holding the position.

All roles are norms, but not all norms are roles. Some norms apply to everyone. Roles are norms for positions and occupations. Roles are expectations about how someone in a certain position or occupation should act. Role behavior is a function of role pairs. For example, there are parent-child, doctor-patient, teacher-student, lawyer-client, and superior-subordinate role pairs. The role pair dictates the behavior of each person (Klein and Ritti 1984).

Why is the Japanese educational system so effective? The teacher-student role pair plays a vital role. Japanese students revere their teachers almost as parents. Students are attentive, and there are few classroom discipline problems. In turn, the teachers regard the opportunity to teach as an honor. In Japan, there are several applicants for each teaching position. Teachers enjoy high social status in Japan. We will now see how ancient India and Japan defined roles. *The basic principle is dharma, Tao, or Dō.*

Dharma or Right Conduct

> Each position or occupation has an inherent right conduct or Way.

Norms and role pairs look like impressive modern management concepts. The ideas, however, are several thousand years old.

Dharma's Origin—Social Castes

> Dharma and Dō came from the caste system; however, they are valid without a caste system.

Long ago, dharma applied to castes, or social classes and occupations. Under the caste system, one's social class and occupation were the same.

Hindu society had four castes. Brahmans were priests, who also served as teachers. The Kshatriyas were rulers and warriors. Vaisyas were merchants, farmers, and townspeople. Sudras were servants and menials. Although Sudras were the lowest caste, they were still Aryans (Indo-Europeans). Men of higher castes could marry Sudra women (Buck 1973). Then there were outcastes, or untouchables. Japan had a similar caste system. The warriors were the highest caste. Next were peasants (farmers), followed by artisans, and then merchants. There also were Eta, or untouchables.

Each caste had its own dharma. The Japanese had the Way of the Farmer, Way of the Carpenter, and Way of the Merchant. These forms of dharma, Tao, or Dō were occupation-specific roles. There also were role-pair dharmas: teacher-student, husband-wife, and so on. Van Nooten refers to dharma as "the doctrine of the moral law. . . . The moral law sustains and favors those creatures that abide by it, while thwarting those that trespass" (Buck 1973, xvii). Dharma has measurable and immediate effects on organizational performance. Sun Tzu cites "moral influence" as one of five critical factors in competition. His use of moral influence implies commitment. Moral influence comes from adherence to dharma. The section on commitment discusses this.

In Asia, dharma, Tao, and Dō promoted and enforced social conformity. Everyone knew his or her place. It was very difficult to cross caste boundaries. In theory, a wealthy merchant could not buy his or her way into the ruling class. (As with all matters involving money, there were doubtlessly exceptions.) The *Bhagavad Gita* says, "And do thy duty, even if it be humble, rather than another's, even if it is great. To die in one's duty is life; to live in another's is death" (Mascaro 1962, 59). Even today, "The typical Japanese is most comfortable knowing exactly where he or she stands relative to people above, below, and on either side" (*Time-Life Library of Nations* 1985, 24).

> Today, dharma goes by names like code of ethics, and occupational myth.

Modern society does not approve of castes or class boundaries. Instead, we admire people who work their way from the lower classes into the upper classes. The term *self-made man* is a compliment. Modern Japan is a meritocracy. Achievement, and not birth, dictates the modern Japanese's social class. Dharma still yields predictability, but in other ways. Today, dharma goes by names like code of ethics and occupational myth. Occupational myths are images of the ideal practitioner of an occupation. They represent the ideals of an occupation or profession (Klein and Ritti 1984). The *code of ethics* and the *occupational myth* are forms of dharma.

Why do most people trust doctors? The Hippocratic oath is part of the dharma of the physician. It requires the doctor to act for the benefit of his or her patient. The Code of Ethics of the National Society of Professional Engineers requires engineers to "hold paramount the public safety." This is part of the dharma of the engineer. All codes of ethics for professionals require the professional to provide clients with loyal service. Codes of ethics promote reliability in behavior. They tell us what to expect from a doctor, lawyer, or other professional.

Dharma in Organic Organizations

> Dharma is the keystone of organic systems. It makes behavior predictable, while allowing flexibility and adaptability.

We will examine mechanistic and organic organizations in detail later. For now, a mechanistic organization works through formal rules and structure. If there is no rule to cover a new situation, personnel must wait until superiors develop one. Such organizations are almost helpless in rapidly changing business environments. Organic organizations are adaptive and creative. Their members react to new problems without waiting for orders. Even the lowest level worker takes initiatives. Suppose a customer complains to a salesclerk. In a mechanistic organization, the clerk must consult the boss or rule book. In an organic organization, the clerk resolves the problem. He or she looks to the organization's culture for guidance.

> Principles (culture, morals, or dharma) are an organization's compass.

But I am constant as the northern star,
Of whose true-fix'd and resting quality
There is no fellow in the firmament.

—William Shakespeare,
Julius Caesar, act III, scene i, line 60

Stephen Covey (1991) compares organizational culture to a compass. Covey says a road map (mechanistic procedure) is useful only when you are on a road (predictable environment). If you are in a wilderness, it is almost useless. A compass, however, always points to true north. If you have a good compass (organizational culture, principles), you can find your way. Covey says today's competitive environment is more like a wilderness than a road. We can recall Tom Peters' discussion of the turbulent, ever-changing environment.

Dharma is the keystone of an organic organization. It replaces or supports the rule book as the source of predictability. It assures predictability of behavior without stifling judgment and initiative. Covey cites the role of this compass in customer service. He went to a hotel and wanted room service. The kitchen was not open, but the employee he spoke to offered to get him something. "Our mission is to serve your needs." Covey said of the employee, "That person had a compass." A sense of mission, and not mechanistic rules, guided the employee's behavior.

Compare the employees of a mechanistic and an organic organization. In the mechanistic organization, the rule book says, "Come to work at 7:00. Assemble widgets by doing A, B, and C. Go home at 3:30." Now consider an organic organization. The dharma of a machinist is to use his or her skills for the organization's benefit. Dharma requires the machinist to do the best work possible. The machinist also learns new skills as the opportunity or need arises. Common terms for the machinist's dharma include *craftsmanship* and *pride in workmanship.*

Specifications, or customer requirements, govern the machinist's work; however, the machinist, and not the rule book, is responsible for working out the details of the job. The machinist may suggest or create ways to improve the job. Dharma, and not a rule book, is the mechanism that controls the machinist's behavior.

The next chapter will examine the role of the manager or leader. Kshatriya Dharma and Bushidō are the Way of management and leadership. The manager who follows this Way leads the organization to success and victory.

2

The Architect of Victory

*By victory gained in crossing swords with individuals, or enjoining bat-
tle with large numbers, we can attain power and fame for ourselves or
our lord. This is the virtue of strategy. . . .The Way of the Ichi School is
the spirit of winning, whatever the weapon and whatever its size.*
— Miyamoto Musashi, *A Book of Five Rings*

A business professional's goal is to win success for employers or
clients. He or she uses appropriate physical, organizational, and
management tools to do this.

THE WAY OF THE WARRIOR

The Way of the warrior is the path to success in business. The Japanese
call this *Bushidō*, the Way of the man of war. India had *Kshatriya Dharma*,
the right conduct of the Kshatriya. The Kshatriyas included the professional, governing, and military occupations. According to the *American
Heritage Dictionary of the English Language*, *ksei*, or "to rule," is the Indo-
European root of Kshatriya. It is the root of *Shah* and *satrap*. It shows up
in chess—the game of kings. Checkmate is *shāh māt*, "the King is dead
(or perplexed)." As the Persian *khshaya*, it became *Xerxes*. We will now
study the Way of the warrior.

Weapons as Instruments of Competition

> Think, "weapon = tool." The tool can be physical, mental, organizational, or managerial.

Musashi's *A Book of Five Rings* often refers to weapons. A weapon need not be a destructive implement. A weapon is an instrumentality. It is any means of achieving a goal. This concept has parallels in classical Western cultures. A Greek hoplite was a soldier, a user of weapons. The word *hoplon*, however, also means tool or implement. The Latin word *armamenta* means implements or equipment. To understand the Way of strategy, think of a weapon as any physical, organizational, or mental resource.

Clausewitz (1976, Book 2, chap. 1) wrote, "The art of war is the art of using the given means in combat. . . . In its wider sense the art of war includes all activities that exist for the sake of war, such as the creation of the fighting forces, their raising, armament, equipment, and training." The conduct of war is "the free use of the given means, appropriate to each individual occasion" (Book 2, chap. 2). This means using appropriate instruments of competition.

Preparing to Wage Competition

> Companies prepare for business campaigns much as nations used to prepare for war.

In business, the given means are organizational, physical, psychological, and managerial tools and resources. A business enterprise raises capital and hires employees. It buys equipment and trains employees. These activities are preparations for competitive activity. A company may sell stocks or bonds to raise money for a competitive venture. If it is a potential competitor, this should alert us to danger. In ancient and medieval times, a sovereign had to raise money before starting a war. He or she could tax subjects, sell assets, ask for donations, take money from the treasury, or borrow money. ("Buy War Bonds!") Businesses cannot levy taxes, and few people will give them money; however, they can sell assets or equity and incur debt. A cash-rich company can strike almost at will. We must ask ourselves what the competitor plans to do with the funds it is raising. Maybe its plans involve our market share.

We wage competition by using and directing the available resources. We match our actions to the situation and environment. In this sense, there is no difference between business and war. The activities Clausewitz describes occur routinely in business.

Musashi shows similarities among the four professions of medieval Japan: warrior, farmer, artisan, and merchant. "Like a trooper, the carpenter sharpens his own tools" (Musashi 1974, Ground Book). The sword is the tool of the warrior. The carpenter uses the axe and plane. The farmer employs agricultural implements and watches the weather. Timing is important to the merchant, in "the rise and fall of capital." Musashi noted this fact hundreds of years before macroeconomics became a recognizable science.

We've examined the tools of competition and preparation for competition. We will now look at management of human and physical resources.

Management of Human and Physical Resources

> Competitions between organizations involve management of human and physical resources.

The Book of Five Rings makes a clear connection between business management and the Way of strategy. Musashi compares the Ways of the warrior and artisan. The artisan is the carpenter or architect (Musashi 1974, Ground Book).

> *The foreman should take into account the abilities and limitations of his men, circulating among them and asking nothing unreasonable. He should know their morale and spirit and encourage them when necessary. This is the same as the principle of strategy. In large-scale strategy the superior man will manage many subordinates dexterously, bear himself correctly, govern the country, and foster the people, thus preserving the ruler's discipline.*

The responsibilities of the architect, business manager, and general are the same. The architect lays plans to construct buildings, and directs their completion. He or she assigns and directs human and physical resources to get the best possible results. A general creates and executes plans to win victories. The business manager develops organizational goals and strategies. He or she then manages human and physical resources to achieve them. Any leader must manage subordinates or followers dexterously. This is the clear connection between the Way of strategy and the work of a business manager or organizational leader.

The Warrior as the Product of a Lifetime of Training

A professional is the product of extensive training and lifelong exercise. Continuous improvement applies to people as well as to organizations.

Bushidō is the Way of the warrior. To the Japanese, a Way is far more than a job or occupation. The Japanese character for Dō is the same as the Chinese *Tao*. It is similar to India's dharma, duty, or right conduct. It means a way of life.

Bushidō governed every aspect of the life of the samurai, or Japanese knight. The samurai began training in boyhood. He exercised with the tools of his profession—the long sword, short sword, dagger, spear, and bow. He learned to fight with or without armor, and with his empty hands if necessary. The Japanese warrior was the product of a lifetime of training, exercise, and discipline.

The samurai's counterpart was the European knight. Like the samurai, a knight began training in boyhood. The squire practiced with sword, axe, and mace on horseback and on foot. He hacked at pels, or wooden stakes, for hours at a time. He practiced with the lance until he could drive it through a tiny ring. He learned to control a horse with his legs to leave both arms free. He learned to fight while wearing 60 or 70 pounds of armor. He also had to distinguish friend from foe through his tiny helmet visor. To encourage knights to maintain their skills, there were tournaments in peacetime.

Common peasant soldiers could not hope to defeat a knight. This wasn't just because the knight had armor. Many infantry weapons could pierce or break armor. The man inside the armor was the reason. The peasants had to work the land for a living. They had little time to practice the martial arts. Although the peasant's weapon could kill, he rarely got the chance to land a solid blow. Professional infantrymen had better training than peasant levies. One knight, however, was still more powerful than several infantrymen. His equipment was usually better, but his training was the decisive factor.

The Welsh archer was the one notable exception. English longbowmen mowed down hundreds of French knights at Agincourt and Crécy. Becoming a longbowman, however, was almost like becoming a knight. A woodsman received his first bow when he was a boy. He learned to judge distances, trajectories, and the characteristics of different arrows. As he grew, he used larger bows. When he became a man, he had developed the strength to draw and fire the powerful six-foot longbow. Like the knight, the archer was the product of a lifetime of training.

How Technology Democratized Warfare

> The gun equalized low-skill troops and knights. A mechanistic system (volley fire) made low-skill troops effective.

Technology, in the form of the musket and crossbow, democratized warfare. Contrary to popular belief, it wasn't because they could penetrate armor at a distance. The Welsh longbow could do this, and do it better than the musket and crossbow. Even in the sixteenth century, armor could stop pistol fire. Many cavalrymen preferred to rely on the lance (Held 1957). The musket and arquebus were deadlier, but they could fire one shot a minute at most. A longbowman might fire 10 aimed shots in the same time.

Prince Louis Napoleon observed, "A first-rate English archer who, in a single minute, was unable to draw and discharge his bow 12 times with a range of 240 yards and who in these 12 shots once missed his man, was very lightly esteemed" (Hardy 1992, 68). Hardy adds, "The Prince's 240 yards is a low estimate of the longbow's extreme range."

Rudyard Kipling composed a poem ("Brown Bess") to honor the tower musket. This was the British infantry musket between 1700 and 1815. Kipling wrote that Brown Bess "danced her last dance" at Waterloo. The loose fit (windage) between the ball and barrel made the weapon easy to load. A soldier could fire six shots each minute; however, he had little chance of hitting an opponent even at 120 yards. A fourteenth century Welsh longbow, therefore, had twice the range and twice the rate of fire as an eighteenth century musket. The bow far outclassed the earlier matchlock muskets. Who would want a musket if he could use a longbow?

The answer is, very few people could use longbows. It took a lifetime of practice to make an archer.

The musket and crossbow were low-skill weapons that gave subprofessionals real combat capability. Infantry commanders could mass-produce death and sell it wholesale. A general no longer needed professional knights or infantry to wage war. He could hire peasants off the streets. He could hand them muskets and give them a few lessons. People with doubtful lineage and perfunctory training could now kill knights, as well as each other. Gunpowder gave everyone a chance to play a meaningful role in the sport of kings.

At Nagashino (1575), Takeda Katsuyori saw his enemy, Oda Nobunaga, form three lines of foot soldiers behind a palisade. Nobunaga's infantrymen were the lowest class of samurai. The Takeda cavalry were probably the best in Japan. Katsuyori ordered an attack, only to see the footmen shoot his men down with arquebus volleys. Katsuyori knew about arquebuses, but did not believe they could be so effective. He expected to lose a few men in the advance. The remainder would obliterate the Oda troops. Nobunaga, however, had organized his semiskilled labor into a lethal assembly line. Mechanistic training in volley fire made up for the arquebusiers' other deficiencies. Nobunaga won through effective use of his human resources.

During the late nineteenth century, assembly line workers didn't need diplomas to do their jobs. They didn't even need to speak English. According to the Taylor management school, all that was needed was a pair of hands and the ability to do a simple task. Workers could leave their brains at the factory gate. Military technology was similar. Soldiers didn't even have to be literate. ("I'm a sergeant. They don't pay me to think.") This approach won't work in modern business.

Does Technology Democratize Business Competition?

> Modern technology and mechanistic systems do *not* equalize skilled and unskilled workers.

Like the medieval knight or samurai, the modern professional is the product of a lifetime of training. The aspirant to a profession must begin to train in early childhood. For example, a prospective engineer or scientist must learn mathematics and science in grade and junior high school.

High school is almost too late to start. The aspirant must work hard in college. Would-be physicians then face another four years of medical school. Scientists and engineers may attend graduate school. Law school takes three years after college. The MBA degree requires about 18 months of study beyond a college degree.

Technology has not democratized business competition. Computers and even expert systems cannot replace human judgment. Businesses need people to whom a profession is a way of life. These are the knights of the twentieth century, today's samurai.

Blue-collar jobs are becoming less democratic too. Modern soldiers must maintain and use complicated machinery and electronics. Illiterate high school dropouts cannot fix modern tanks or jet aircraft. Today's military forces want recruits with high school diplomas. In industry, robots are now the pairs of hands. Workers must repair the robots and maintain pneumatic, hydraulic, and electronic systems. Dropouts cannot do these jobs.

Tom Peters and Robert Waterman, the authors of *In Search of Excellence* (1982), stand Taylorism on its head. The frontline service provider knows the most about the job he or she is doing. Peters (1989) uses the example of a team of hourly workers at Johnsonville Sausage. The team had the authority to recruit, hire, appraise, and dismiss its own members. Members learned new skills as necessary. The team

- Formulated and tracked annual budgets
- Made capital investment proposals
- Assumed full responsibility for quality control
- Monitored and improved productivity and quality
- Developed new products and packages

The modern blue- or grey-collar worker is the organization's man- or woman-at-arms. Although he or she is not a professional, this person has a critical role to play. The frontline service provider is the body of the organization, and is its strength.

The skill and experience of the frontline worker is a critical resource. Feigenbaum (1991, 207) writes, "the most underutilized resource of many companies is the knowledge and skill of employees." Remember that a weapon is an organizational resource. Musashi (1974, Ground Book) wrote, "you must make fullest use of your weaponry. It is false not to do so, and to die with a weapon yet undrawn." The Way of strategy requires that organizations avoid wasting, or leaving unused, the experience and knowledge of frontline workers.

The Need for Ongoing Professional Development

No one is a master of anything. Only a dead person has nothing more to learn. Life itself is a continuous struggle for self-improvement.

A student once asked the Zen master Deshimaru Taisen, "How many years must I practice *zazen* (Zen meditation)?"

The master replied "Until you die." (Deshimaru 1982, 3).

The need for ceaseless, unremitting training and practice pervades the Japanese attitude toward all arts and disciplines. Only a fool regards himself or herself as a master of anything, with nothing more to learn. This book sometimes refers to "masters of strategy." The word master is only comparative. What we call a master is an extremely advanced student of an art. He or she can teach others; however, if the master ceases to learn, others may surpass him or her. The Japanese view life itself as "a battle to achieve constant improvement" (Peters 1987, 272).

In the Asian martial arts, a black belt does not mean that one is an expert. The word for first degree black belt, *sho dan*, means "first step." Even the headmaster of a style continues to practice. He practices even if he holds a seventh or eighth degree black belt. Only a dead person has nothing more to learn. This is especially true in today's rapidly changing technological environment.

Changing technology can make much of what you learned in college obsolete in a few years. Only the basic principles remain the same. School provides these principles and teaches learning skills. This allows the professional to learn new technology throughout his or her working life.

Continual Learning and Improvement in Organizations

Constant improvement applies to organizations. The Japanese word *kaizen* means continual improvement. "The final unifying theme underlying manufacturing competitiveness is the *centrality of continual learning and improving*" (Hayes, Wheelwright, and Clark 1988, 342). Three of Deming's 14 points focus on constant improvement. (See the introduction for a list of the 14 points.) Continual improvement and willingness to learn are major factors in Japan's success.

Japanese characters for kaizen.

Japan: Openness to New Ideas

> Willingness to learn from outsiders is among Japan's principal success secrets. It yielded phenomenal results in the nineteenth and twentieth centuries.

Constant improvement and willingness to learn are major factors in Japan's economic success. Consider the founding of the Tokugawa Shōgunate at the start of the seventeenth century. The first Tokugawa Shōguns wanted to exclude foreign social influences and religions from Japan. They expelled all westerners, and forbade Japanese to travel abroad. All trade went through an island off Nagasaki. This protected Japanese culture from foreign influences, however, it also kept out technological advances. These included military advantages.

In 1853, Commodore Perry showed up at Edo (Tokyo) with several warships. He brought demands from President Millard Fillmore. The United States reasonably asked that Japan treat shipwrecked sailors humanely. A more onerous demand was that Japan open its ports to American ships. The Japanese noticed that Perry's steam-powered warships moved without benefit of wind or oars. They also saw modern cannon for the first time. Japanese small arms technology was still in the seventeenth century.

Many Japanese realized their country had to change. Otherwise the Europeans would dominate it, as they were doing to China. The Chinese regarded the "western barbarians" as racially and culturally inferior. They refused to learn from them. Feelings of superiority, however, were no match for modern weapons. The Japanese did not like barbarians either, but they recognized the West's superior technology. In a brief civil war, the Japanese overthrew the Shōgunate, and restored Imperial rule. The new government abolished the special privileges of the samurai class. In the early 1870s, Japan sent a delegation to study Europe.

Japan swiftly introduced Western technology and a compulsory educational system. By 1879, Japanese children were singing a "Civilization Ball Song." The song included desirable technological benefits—gas lamps, steam engines, carriages, cameras, telegraphs, newspapers, lightning rods, schools, and a postal system (*Time-Life Library of Nations* 1985).

The military saw other benefits, like ironclad battleships and machine guns. It adopted the best organizational structures Europe could offer: Prussian for the army and British for the navy. By 1894, the Japanese were ready to go to war. They defeated China in the Sino-Japanese War. Russia was the next victim. In 1905, the Japanese defeated the Russian Baltic Fleet at Tsushima. This was only 52 years after the arrival of Perry's ships in Japan. The Japanese admiral, Togo Heihachiro (1849–1934), began life as a samurai. As a young boy, he expected to grow up to carry two swords. At the height of his career, he commanded weapons no Japanese could have imagined in 1850. Japan went from a medieval country to a modern nation in less than 50 years.

After World War II, Japan's and most of Europe's industry lay in rubble. American companies could sell anything they made. There was a backlog of consumer demand from the war and little foreign competition. American businesses saw no need to listen to quality expert W. Edwards Deming. Some had used the quality management techniques of Walter Shewhart, Joseph Juran, and Deming for wartime production. Many of them discarded or forgot these techniques after the war. When Deming visited Japan in 1950, the Japanese listened enthusiastically. They began using his methods, including statistical process control. Within six weeks, some industrialists reported 30 percent productivity gains without new capital investment (Tribus 1992). Within 25 years, Japanese products were serious challengers in the United States. By 1992 (42 years later), they had taken over most of the consumer electronics market. Japanese automakers have a respectable share of the American auto market. Without import quotas, they would have more. We again see the results of Japan's belief in continuous learning and improvement.

During the past few years, American industry has been waking up. Managers are asking, "Who was this Deming fellow? What is statistical process control?" More Japanese than Americans can answer this question. Since 1951, the Union of Japanese Scientists and Engineers (JUSE) has awarded a Deming Prize for individual and corporate achievements in quality control.

THE MIND OF THE WARRIOR

Organizational Performance Begins in the Leader's Mind

> Quality, productivity, and competitiveness begin in the leader's mind. The intellect of the leader is the keystone of performance. Excellence depends on the leader's attitudes, values, beliefs, and conduct. This must be the right conduct of the leader. This is Bushidō, or *Kshatriya Dharma*—the Way of the warrior and king.

Masters of strategy have recognized this principle for thousands of years. Wu Ch'i (430–381 B.C.E.) said it concisely. "The responsibility for a martial host of a million lies in one man. He is the trigger of its spirit" (Sun Tzu 1963, 108).

Firearms expert Jeff Cooper (1990, 20) writes, "Man fights with his mind. His hands and weapons are simply extensions of his will, and one of the fallacies of our era is that equipment is the equivalent of force." The sword master Yagyu Munenori compared an army to the arms and legs of its general in *The Sword and the Mind* (1986).

> *Winning a battle by commanding a great army should be no different from winning a sword fight in a one-to-one combat. . . . Winning or losing by the sword depends on the mind. It is with the mind that you move your arms and legs. . . . The various armies are the general's arms and legs. Making the various forces work well means making the general's arms and legs work well.* (p. 51)

Armand Feigenbaum defines good management as *personal leadership in mobilizing the knowledge, skills, and positive attitudes of everyone.* Feigenbaum says quality is a way of managing an organization (Dooley 1990). Quality begins in the mind of the leader.

A human body is an organization. The brain is the general and the arms and legs are the soldiers. Conversely, the general is the brain of the army. A good general can move the army's units as if they were his or her arms and legs. In either case, organizational performance begins in the mind of the commander.

The Japanese martial arts emphasize mental training in addition to physical skills. The swordsman had to control his mind before he could govern a sword. Once he learned to rule his own mind, he could govern others effectively. Yagyu Muneyoshi (1986, 16) said, "Among those who control the world and protect the state, there's no one who doesn't employ swordsmanship in his mind." This principle makes the commander's mind itself a military target.

The Mind as a Target: Checkmating the Opponent

> The intellect of the leader is the keystone of performance. Checkmate, or *shAh mAt*, means destruction of this keystone.

"His [the general's] primary target is the mind of the opposing commander; the victorious situation, a product of his creative imagination. Sun Tzu realized that an indispensable preliminary to battle was to attack the mind of the enemy" (Sun Tzu 1963, 41). Remember that *checkmate* means, "the King is dead, or perplexed." Checkmate ends a chess game, no matter how many pieces the losing side has.

In ancient and medieval warfare, the king's death or discomfiture often ended a battle. The Normans won the Battle of Hastings (1066 C.E.) by killing King Harold. At Okehazama (1560 C.E.), Imagawa Yoshimoto had eight-to-one numerical superiority over Oda Nobunaga. Nobunaga's troops surprised the enemy's headquarters during a thunderstorm and killed Yoshimoto. The Imagawa Army simply dispersed (Turnbull 1987). King Darius lost the Battle of Arbela (331 B.C.E.) to Alexander of Macedon by fleeing the field. Had he stayed, he would have encouraged the parts of his army that were standing firm. A strong organization, however, always has a qualified successor. Nelson's death at Trafalgar (1805) did not put the English out of business.

The *Mahabharata*, an ancient Sanskrit epic, provides an outstanding example of attacking the opponent's mind. The Battle of Kurukshetra was India's Ragnarok, or Armageddon. There, the Pandavas met the Kauravas for a final settlement of their differences. Drona, the Kaurava commander, was unkillable as long as he held a weapon. Bhima, a Pandava, cried out that Aswatthaman (Drona's son) was dead. This was a lie, but Drona threw down his weapons in complete dejection. Then Drishtadyumna, Bhima's brother-in-law, killed him. No one could kill Drona in battle, but Bhima struck him down by attacking his spirit (Buck 1973).

Attacking the opponent's self-confidence is often more effective than attacking his or her soldiers. Once the opposing general suffers confusion, fear, or apprehension, you can easily beat his or her army. Modern football coaches sometimes call a time-out just before the opponents try a field goal. The idea is to make the placekicker wait and worry about the kick.

In a civilian organization, checkmate rarely involves the death of the leader. The leader does not fall like Harold at Hastings, or Nelson at Trafalgar. He or she flees—usually mentally—like Darius. Checkmate means the king is irresolute, indecisive, disoriented, or perplexed. *Checkmate does not require the services of an opponent.*

Organizational and Personal Morale

> *Weapons change but man who uses them changes not at all. To win battles you do not beat weapons—you beat the soul of man of the enemy man.*
>
> —General George S. Patton

The Book of Five Rings discusses the concept, "To Penetrate the Depths." It means destroying the enemies' spirit and demoralizing them. Clausewitz (1976) wrote that demoralization of the enemy is often more important than destruction of his or her assets. The effect of battle "is rather a killing of the enemy's spirit than of his men" (Book 4, chap. 11). "In the engagement, the loss of morale has proved the major decisive factor" (Book 4, chap. 4). Setbacks in battle, whether real or imaginary, affect the commander's personal morale.

In the play *Julius Caesar*, Cassius' death at Phillipi comes from an imaginary setback. It is an example of checkmate without the services of an opponent. Cassius' servant thinks he sees enemy horsemen capture Titinius, Cassius' friend. Cassius thinks his side has lost the battle, and orders the servant to kill him. The horsemen are actually Brutus' men. They were giving Titinius a victory wreath for Cassius. Brutus says of Cassius' suicide, "O Julius Caesar, thou art mighty yet! Thy spirit walks abroad, and turns our swords/ In[to] our own proper entrails" (act v, scene iii, line 95).

Does psychology play a role in business? The Japanese know Americans are often impatient. They take advantage of this when negotiating with Americans. For example, they may serve tea, sit, wait, and say nothing. The Americans are in a hurry to get down to business. They will often make the first move and give away their position (Musashi 1982). The Americans checkmate themselves, even if they have more pieces on the board.

Dangers of Emotion and Ego

The leader or manager must rule his or her own mind to command effectively. Emotion and ego have no place in strategy. Sun Tzu (1963) warned against recklessness, cowardice, quick temper, a delicate sense of honor, and excessive compassion. These character defects "inevitably" cause the army's defeat and the general's death.

The commentator Tu Mu gave an example in which a commander's temper got the better of him. The Emperor T'ai Wu was besieging the Sung general Tsang Chih in a fortified city. By custom, generals exchanged gifts and compliments before a battle. The Emperor asked his opponent for a pot of wine. Tsang Chih sent a pot, but it did not contain wine. It was a full chamber pot. The insult enraged T'ai Wu, who ordered his soldiers to scale the city's walls. Thirty days of these attacks cost him half his men (Sun Tzu 1963).

Lawyers sometimes badger witnesses to unsettle or enrage them. This is important to remember if you are serving as an expert witness. If you are quick-tempered, the lawyer can make a fool of you. Just remember that it's nothing personal. It's the art of war.

Wield the Spear with Empty Hands

> The Japanese martial arts are tools for disciplining the mind. No adversary can checkmate a warrior who can wield a spear with empty hands.

He spent hours fencing as he sat in moveless meditation, hours in practice as he slept, and the untouched sword upon the tokonoma *rack never left his hands by night or day.*

—William Dale Jennings, *The Ronin*

Even his thoughts are arrows.

—Jean-Claude Carrière, *Mahabharata*

The Japanese martial arts go far beyond physical fighting techniques. Musashi makes this very clear. "Recently there have been people getting on in the world as strategists, but they are usually just sword-fencers" (Musashi 1974, Ground Book). Japanese warriors practiced martial arts to discipline their minds as well as their bodies. The Zen priest Gio spoke to a spear master about wielding a spear with empty hands. The spear master did not understand. Gio said, "If you don't understand, your art of the spear is a little affair of the hands alone" (Newman 1989, 78).

This takes us back to Yagyu Muneyoshi's statement. "Among those who control the world and protect the state, there's no one who doesn't employ swordsmanship in his mind" (1986, 16). To control an organization, you must control your mind. Martial arts like karate, kendō (swordsmanship), and *kyudō* (archery) teach mental discipline. Controlling the mind is then like wielding a sword or spear with empty hands. Tricks, deceptions, and real or imaginary fears will not shake such an intellect. No one can checkmate this warrior. Enemies who cannot win in their opponent's mind must win on the field. This is a hard path to victory, and an easy road to failure.

Personal Detachment in Strategy

> To succeed, we must not care if we fail.

If you can meet with Triumph and Disaster
And treat those two impostors just the same. . . .
　　　　　　　　　　　　—Rudyard Kipling, "If"

Set thy heart upon thy work, but never on its reward. Work not for a reward; but never cease to do thy work. Do thy work in the peace of Yoga and, free from selfish desires, be not moved in success or in failure.
　　　　　　　　　　　　—The Bhagavad Gita

If the warrior proceeds by casting aside the two things, life and death, nothing at all can best his mind.
　　　　　　　　　　　　—Tsukahara Bokuden (1490–1571)

Tsukahara Bokuden did not care whether he won, lost, or died in battle. He felled 212 opponents during his career. No sword ever touched him.

Not caring about your goals is the key to success. If you worry about your aims, you will not achieve them. The surgeon in the operating room must not care whether the patient lives or dies. The sales representative must not care whether he or she makes the sale. The attorney must not care about winning or losing the case. A student taking an exam must not think about passing or failing. To survive a physical battle, the combatant must write himself off as dead. This is the essence of personal detachment.

Would you hire a surgeon who doesn't care if you live or die? Would you want a lawyer, general, or coach who doesn't care about winning or losing? The professional must care, but not while he or she is acting. This is a theme of the warrior rune, Teiwaz. Teiwaz's message is to focus on a task for its own sake, and not worry about the outcome (Blum 1987).

A professional acts because of the goal. The goal is an extrinsic factor. The surgeon enters the operating room to help the patient. The lawyer enters the courtroom to aid a client. The student enters the examination hall to earn a grade. The warrior goes into battle to support his or her comrades and the cause. Once action begins, however, all extrinsic thoughts must stop.

Consider a football placekicker who is trying to get a field goal. He must think only of kicking the ball. Suppose he looks up to see where the ball goes as he is kicking. He will probably miss. Caring about the field goal could easily prevent him from making it. He must not look until the ball is on its way.

Dash Forward and Don't Look Around

In the "Bhagavad Gita" chapter of the *Mahabharata*, Krishna counsels the warrior Arjuna before the Battle of Kurukshetra (Carrière 1987, 159). He says, "Victory and defeat, pleasure and pain are all the same. Act, but don't reflect on the fruits of the act. Forget desire; seek detachment. . . . You must rise up free from hope and throw yourself into the battle." This story is at least 2500 years old. This scene recurred in thirteenth century Japan, but the characters were real.

In May of 1268, Hojo Tokimune received the news that Kublai Khan had ordered an armada to attack Japan. He went in full armor to see his Zen teacher, the priest Bukko. Tokimune said, "The great thing has come."

Bukko asked, "Can you somehow avoid it?"

Tokimune stamped his feet and gave a great *Katzu* (shout).

The teacher said, "A real lion cub; a real lion roar. Dash straight forward and don't look around!" (Newman 1989, 78).

The mythical Krishna told Arjuna, "Rise up free from hope and throw yourself into the battle." The historical figure Bukko advised Tokimune, "Dash straight forward and don't look around." Action follows the extrinsic decision. There are no second thoughts, and no regrets. This does not mean we dash forward recklessly. It does not mean we can't change course if our decision was wrong. It means we weigh our options carefully before acting. Arjuna and Tokimune did this, and committed themselves. Then they acted on their choices without regrets.

Resolute Acceptance of Death

> To live, write yourself off as dead.

> *And whether we shall meet again I know not. Therefore our everlasting farewell take: For ever, and for ever, farewell, Cassius! If we do meet again, why, we shall smile. If not, why, then, this parting was well made.*
> —William Shakespeare, *Julius Caesar* act v, scene i, lines 114–118 (the parting of Brutus and Cassius at the Plains of Philippi)

Samurai commanders often shared a farewell meal before battle. They assumed it would be their last meal together. In the *Mahabharata*, the Trigartas perform their own funerals before battle (Buck 1973). This is the essence of personal detachment. Miyamoto Musashi discusses the warrior's need for "resolute acceptance of death." This has nothing to do with fanaticism, ritual suicide, or kamikaze attacks. Musashi explains that anyone can choose to risk death or commit suicide. What sets the warrior apart is his state of personal detachment. This is not a desire for death. It is the most effective way of staying alive and winning.

Takeda Shingen's famous rival Uesugi Kenshin (1530–1578) said,

> *Go to the battlefield firmly confident of victory, and you will come home with no wounds whatever. Engage in combat fully determined to die and you will be alive; wish to survive the battle and you will surely meet death. When you leave the house determined not to see it again you will come home safely; when you have any thought of returning you will not return. (Storry 1978, 49–50)*

Wu Ch'i (430–381 B.C.E.) wrote almost exactly the same words in his *Art of War*. The New Testament contains an almost identical passage in Luke 17:33. Wu Ch'i said, "Now the field of battle is a land of standing corpses; those determined to die will live; those who hope to escape with their lives will die" (Sun Tzu 1963, 159).

The war banner of Uesugi Kenshin.

Takeda Shingen and Uesugi Kenshin faced each other at the Fourth Battle of Kawanakajima (1561). During the battle, Kenshin personally tried to kill Shingen. As he attacked, Kenshin presented a *koan*, or Zen riddle. "What do you say at this moment?"

As Shingen parried the blow with his iron war fan, he calmly answered, "A snowflake on a red-hot furnace!" Shingen and Kenshin were Zen Buddhist monks. One should answer a *koan* without pausing to think. One who can reply while fighting for his life has certainly achieved the ultimate level of personal detachment. In Rostand's *Cyrano de Bergerac*, the hero composes and recites poetry while fighting a duel. The idea is the same.

"Resolute acceptance of death" is part of detachment. The swordsman's intellect, arm, and sword must join as a single entity. As soon as the mind goes elsewhere—into thinking about staying alive—this entity collapses. This swordsman will probably die. When the swordsman writes himself off as dead, his mind stays where it belongs. He is more likely to live, and win.

Cutting Off Your Own Escape Route

> An intelligent rat sometimes corners itself.

Sun Tzu (1963) even suggested putting yourself in a position where you must win or die. This might include cutting off your own army's escape route when facing a superior force. Then the soldiers will fight to the death and obey every command. Machiavelli gave similar advice in his *Art of War*. The corollary is the aphorism, "Never corner a rat."

The Japanese general Shibata Katsuie put this advice to good use at the siege of Chokoji Castle in 1570. An enemy army that outnumbered him 10 to 1 surrounded him and cut the castle's aqueduct. The castle's water supplies were running out. Katsuie realized that he and his men could last only a few more days. He assembled his samurai in the castle courtyard. There, he took his spear and smashed the remaining water jars. He shouted, "Sooner a quick death in battle than a slow death from thirst!" He then opened the gates and led an attack that routed the besiegers (Turnbull 1987).

How would Sun Tzu have advised the besiegers? Give the trapped enemy a way out! Seeing a hope of escape, they will seek to live by fleeing. This will break their organization and battle order. Then you can destroy them. Their hope of life becomes their death and your victory. Their expectation of certain death is their salvation and your destruction.

Opponents Are Not Enemies

> A warrior has opponents, not enemies.

Detachment also includes lack of enmity. Competition does not require animosity, or even a contest of egos. The opponent is doing his or her job, just like you. In ancient times, opposing commanders often exchanged gifts before battle.

In the *Mahabharata*, the Pandava leader Yudhisthira sees friends in the enemy ranks. Duty has bound his foster grandfather Bhishma to the Kauravas. His teacher Drona also is with the Kauravas. In Asia, a teacher deserves almost as much reverence as a father or uncle. Before the battle, Yudhisthira approaches both men and asks leave to fight against them. Each says, "Had you not come to me, I would have cursed you." Each wishes Yudhisthira success in battle. They recognize that it is Yudhisthira's duty to fight them, however, they would have despised him for not greeting them before the battle.

Christian philosophy includes a similar concept. According to C. S. Lewis (1952, 3:107),

I have often thought to myself how it would have been if, when I served in the first world war, I and some young German had killed each other simultaneously and found ourselves together a moment after death. I cannot imagine that either of us would have felt any resentment or even any embarrassment. I think we might have laughed over it. . . . We may kill if necessary, but we must not hate and enjoy hating.

Johann Tserclaes, Graf von Tilly (1559–1632) was a general for the Holy Roman Empire in the Thirty Years' War. At the River Lech, he suffered a mortal wound while fighting the Swedes. He asked the Swedish King, Gustavus Adolphus, for a famous surgeon. Adolphus sent the surgeon, although in vain. The two commanders did not see each other as enemies. Their relationship was more like that of opposing football coaches. Even into the twentieth century commanders saw war as the ultimate sport, and their opponents as "the ultimate sportsmen" (Spector 1991).

The Itto Ryu kendo school teaches *Ai Uchi*. This means "to cut the opponent just as he cuts you. This is the ultimate timing. . . . it is lack of anger. It means to treat your enemy as an honoured guest" (Musashi 1974, 7). In the *Mahabharata*, Arjuna challenges Karna, his rival. "If I am a worthy guest, grant me the hospitality of battle!"

Karna replies, "I am honored. I could never turn you away!"

The story proceeds, "Karna gave that desirable guest a million arrows striking all at once to pierce his armor, like the charity of a perfect host who offers all his home to a wayfarer" (Buck 1973, 290). Hatred and anger play no role in the martial philosophies of India and Japan. The concept repeats itself in Western Christian thought. This is not the pacifist or turn-the-other-cheek version of forgiveness. It is the personal detachment of the professional warrior.

Avoiding the Peter Principle—The Sword of the Intellect

> Miyamoto Musashi was ahead of Myers and Briggs by three centuries. He also showed how to avoid the Peter Principle.

Progressive career stages require different sets of problem-solving skills (Schermerhorn, Hunt, and Osborn 1985). Sensation is direct observation.

Intuition includes inference and perception. Thinking is the application of consistent rules and principles. Feeling is empathy.

The Myers-Briggs Type Indicator (MBTI) describes a person's thought preferences. The test shows each person's Jungian type as follows:

- Introverted/Extroverted (I/E)
- Sensing/iNtuitive (S/N)
- Thinking/Feeling (T/F)
- Judging/Perceiving (J/P)

An MBTI class dramatically shows the differences between types. The trainer forms groups according to type. There are profound differences in the ways groups do tasks and answer questions. For example, the trainer asks groups of thinkers and feelers to define time. Thinkers look for scientific definitions. The feelers describe time's effects and how it makes them feel. Miyamoto Musashi was far ahead of the psychologists.

The Peter Principle

> Carl von Clausewitz recognized the Peter Principle long before Laurence Peter's birth.

The Peter Principle says people often "rise to their levels of incompetence" (Klein and Ritti 1984, 327). Dr. Laurence Peter was not the first person to recognize this principle. Carl von Clausewitz wrote, "There are commanders-in-chief who could not have led a cavalry regiment with distinction, and cavalry commanders who could not have led armies" (1976, Book 2, chap. 2).

Performing well in one job may earn a promotion to a position the employee cannot handle. Scientists rely heavily on direct observation and physical laws. Scientists are usually sensing-thinking (ST) personalities. Marketing and sales personnel use intuitive and feeling skills (NF). Direct management, however, requires sensation and feeling (SF). Becoming and succeeding as a direct manager thus requires at least three skills. Middle and upper management require intuitive and thinking skills (NT). Progression to and success in these levels require all four skills. Clausewitz's field marshal, like the upper manager, needed intuitive and thinking skills. He needed an intuitive grasp of the big picture. He had to perceive the overall situation through the fog of war. The regimental colonel, like the direct manager, needed sensation and feeling. He had to inspire his soldiers in battle.

Suppose a professional is strong in thinking and sensation, but not in feeling. He or she will succeed as a technical professional, but not as a group manager or leader. This is the Peter Principle at work. The person rises to his or her level of incompetence.

Miyamoto Musashi showed the key to defeating the Peter Principle 350 years ago. He identified the basic skills long before business management became a science. He wrote, "Polish the twofold spirit heart and mind, and sharpen the twofold gaze perception and sight."

Heart and mind are feeling and thinking. Sight is direct observation, and perception is intuition. (It is not the MBTI "perceiving." *The Book of Five Rings* says, "Perceive that which cannot be seen." This suggests inference or intuition.) The words *polish* and *sharpen* are especially significant. Polishing and sharpening were vital operations in the care of the Japanese sword. The sword was the soul of the Japanese warrior. Musashi tells us how to polish and sharpen the sword of the intellect. This is the instrument of all victories.

Adapt to the Situation

Choose the right organizational or managerial tool for the situation.

Is there a best management style or a best way to approach problems? Remember that a weapon is a physical, organizational, or mental resource. Such weapons include management and problem-solving techniques. Miyamoto Musashi wrote in the *A Book of Five Rings* (1974, Ground Book).

> *You should not have a favorite weapon. To become overfamiliar with one weapon is as much a fault as not knowing it sufficiently well. You should not copy others, but use weapons which you can handle properly. It is bad for commanders and troopers to have likes and dislikes.*

The contingency theory of leadership says there is no one best way to lead people. The best method will depend on the situation. This includes the types of followers (Schermerhorn, Hunt, and Osborn 1985). A good leader can use a task-oriented or relationship-oriented approach, or a combination of the two. A good manager can use directive, participative, and delegative styles. The following factors determine the proper style.

- Good or poor leader-follower relations
- High or low task structure
- The degree of the leader's authority
- Ability and willingness of the followers to accept responsibility for task outcomes

A warrior should not have a favorite weapon. A leader should not have a favorite leadership style. Musashi criticized the fencing schools that taught students to rely on a particular weapon. Some schools promoted the virtues of the extra-long sword. Musashi replied as follows:

> *Your strategy is of no account if when called upon to fight in a confined space your heart is inclined to the long sword, or if you are in a house armed only with your companion [short] sword. (1974, Wind Book)*

There is no best management or leadership style. Successful leaders adapt their approach to the situation of the followers or subordinates. Similarly, successul leaders must adapt their external competitive strategy to the situations of customers and competitors. We will return to this principle later.

Acceptance of Change and New Ideas

Openness to change and new ideas is critical for individual and organizational success.

Niccolò Machiavelli (1965, 122) wrote, "I conclude, then, inasmuch as Fortune is changeable, that men who persist obstinately in their own ways will be successful only so long as those ways coincide with those of Fortune; and whenever these differ, they fail."

Why do people cling to outmoded ways of thinking or to rigid attitudes and beliefs? To cast these away is to admit that one has been wrong for years or decades. It is far more comfortable to hold on to the old ways, although they may be wrong. We must remember the management concept of sunk costs. A sunk cost is money that we have already spent, for good or for bad. We don't account for sunk costs in decision making. We recognize the error of sending good money after bad.

There is a story that shows this concept. The headmaster of a Zen monastery was dying. He held a ceremony to confirm his successor. He handed the monk a scroll. "This scroll contains all the wisdom I have gathered over these years." The monk instantly threw the scroll into the fire. The headmaster said, "Well done!" The scroll was a test. The master did not want dogma to bind his successor.

Frederick the Great's successors did not do as the monk did. This was unfortunate for Prussia. The generals had inherited Frederick's oblique order battle tactic. Instead of treating it as one of many tools, they saw it as a sacred mantra. King Frederick had won many victories with it. It would always work, wouldn't it? This attitude resulted in the disaster of Jena in 1806. Clausewitz wrote, "It was not just a case of a style that had outlived its usefulness but the most extreme poverty of the imagination to which routine has ever led" (1976, Book 2, chap. 4). The oblique order was a useful tool for an able commander. It was not an adequate substitute for thinking.

How many American management teams have sacred mantras? "The founder always did it that way." "It worked for the old man years ago." "We've always done it that way." We must be sure this dogma does not become our oblique battle order when we face a corporate Napoleon.

Parallels in Religion and Philosophy

> We must learn from the past without becoming its prisoner. To cling to the past is to defend what we no longer have.

Marcus Aurelius wrote that the longest and shortest lives are equal. Everyone owns the passing minute. The past has gone, and the future has not come. Death deprives us only of the present moment. We cannot lose what we don't have. Gautama Buddha taught a similar concept. He taught that we live in the present-one breath. We do not have what is past. To cling to obsolete methods and attitudes is to defend what we no longer have. We must learn from experience, but we must not be its slave.

There is a striking similarity between Asian and Christian philosophy. The Christian "dies in Christ" and undergoes a rebirth. This involves the forgiveness of his or her sins. This spiritual death means the death of the past. The Christian cannot undo the sins, however, he or she realizes that they are in the past. (The same applies to good deeds.) The Zen Buddhist also seeks the death of the past.

Two Zen monks were traveling. They came to a river and found a young woman, who was unable to cross. The older monk picked her up and carried her across. Afterward, the younger monk admonished him. "How could you, a monk, even consider holding a woman in your arms, much less a young and beautiful one? It is against our teachings. It is dangerous."

"I put her down at the roadside," said the older monk. "Are you still carrying her?" (Musashi 1982, xxvi).

The old monk did not feel shame for breaking the rules of his order. He did not praise himself for doing a good deed. This is what the strategist does with successes and failures. He or she does not exult over good decisions or agonize over mistakes. The strategist learns from the past, but concentrates on today's battle.

The idea of psychological death and rebirth appears in medieval Tarot cards. One of the Major Arcana is the card for death. It shows a skeletal knight with a banner bearing a black flower. Its description is, "Death, rebirth, generally in areas of one's consciousness. Great change in one's life." Its reverse is "Stagnation, tendency to lethargy" (Aquarian Tarot 1975). Individuals and organizations that accept and welcome change can adapt to changing circumstances. Those that cannot, stagnate and become lethargic. The rush of changing events overtakes them. They drown in the tide of chaos.

Be Open-Minded, Avoid Preconceptions

> Prejudices and preconceptions are self-limiting. The true strategist avoids them.

Perception means receiving, interpreting, and organizing information. Perceptual distortions are obstacles to understanding the competitive environment. They are a major barrier to effective verbal and written communication. Our attitudes, expectations, and beliefs affect our perceptions (Klein and Ritti 1984). When we put aside our preconceived ideas, expectations, and prejudices, we can see past superficial appearances. Open-mindedness allows us to see situations as they really are.

The following Zen example shows the desirable frame of mind (Musashi 1982, xx).

The mind of an infant is empty. It has no preconceived ideas; it sees things as they are. It is free from the habits of experience and is therefore open to all possibilities. It makes no judgements, no distinctions.

Christianity apparently calls for a similar absence of preconceptions. "Whosoever shall not receive the kingdom of God as a little child shall in no wise enter therein" (Luke 18:17). This could mean that prejudices or preconceptions are obstacles to understanding and practicing the religion.

A very effective legendary magical deception made the subject see what he or she expected or hoped to see. The magic relied on the subject's own preconceptions and prejudices. In the *Iliad*, Athena appeared as Hector's brother Deiphobus. This ruse tricked Hector into fighting Achilles. She appeared as what Hector expected or hoped to see. The ruse was successful, and Hector fell to Achilles' spear.

Francis Bacon (1561–1626) wrote, "For what a man would like to be true, he more readily believes." Julius Caesar also knew how easy it is to fall prey to one's own expectations. He said, "men willingly believe what they wish."

Our Own Preconceptions Can Checkmate Us

> We can defeat the opposing leader's mind by exploiting his or her prejudices.

Showing your opponent what he or she expects to see can be devastating. The enemies' own prejudices and expectations trick them. They become their own assassins. This is how Sun Pin won a victory and gained revenge on P'ang Chuan (Sun Tzu 1963).

Sun Pin was a descendent of Sun Tzu. He began his career in the country of Wei. P'ang Chuan falsely accused Sun Pin of a crime to advance his own military career. This resulted in Sun Pin's mutilation and banishment. Sun Pin then became military chief of staff to the state of Ch'i.

Some time later Wei and Ch'i fought. Sun Pin knew that the enemy thought the Ch'i troops were cowardly. He ordered his men to build 100,000 fires the first night, 50,000 the second, and 30,000 the third. The Wei scouts dutifully counted the fires and reported to P'ang Chuan. P'ang Chuan exulted. He assumed the dwindling number of fires meant the cowardly Ch'i troops were deserting. To exploit his supposed advantage, he set off after the Ch'i Army with light shock troops.

Sun Pin laid an ambush. He deployed 10,000 crossbowmen on both sides of the road. He cut the bark off a tree and wrote, "P'ang Chuan will die under this tree." He ordered his men to shoot at any light that appeared that night.

P'ang Chuan arrived that night. He saw writing on the tree and lit a torch to see the words. He did not die in the volley of arrows, but his army panicked. P'ang Chuan realized that he had lost. He committed suicide, saying, "So I have contributed to the fame of that wretch!"

> This form of checkmate does not, however, require the services of an adversary. Some people do it to themselves without any help.

Can our prejudices and preconceptions assassinate us or our organizations? The answer is yes, and very easily. *Groupthink* occurs when a highly cohesive group loses its capacity of critical self-evaluation. Irving Janus thinks this organizational dysfunction helped cause Pearl Harbor, the Bay of Pigs, and the Vietnam fiasco (Schermerhorn, Hunt, and Osborn 1985). Symptoms of groupthink include writing opponents or competitors off as inferior, evil, or immoral. Believing one's own organization to be invincible or infallible is another. Hitler and his henchmen may have actually convinced themselves that they were supermen and their enemies subhuman. This was groupthink at its finest, and it led to disasters such as Stalingrad. American automakers were the master race of the 1950s and 1960s. The "little yellow men" across the Pacific could never be a threat. The United States had the same belief on December 6, 1941. In turn, the Japanese believed the "round-eyed Western barbarians" were weaklings. Japan thought the United States would fold up after one solid blow. Each side misjudged the other.

A Scottish Army captain, Patrick Ferguson, invented and demonstrated a breechloading rifle during the American Revolution. Fortunately for the United States, the British did not adopt the Ferguson rifle. Richard Gatling attached an electric motor to his gun in the late nineteenth century, thus anticipating Puff the Magic Dragon by several decades. The U.S.'s Project Vulcan rediscovered Gatling's idea in the 1940s.

Even famous business leaders have fallen prey to preconceptions, prejudices, and paradigms. Tom Peters (1987) provides some examples. In 1925, the editor of London's *Daily Express* refused to see a lunatic who had a machine for seeing by wireless. The "lunatic" was John Baird, the inventor of television. In 1927, Harry Warner, founder of Warner Brothers Studio, said this about soundtracks. "Who in the hell wants to hear actors talk?" Even IBM's patriarch, Thomas Watson Sr., misjudged the future. In 1943, he predicted, "I think there is a world market for about five computers." Digital Equipment's Ken Olsen said the following about home computers in 1973. "There is no reason for any individual to have a computer in their home." Five years later, Apple released its first desktop computer.

Swiss watchmakers invented the quartz watch movement. It is 1000 times as accurate as a mechanical movement. The Swiss didn't even bother to patent it. Everyone "knew" mechanical Swiss watches were superior. Texas Instruments and Seiko quickly exploited the idea. The Swiss market share dropped from 80 percent to 10 percent ("Paradigm pioneers" 1992).

The strategist does not make these mistakes. He or she sees the situation as it really is. An organization can protect itself too. Hiring outside consultants, and listening to them, can dispel comfortable illusions. Another technique is to assign group members to play devil's advocate. This person's role is to do his or her best to show what can go wrong with a plan or policy.

Self-Reliance—Internal Locus of Control

> The strategist must have an internal locus of control. He or she must have virtù—boldness, bravery, resolution, and decisiveness.

> *The fault, dear Brutus, is not in our stars*
> *But in ourselves, that we are underlings*
> —William Shakespeare, *Julius Caesar,* act I, scene II,
> lines 140–141

A person with an internal locus of control feels responsible for his or her own destiny. Those with an external locus of control believe outside forces control their destinies (Schermerhorn, Hunt, and Osborn 1985).

Niccolò Machiavelli uses the words *virtù* and *fortuna* in his *Art of War* (1965, 7–8). Fortuna is what it sounds like—fortune, fate, and external circumstances. Virtù looks like the word *virtue,* and its meaning is similar. It includes boldness, bravery, resolution, and decisiveness. Its opposite (*ozio*) includes inaction, indolence, and lack of energy. "Fortune may place us in particular circumstances, but whether we exert some control over our lives, instead of becoming the plaything of chance, depends upon our virtù." Appius Claudius Caecus (312–279 B.C.E.) wrote, *Faber est suae quisque fortunae*. "Each man is the smith of his own fortune."

The Tarot deck includes a card for strength. It means, "Courage, magnanimity, persistence, patience, spiritual power. Able to offset any bad luck in surrounding cards" (Aquarian Tarot 1975). Its attributes are those of virtù. Like virtù, it can offset bad luck or the whims of fortune. Its reverse means "weakness, possible loss of honor, and discord." Thus, we have the two opposites—virtù and ozio.

The wheel of fortune is another of the Tarot's Major Arcana. It means, "the ups and downs of life, constant change." Its reverse means, "the quality of your involvement will be the measure of your reward." Again we see two opposites—external and internal locus of control.

The Sword and the Anvil: An Illustration

> Siegfried became a hero by being the smith of his own fortune.

The idea of self-reliance appears in Wagner's opera *Siegfried*. Siegfried is a good Germanic hero. He doesn't know what fear is. He starts with a lot of potential because he is a Volsung—the race of heroes. He cannot succeed, however, unless he takes destiny into his own hands. He has no sword! The Nibelung blacksmith Mime has the pieces of the sword Nothung, or "Needful." Nothung once belonged to Siegfried's father, Siegmund. The god Wotan had broken it with his spear. Mime, however, lacks the skill to repair Nothung.

Mime wants Siegfried to kill the dragon Fafnir. Mime wants Fafnir's treasure, and he plans to poison Siegfried after Fafnir is dead. Mime tries to make a sword for Siegfried. Siegfried tests the quality of Mime's work by striking the anvil. The sword shatters, and he berates Mime as an incompetent bungler. Finally, Siegfried can stand no more. "My father's steel yields but to me. Let me fashion the sword!"

Mime urges Siegfried to solder Nothung's fragments together. Solder, an alloy of lead and tin, is soft and weak. It is no material for a hero's sword! Siegfried refuses this easy path, and does the job properly. He melts Nothung's fragments and pours them into a mold. Sparks fly as he hammers the blade. "Hammering blows make you strong and hard!" Finally, he plunges the blade into water. He applies the same quality test he used for Mime's work. "See, Mime, you smith, see how my sword can cleave!" The anvil splits in half under Nothung's edge.

This is a good lesson in self-reliance. Siegfried is indeed the smith of his own fortune. He slays Fafnir and wins the treasure. When Mime tries to poison him, he runs him through. Finally, Siegfried meets Wotan. Wotan challenges him, but this time his spear shatters under Nothung's blow.

The following story from *Hagakure* ("Hidden Leaves") summarizes the attitude that is proper for a warrior (Yamamoto 1979). It clearly shows the difference between an internal and an external locus of control. Lord Nabeshima Shima tells his father he wants to make a pilgrimage to the Atago Shrine. He wants to pray to the archery god for success in battle. Lord Nabeshima Aki angrily replies that this is worthless. If the god sides with the enemy, the Nabeshima vanguard should cut him in two!

Vitality

> Successful individuals and organizations have vitality—a bias for action.

> *The world continues to offer glittering prizes to those who have stout hearts and sharp swords.*
> —F. E. Smith, Earl of Birkenhead (1872–1930) in his Rectorial Address at Glasgow University, November 7, 1923

Machiavelli's terms *virtù* and *ozio* apply to Tom Peters' "bias for action." Deficient leadership comes when the leaders see themselves as financial analysts, technological innovators, marketers, or statisticians. The leader should understand these disciplines, but not rely on them blindly. Hayes, Wheelwright, and Clark (1988) cite this deficiency in many American businesses. Carl von Clausewitz noted a similar deficiency in many European nations.

> *When business becomes too analytical, too concerned with the calculus of costs versus benefits and risks versus returns, it becomes prey to those who seek market share, the dynamics of growth, and a place in the sun.* (Hayes, Wheelwright, and Clark 1988, 30)

> *Woe to the government which, relying on half-hearted politics and a shackled military policy, meets a foe who, like the untamed elements, knows no law other than his own power! Any defect of action and effort will turn to the advantage of the enemy [author's emphasis].* (Clausewitz 1976, Book 3, chap. 16)

A bias for action is "a preference for doing something—anything—rather than sending a question through cycles and cycles of analyses and committee reports" (Peters and Waterman 1982). John Maynard Keynes (1936, 161–162) notes, "Our decisions to do something positive, the full consequences of which will be drawn out over many days to come, can only be taken as a result of animal spirits—of a spontaneous urge to action rather than inaction." Clausewitz (1976, Book 3, chap. 16) also knew the value of a bias for action.

> *Unless an enterprising martial spirit is in command, a man who is as much at home in war as a fish is in water, or unless great responsibilities exert a pressure, inactivity will be the rule and progress the exception. . . . The first of these [determinants], which creates a permanent tendency toward delay and thus becomes a retarding influence, is the fear and indecision native to the human mind. It is a sort of moral force of gravity, which, however, works by repulsion rather than attraction: namely, aversion to danger and responsibility.*

In modern management theory terms, we would say this is risk-averse behavior. The leaders do not want to take risks; however, doing nothing is a decision, and it can often be fatal. Recall Machiavelli's discussion of virtù and ozio. The organizations Hayes, Wheelwright, and Clark mention, which place too much reliance on analysis, show ozio. The "decision to do something positive" shows virtù (Keynes 1936). Ozio places us at the mercy of the winds of fortune and our opponents. Virtù gives us some control of our destiny.

Conclusion

This chapter has addressed the desirable characteristics and attributes of an organizational leader. These include the following:

1. *Genuine concern for the welfare of subordinates, superiors, the organization, and customers.* Stewardship is a key concept, as discussed in chapter 1. Sun Tzu's ideal general does not advance to seek fame. He does not retreat to avoid punishment. He seeks only to protect the interests of the people (employees) and sovereign (stockholders).

   Serving others is the essence of Kshatriya Dharma and Bushidō. This service orientation makes the leader more valuable to the organization. It helps him or her command the respect and loyalty of subordinates. This makes the leader effective. The section on commitment in chapter 3 will discuss this further. Even the owner of a company serves others by fostering the welfare of customers and employees. In turn, they give the owner continuing patronage and loyal service.

2. *Ongoing, lifelong professional development.* The ending of Anthony Hope's Prisoner of Zenda (1967) shows an incentive for lifelong practice. The hero, Rudolf Rassendyll, had a sword fight with the villain, Rupert Hentzau. The fight was inconclusive, and Hentzau escaped. "[Perhaps] I have yet a hand to play with young Rupert; therefore I exercise myself in arms, and seek to put off the day when the vigor of youth must leave me" (p. 158).

   In business, Rupert Hentzau is the competitor who wants your market share. He may be a younger employee who wants your job. Through continuing professional development, you can stay ahead of him.

3. *Personal detachment.* While acting, the warrior does not think about the good or bad results. Personal detachment makes him or her more effective.

4. *Willingness to abandon past methods in adapting to changing circumstances. Avoidance of prejudices and preconceptions.* Preconceived ideas, attitudes, and prejudices are self-constraints. The competitive environment and opposition create enough constraints and barriers. Preconceptions and attitudes exist only in one's mind. The strategist does not create barriers and constraints where none exist.

5. *Self-reliance or internal locus of control, and a bias for action (Tom Peters) or virtù (Machiavelli).* As written in the song "Fortuna Imperatrix Mundi" (Fortune, Empress of the World) from Carmina Burana by Carl Orff,

> *Oh Fortune, as the moon everchanging you are always waxing or waning. . . . The wheel of Fortune turns.*

Sun Tzu also wrote of changing circumstances, and the cycles of the moon. Miyamoto Musashi noted the rise and fall of capital in the Way of the merchant. Tom Peters tells of the oncoming tide of chaos. Fortune's wheel turns more quickly now. Virtù is the strong hand at the tiller that lets us navigate the storm. An internal locus of control helps us sail the tempest and fight our guns in it as well.

3

Managing the Organization

A business organization, like an army, is a living system. It develops traditions and customs. Regiments have long traditions and histories, and so do companies. A good leader can make the organization respond like his or her own arms and legs. Yet we know how difficult it sometimes is to make the organization respond. Sometimes, it fights the leader or even itself. The Way of strategy teaches how to overcome these obstacles.

COMMITMENT

> Commitment means mutual trust and loyalty between people and an organization. Commitment is a priceless asset. Perceived equity, mutual trust, and adherence to psychological contracts are vital contributors to commitment.

My castle is in the hearts of my people.
—Takeda Shingen (1521–1573)

The best fortress which a prince can possess is the affection of his people; for even if he has fortresses, and is hated by his people, the fortresses will not save him; for when a people have once risen in arms against their prince, there will be no lack of strangers who will aid them.

—Niccolò Machiavelli, *The Prince*

Takeda Shingen's son Katsuyori liked castles. He built many fortresses during his brief career. Meanwhile, he lost the commitment of his followers. His vassals, including some of his father's Twenty-Four Generals, deserted him one by one. Some even went over to his enemies. Katsuyori could not defend his land. He had to burn his fine new castle of Shimpu-jo the year after its completion to prevent its capture. By 1582, the Takeda Army had shrunk from tens of thousands to 300. Katsuyori's enemies surrounded his small band at Temmoku-zan, where he committed ritual suicide (Turnbull 1987).

American firms build fortresses. They call them poison pills, labor contracts, work rules, and so on. The poison pill protects management from the stockholders by discouraging buyouts. Work rules protect union jobs. Labor contracts hold off strikes until it is time to negotiate the next contract. Everyone wants a castle of laws, rules, or contracts. These castles are no defense against a competitor. While the stockholders, managers, and union employees are defending themselves against each other, the real adversaries are destroying all of them. Rudyard Kipling's poem, "Together—England at War," is worth posting in the corporate boardroom and on the shop floor. Here is its conclusion.

> *It is not wealth, nor talk, nor trade, nor schools, nor even the Vote,*
> *Will save your land when the enemy's hand is tightening round your*
>   *throat.*
> *But a King and a People who thoroughly trust each other in all that is*
>   *done*
> *Can sleep on their bed without any dread—for the world will leave*
>   *'em alone!*

Sun Tzu cites commitment as one of the five basic factors that decide victory or defeat. "Moral influence" promotes harmony between the people and their leaders. When commitment is strong, the people will follow the leaders in life and death. Recall that Tao, or the Way, is another word for moral influence. Following *Kshatriya Dharma* or *Bushidō* earns and keeps the commitment of our followers. The section "Perceived Equity" discusses this.

What is commitment? Commitment is personal identification with an organization. It makes the participant willing to endure personal reversals or hardships (Schermerhorn, Hunt, and Osborn 1985; Miller 1985–1986). The organization could be a military unit, company, or work group. If the participants value the group, they will make sacrifices for it. If it is a military unit, they will endure long marches, poor living quarters, and danger. At Valley Forge, committed American Revolutionaries endured cold and hunger. Those who did not feel commitment deserted. General Patton enjoyed the commitment of his soldiers. A reporter asked one man if he thought Patton might not go to heaven after death. The soldier replied, "If General Patton decided to go to hell, I would sure like to go along!" (Williamson 1979, 152). Patton's soldiers were willing to follow him even to hell. It is no surprise that Patton earned a place as one of America's greatest generals.

It is the same in business. Committed employees work extra hours without pay. In extreme cases, they continue to work when the company cannot pay them. Instead, they accept the company's stock as payment. They pool their fortunes with those of the company. If the company thrives, they become rich. If the company fails, they lose their entire investment.

Benefits of Commitment

> Committed organizational members will make exceptional efforts and sacrifices for the organization.

An army that maintains its cohesion under the most murderous fire; that cannot be shaken by imaginary fears and resists well-founded ones with all its might; that, proud of its victories, will not lose the strength to obey orders and its respect and trust for its officers even in defeat . . . such an army is imbued with the true military spirit.
—*(Clausewitz 1976, Book 3, chap. 5)*

Modern companies do not ask employees to face enemy gunfire. They may ask them for exceptional efforts. Employees show commitment by working extra hours without pay. Commitment also helps companies keep experienced employees. "Obviously, a company would be reluctant to invest in expanded job definitions, technical training, and problem-solving skills if it faced high turnover among its people" (Hayes, Wheelwright, and Clark 1988, 263).

Commitment as a Keystone of Napoleon's Victories

Commitment helped Napoleon Bonaparte conquer most of Europe. Anyone who wants to be a corporate Napoleon must follow this example.

Carl von Clausewitz, who fought in the Napoleonic Wars, studied the organizational structure of the French State. He wrote the following analysis.

> *A government behaved as though it owned and managed a great estate that it constantly endeavored to enlarge—an effort in which the inhabitants were not expected to show any particular interest. . . . War thus became solely the concern of the government [upper management/owners] to the extent that governments parted company with their peoples and behaved as if they were themselves the state. Their means of waging war came to consist of the money in their coffers [cash, short-term assets] and of such idle vagabonds as they could lay their hands on, either at home or abroad. In consequence the means they had available were fairly well defined, and each could gauge the other side's potential in terms both of numbers and time. War was thus deprived of its most dangerous feature—its tendency toward the extreme, and of the whole chain of unknown possibilities which would follow.*
>
> *The enemy's cash resources, his treasury, and his credit, were all approximately known; so was the size of his fighting forces. [Today we can read his annual report.] . . . [After 1793,] Suddenly war again became the business of the people—a people of thirty millions, all of whom considered themselves to be citizens. . . . The people became a participant in war; instead of governments and armies as heretofore, the full weight of the nation was thrown into the balance. The resources and efforts now available for use surpassed all conventional limits; nothing now impeded the vigor with which war could be waged, and consequently the opponents of the French faced the utmost peril. (Clausewitz 1976, Book 8, chap. 3)*

The French Army under the Revolutionary government was less effective than it could have been. Commissars, or political officers, accompanied the armies and shared authority with the military commanders. Commissars could arrest officers, many of whom ended up in the guillotine. Discipline was poor, and many soldiers wore rags (Koch 1982). Once Lazare Carnot and Napoleon corrected these management deficiencies, the French Army became an unstoppable juggernaut. It crushed everything and everyone in its path.

Eventually, France's opponents recognized the value of popular commitment. Spanish partisans began resisting the French. They saw themselves fighting for Spain, not for the king. Under the direction of General Gerhard von Scharnhorst, Prussia developed its *Landwehr,* or militia. Scharnhorst also supported making commoners eligible for commissions. Promotions were to depend on ability and merit instead of noble birth (Koch 1982).

Like Napoleon's opponents, American companies now face "the utmost peril" from competitors. Commitment helps a company "surpass all conventional limits." Everything and anything are possible to such an organization.

Commitment in Industry

Matsushita workers recite their company creed daily. "Alone we are weak, together we are strong. We shall work together as a family in mutual trust and responsibility." Their company song says, "Sending our goods to the people of the world/ Endlessly and continuously/ Like water gushing from a fountain/ Grow, industry, grow, grow, grow!" Toyota's company newsletter urges workers to "challenge the highest peaks with our all-out efforts. . . . With ingenuity and good ideas, we can find a solution to increased orders even beyond our present full capacity." At Nissan, workers, and not efficiency experts, experiment with process improvements. "First we work one machine with the left hand, then another with the right. Then we put one machine in front and another behind and work them simultaneously" (*Time-Life Library of Nations* 1985, 21–23).

Japanese companies have gained similar commitment from American workers. Honda's plant in Marysville, Ohio, has no labor union (Brown 1987). The United Auto Workers have been unable to unionize the Nissan plant in Smyrna, Tennessee (Buckley1988). Commitment does not depend on nationality or even national culture. Excellent leadership can evoke it anywhere.

Loss of Commitment

> Demoralization is survivable. Loss of commitment is a death sentence.

Commitment is probably the most important of Sun Tzu's five factors. A defeated organization may suffer demoralization, however, its members can still feel commitment. Such an organization can regroup and fight again. Loss of commitment is far worse than demoralization. It means a breakdown in trust between the leaders and the followers. Unfortunately, this characterizes the relationship between stockholders, employees, and managers at many American companies.

American stockholders pay close attention to the quarterly report. If the quarterly report disappoints them, they pressure the directors for action. Such action often includes layoffs and restructuring. Meanwhile, there is union-management friction. The union seeks to take as much as it can while delivering as little as possible. The union imposes restrictive work rules. For example, only a union mechanic can touch a machine. If an engineer or manager does so, it is a violation of the work rules. Management behaves similarly. To management, workers are not trustworthy. They are assets one hires when necessary. One dismisses them when they are unnecessary. Meanwhile, professionals and managers respond to the headhunter's call. The way to advance is to change jobs for salary increases.

Clausewitz (1976) described the terrible results of demoralization. "In the engagement, the loss of morale has proved the major decisive factor"(Book 4, chap. 4).Demoralization, not physical destruction, is the decisive element. Demoralized troops (1) lose confidence in the leaders' ability and (2) recognize that the enemy is stronger (Book 4, chap. 10). Now consider that *loss of commitment is even worse than demoralization.* Loss of commitment means a breakdown in the trust and loyalty between superiors and subordinates (Klein and Ritti 1984). Its results include: (1) perfunctory performance of duties; (2) turnover; and (3) a narrow zone of indifference (willingness to accept duties that are outside one's job description). People say, "It's not my job." They watch the clock.

Henry Ford Sr. recognized this prinicple. "It is a reciprocal relation—the boss is the partner of his worker, the worker is partner of his boss. . . . Both are indispensable. . . . It is utterly foolish for capital or for labor to think of themselves as groups. They are partners" (Stuelpnagel 1993, 93).

Henry Ford wrote this in *My Life and Work* in 1926. Ford also foresaw design for manufacture (DFM) and just-in-time (JIT) manufacturing.

Unfortunately, Ford's successors forgot his principles. In 1982, a group of Ford executives visited Japan to learn about Japanese management principles. "One Japanese executive referred repeatedly to 'the book.' When Ford executives asked about the book, he responded: 'It's Henry Ford's book of course—your company's book'" (Stuelpnagel 1993, 91).

Now consider the Japanese company. It is often like an extended family. Stockholders are patient and look for long-term results. They don't worry too much about a bad quarter or two. Labor relations are like the ancient lord-retainer relationship, with its code of mutual loyalty. The "Way of Lord and Retainer" is a basic concept (Sōhō 1986). The employer is more than a source of money to the employee. The employee is not a mere hired hand to the employer. In ancient times, samurai families were proud to serve a given lord for many generations.

Organizations as Extended Families

Compare these organizations. In one, money is the only consideration. The other is like an extended family. Sun Tzu was fond of the visual picture of a grindstone striking an eggshell. This is a good image of a cohesive organization with committed members meeting one that lacks these qualities. We've seen what the Japanese automakers have done to America's Big Three. Now let's consider the example of Delta and Eastern Airlines.

Eastern's recent history included severe labor-management friction. Eastern is no longer a major competitor in the airline industry. Tom Peters and Robert Waterman (1982) identify Delta Airlines and American Airlines as the top competitors. Delta's last strike was in 1942. Its last union vote was in 1955. Delta "promotes from within, pays better than most airlines, and goes to any length to avoid laying workers off in a traditionally cyclic industry" (p. 253). During a recession, Delta's management told its stockholders to expect some losses. Delta would not dismiss workers to improve short-term earnings. It would cut dividends if that is what it took to keep full employment (Deal and Kennedy 1982). It is easy to talk about an extended-family culture in good economic times. Living up to this culture in hard times keeps and strengthens commitment.

Peters and Waterman state, "Many of the best companies really do view themselves as an extended family. We found prevalent use of the specific terms 'family', 'extended family', or 'family feeling' at Wal-Mart, Tandem, HP, Disney, Dana, Tupperware, McDonald's, Delta, IBM, TI, Levi Strauss, Blue Bell, Kodak, and Procter & Gamble" (p. 261).

Peters and Waterman suggest, "Treat people as adults. Treat them as partners; treat them with dignity; treat them with respect. Treat *them*—not capital spending and automation—as the primary source of productivity gains. . . . If you want productivity and the financial reward that goes with it, you must treat your workers as your most important asset" (p. 238). Sun Tzu recognized this principle 2500 years ago. Takeda Shingen and Niccolò Machiavelli knew it too. Takeda Katsuyori forgot it and died. So have many American businesses and other organizations. Now let's consider how we can build and maintain this "castle in the hearts of our followers."

Perceived Equity

> Rank has duties and responsibilities as well as privileges. Treating everyone fairly promotes commitment.

During eighteenth and nineteenth century naval warfare, there was an incentive for capturing an enemy ship instead of sinking it. If the crew brought a captive vessel into port, the navy paid the victors for the prize. In the Royal Navy, the captain and officers got most of the money. The crew had to share a small portion of the prize money.

A British cartoon commented on this inequity. It showed an English sailor praying before a naval battle. An officer asked him, "Why are you praying? Are you afraid of the French who are bearing down on us?"

The sailor replied, "Not at all, Sir. I'm just asking for our shares of the enemy fire to come in the same proportions as the prize money."

This little story could describe the bonus and profit-sharing systems in many modern corporations. In some cases, the captain and senior officers have an even better bargain. They receive a bonus even when they have taken no prizes. If the ship is sinking, they are the first ones into "golden lifeboats." This does little to earn the commitment and loyalty of the crew. It is a long way from this to the majesty of Julius Caesar. Shakespeare has Caesar say of his personal welfare, "What touches ourself shall be last serv'd" (*Julius Caesar,* act III, scene i, line 8).

Perceived equity is an important part of commitment. "A felt negative inequity exists when an individual feels that he or she has received relatively less than others in proportion to work inputs. Felt positive inequity exists when an individual feels he or she has received relatively more than others" (Schermerhorn, Hunt, and Osborn 1985, 140–141). The following reference shows some possible employee responses to perceived inequities.

Perceived negative inequity   • Decreases efforts
                                          • Asks for a raise
                                          • Quits
                                          • Rationalizes the inequity

Perceived positive inequity   • Increases efforts

Does equity require the company president and the janitor to have the same pay? It is proper to recognize the president's greater responsibility with greater compensation; however, responsibility, authority, and compensation must go together. Rank has privileges but also obligations. The authority to give orders goes with a greater duty to the welfare of the organization. In short, *noblesse oblige,* or "nobility obligates." We expect those of high position to care for the welfare of subordinates. This is fully in line with *Bushidō* and *Kshatriya Dharma.*

Concern for the Welfare of Subordinates
A portion of the *Mahabharata* shows the proper behavior of a ruler. King Yudhisthira, the leader of the Pandavas, dreams that he has lost his family in a desert. A little brown dog had joined his party earlier. Now the dog is his only companion. Indra, the ruler of the gods, appears. He offers to rescue Yudhisthira from the desert, but he cannot take the dog. "There is no place for dogs in heaven. They are unclean. It cannot be."

Yudhisthira refuses to go to heaven with Indra. "I will not surrender a faithful dog to you. . . . Whoever comes to me from fright or from disaster or from friendship—I never give him up." Of course, this is a test. The dog is Dharma, god of justice (or right conduct), and Yudhisthira's father (Buck 1973, 363–369).

The leader does not regard his or her subordinates as assets or disposable machinery. He or she looks on them as valuable retainers. Sun Tzu said the able general treats his men as his own sons. This makes them willing to follow him and die with him.

Sun Tzu's *The Art of War* features examples and comments by later Chinese scholars. These comments amplify Sun Tzu's principles. Tu Mu (803–852 c.e.) described how General Wu Ch'i (430–381 b.c.e.) ate the same food and wore the same clothing as his soldiers. He carried his own rations, and shared hardships with his men. Once he personally treated a common soldier's abcess. The soldier's mother began lamenting and wailing. Wu Chi had performed a similar service for her husband. He never left Wu Chi's side, and finally died in battle. The woman expected the same fate for her son (Clavell 1983). Chang Yu (Sung Dynasty) echoed the following words of Zhuge Liang.

Zhuge Liang (born ca. 180 C.E.) wrote "The Way of The General— Essays on Leadership and Crisis Management" (Cleary 1989b, 52).

> *According to the code of generalship, generals do not say they are thirsty before the soldiers have drawn from the well; generals do not say they are hungry before the soldiers' food is cooked; generals do not say they are cold before the soldiers' fires are kindled; generals do not say they are hot before the soldiers' canopies are drawn. Generals do not use fans in summer, do not wear leather in winter, do not use umbrellas in the rain. They do as everyone does.*

Corporate Examples

The engineering firm of Berson, Ackermann & Associates exemplifies this code. The recession of 1991–1992 forced the company to lay off some employees. Those who remained took salary cuts of 5 percent to 12 percent. The 5 percent applied to the low end of the salary scale, and the 12 percent applied to managers. The president and CEO, Bernard Berson, P.E., stopped his own salary completely. He also loaned money to the company from his own pocket (Chappie 1992). This conduct is a welcome contrast with what we see in many American companies.

The worldwide 1929 depression threatened the Matsushita Electric Works with bankruptcy. Two senior managers advised the founder, Matsushita Konosuke, to dismiss half his employees. Konosuke refused. Instead, he halved production and told the employees to help sell the products. Within a few months, sales improved and the company was back at full production (Koren 1990).

IBM's Thomas Watson Jr. went a step further. He cut his own pay when IBM was at the height of its power, simply because he felt "his [stock] options were becoming indecently lucrative" (Carroll 1993, 53).

Generals who acted this way gained the respect and commitment of their followers. Ross Perot said, "You can't look the troops in the eye and say, 'It's been a bad year; we can't do anything for you;' but then say, 'By the way, we're going to pay ourselves a $1 million bonus'" (Peters 1987, 459). Perot understands *Kshatriya Dharma*, the duty of the ruler. Many executives don't.

Peters continues, "Roger Smith announces eleven plant closings and 27,000 more potential layoffs [at General Motors]—then retreats behind double-locked or triple-locked—(depending on whose story you believe)—glass doors to contemplate the wasteland he's created (his $1.4

million compensation in 1986 doubtless eased the pain a bit)" (p. 459). In early 1992, General Motors announced more plant closings.

Peters specifically cites perceived equity. "Paying bonuses to management and withholding worker bonuses in a problematic year is perceived to be unfair, regardless of the extenuating circumstances. . . . In general, the wisest firms avoid excessive executive perks and even the appearance of minor impropriety" (p. 629).

Peters also suggests getting rid of executive perquisites that merely demean other employees. These include special parking spaces, washrooms, and dining facilities. "I don't care if you've waited twenty-seven years for it, get rid of the damned reserved parking spot right this bloody minute. (*Then* you can consider asking 'them' to 'do it right the first time')" (p. 10).

Machiavelli (1965) also opposed unnecessary executive perquisites.

> *In the first place, no captain or corporal should be permitted to ride during a march: and if the lieutenant colonel wanted to ride, it should be upon a mule, and not upon a horse.* (p. 74)

We can conclude that perceived equity is critical in maintaining employee commitment and loyalty. The leader must show genuine concern for the welfare of his or her subordinates. This is the Way of lord and retainer.

Mutual Trust

Commitment depends on integrity, honesty, and trust.

> *Say 'we', 'us', and 'ours' when you're talking,*
>   *instead of 'you fellows' and 'I.'*
> *Don't ride over seeds; keep your temper;*
>   *and never you tell 'em a lie!*
>   —Rudyard Kipling, "Norman and Saxon"

Tom Peters (1987, 626–627) says, "Integrity has been the hallmark of the superior organization through the ages. . . . The uncertainty of the environment can be swiftly dealt with only if the firm can fall back upon the certainty of relationships among people and among groups—in other words, upon trust and integrity."

Stephen Covey (1991) compares principles and organizational culture to the human immune system. A host of diseases threatens us every day. The immune system adapts to these changing threats and defeats them. A strong culture plays the same role in business. It lets the organization react to the uncertain environment Tom Peters mentioned. Covey says a breakdown in trust is the organizational version of AIDS. AIDS is a failure of the human immune system. AIDS allows diseases to ravage and kill the body. When trust and commitment break down, the organizational immune system goes with them. Covey compares untrustworthy employees to AIDS carriers. Recall the discussion in the introduction. "When you protect dharma, dharma protects you. When you violate dharma, dharma destroys you." In the Indian epic, *Ramayana*, Rama says every broken promise destroys a little piece of dharma (Buck 1991). In Wagner's *Siegfried* (1972), Wotan's word is the foundation of his power. If he breaks his word, his spear will shatter.

There is no substitute for total integrity. The U.S. Military Academy will dismiss a cadet for lying, cheating, or stealing. These are integrity defects that would disqualify someone as a military officer. IBM's Buck Rogers says, "If you lose your character and integrity, you have lost everything." People must be able to count on what you tell them. This is obvious in wartime. An officer who inflates victory claims endangers others who rely on the information. "Those airplanes you shot down just strafed my column!"

Deceiving the enemy (competitor) is another matter. During wartime, military organizations censor news reports. They may deny losses to keep the enemy from knowing how effective its actions were. Their goal is to deceive outsiders, not superiors or subordinates. The option of denying losses may not be practical or legal in business. If the public owns stock, the company's financial performance is a matter of public record. Similarly, a company cannot hide its financial condition from creditors.

A legal, but stupid, way of denying business losses is the dividend potlatch. According to the *American Heritage Dictionary of the English Language*, a potlatch is "a ceremonial feast among (American) Indians living on the Pacific Coasts of Washington, British Columbia, and Alaska, at the end of which the host gives valuable material goods to the guests who belong to other kin groups or destroys property to show that he can afford to do so." A company in financial trouble may continue to pay a dividend to convince stockholders that all is well. It may even increase its dividend. This may please the stockholders for a while; however, it has two serious disadvantages. The annual and quarterly reports are public records. The dividend potlatch cannot fool a serious opponent. It also dissipates the company's equity and aggravates its financial problems.

There was once a W. T. Grant chain store. Even during the last few years of its existence, it was incurring debt and paying dividends. In 1974, it borrowed $100 million and paid $21 million in dividends. The dividends exceeded the total funds from current operations. Many readers may be old enough to remember W. T. Grant. Those who aren't will never see a Grant store, for the chain went bankrupt in 1975 (Anthony and Reece 1983). The reference does not suggest a dividend potlatch occurred; however, why was the company borrowing money and paying dividends? The explanation that debt is cheaper than equity does not work. If the idea was to replace equity with debt, the company would have repurchased stock. It did buy some treasury stock, but not enough to justify the amount of debt.

Here's another example of lack of integrity. A sales force may place orders at the end of the accounting period to inflate the sales figures. Order cancellations will happen in the next accounting period (Peters 1987). If superiors and others believe the inflated figures, it will disrupt planning. Phony information may affect manufacturing schedules. Manufacturing may place orders with suppliers to meet the "product demand." Manufacturing will have to cancel these orders when the truth comes out. Imagine the effect on the material requirements planning (MRP) system. If the sales department has done this in the past, no one will believe it. How should the company then plan its strategies and manufacturing schedules? Remember, however, that this behavior may result from a dysfunctional performance measurement system. We will examine this later.

Deficiencies of "Machiavellianism"
Here is one place where Machiavelli's advice breaks down. In the "notorious" 18th chapter of *The Prince* (1965), Machiavelli wrote,

> *A sagacious prince then cannot and should not fulfill his pledges when their observance is contrary to his interest, and when the causes that induced him to pledge his faith no longer exist. If men were all good, then indeed this precept would be bad; but as men are naturally bad, and will not observe their faith toward you, you must, in the same way, not observe yours to them; and no prince ever yet lacked legitimate reasons with which to color his want of good faith. (p.86)*

This is a self-fulfilling prophecy. If everyone in an organization acts on Machiavelli's advice, here is what will happen. People will behave dishonestly and use others' dishonesty as an excuse. They will naturally erect defenses against the dishonesty of others. This will have two very negative results.

1. Effort will go into defenses instead of toward achieving organizational goals.
2. Acts of dishonesty will damage the organization. These include more than illegal acts like stealing. Falsifying or embellishing reports is an example.

It is better to be honest, and assume others are honest, unless they show otherwise. Any organization will contain about 5 percent bad apples. Peters (1987) recommends that lack of integrity be grounds for dismissal, and provides some examples. Lack of integrity is one of the very few reasons for which Peters would fire someone.

The Culture Must Promote Integrity

Organizations must demand total integrity from their members. The organizational culture must not make people afraid to admit mistakes or report problems. The king must not react to bad news or even criticism by killing the messenger. Unfortunately, many executives make this mistake. "Kill thy physician, and the fee bestow/ Upon the foul disease" (Shakespeare, *King Lear,* act I, scene i, line 166). In the *Mahabharata,* a messenger begs King Virata to spare his life. "Spare me, I bring bad news. Your lands have been invaded, your crops carted away" (Carrière 1987, 124). Should the king *not* want to know about an enemy invasion? Paul Carroll (1993, 56) writes of IBM chairpersons Frank Cary and Thomas Watson Jr., "Cary, like Watson before him, decided to surround himself with people who would tell him what was really going on."

One of Deming's 14 points is, "Eliminate fear. Encourage two-way communication" (Tribus 1992, 31). If the culture penalizes people for admitting mistakes, they will sweep them under the rug. Unfortunately, hiding mistakes does not make them go away. It allows them to continue or worsen.

Keeping secrets from the workforce does not promote openness and trust. Peters (1987) says that only confidential personnel records, patent information, and acquisition plans should be secret.

The Psychological Contract

A psychological contract is an unspoken set of mutual expectations.

A psychological contract is an unspoken but shared understanding. "The employee expects to give something—compliance to authority, for example—in return for organizational rewards. Management expects a certain amount of production in return for a certain amount of reward. When either party gives or receives less than is called for by the implicit contract, feelings of inequity may follow" (Klein and Ritti 1984, 266).

In 1971, the General Motors Assembly Division (GMAD) changed the work standards for the Chevy Vega. It discharged several hundred autoworkers and distributed the workload among the rest. The remaining workers quickly realized they were turning out the same amount of work with fewer people, but without more pay. Grievances increased by 1700 percent. Sabotage occurred, followed by disciplinary layoffs, followed by a strike (Klein and Ritti 1984). This is an example of the results of violating a psychological contract. In this case, higher contribution by the workers did not result in greater rewards.

LEADERSHIP

> Leaders' behavior must convey desirable attitudes and values to their followers. Leaders' actions must accord with their statements.

Managing an Organization Is Like Riding a Horse

> The leader must impart confidence to his or her followers. To do this, the leader must have genuine self-confidence. Pretensions are not enough.

It often happens that a brave and spirited fellow is put upon a pitiful horse and a coward upon one that is unruly and ungovernable, and in either of these cases some disorder must ensue.

—Niccolò Machiavelli, *The Art of War*

When troops are strong and officers weak the army is insubordinate. When the officers are valiant and the troops ineffective the army is in distress.

—Sun Tzu, *The Art of War*

Jumping a fence or other obstacle is a standard challenge in classical English-style equitation. To jump an obstacle successfully, the rider must really want to do it. The rider must be confident that he or she can succeed. A common saying is, "Throw your heart over the fence and the horse will follow." It is not enough to point the horse at the fence and go along for the ride. Horses are emotionally sensitive animals. They can sense when the rider is unsure. If the rider is unsure, the horse will not respond.

Rudyard Kipling (1982, 870) summarized the idea. "They felt that the men on their backs were afraid of something. When horses once know *that*, all is over except the butchery."

The same principle applies in karate. Here, the hands and feet are the soldiers and the mind is the general. To break a board, the karate practitioner must think of hitting *through* the board. This thinking must go far beyond mere intellectual or technical understanding. There must be no doubt that the blow will extend an inch or two past the target. The idea is to aim at this imaginary point and forget that the obstacle exists. "Throw your mind through the target, and your punch or kick will follow."

Pretensions of confidence are not enough. These outward pretensions will not fool a horse, and they will not fool one's own limbs. Humans also can sense when the leader is unsure.

In ancient times, commanders had to interpret bad omens so they looked favorable. Julius Caesar once stumbled and fell in full view of his men, while disembarking in Africa. This may have been an accident or a result of the epilepsy that afflicted him. A commander's clumsiness or physical infirmity does not inspire confidence. Caesar, however, had the presence of mind to cry out, "Africa, I take possession of thee!" (Machiavelli 1965, 175–176). His men thought he had deliberately fallen to embrace the ground.

During the naval battles of the eighteenth and nineteenth century, the captain normally stood on the upper deck. He had to do so even under a hail of enemy fire. When the crew saw the captain walking the deck, their morale went up. "If the captain is confident enough to walk the deck in full view of the enemy, we must be winning the battle."

Such confidence can count for more than sheer physical strength. Predatory animals feel their prey should run away. In the animal kingdom, a weaker animal always runs away. When the target stands its ground, something is wrong. Prey that stands fast must believe it can hurt the predator. Charging the predator conveys a greater psychological advantage. Only powerful animals like the rhinoceros, elephant, and bull defend themselves this way.

Prussia's Frederick II gave orders that Prussian cavalry must always charge the enemy. He threatened to cashier any cavalry officer who allowed the enemy to charge first. "Any commander allowing himself to be attacked would be discharged with infamy: 'The Prussians shall always attack the enemy'" (Asprey 1986, 284). Attacking or seeking the engagement provides an immediate psychological advantage over the enemy.

Does displaying confidence work in human competitions? Everyone knows about acting and "putting on a brave front." Acting confident, however, can still reduce the opponent's self-assurance. Also, showing confidence is vital in maintaining the morale of one's own organization.

Leaders Must Show Commitment to Goals

> Leadership is through action, not exhortation and slogans.

For any program to succeed, managers must show commitment and support. Executives must genuinely want subordinates to make the program work. The executives' role can be supportive instead of directive. This means supplying resources and recognizing successful efforts. It also means not abandoning the program for "business as usual." Tom Peters (1987) gives the following example about quality improvement programs. "Top quality also means, of course, not skimping or taking shortcuts in order to meet a production schedule, especially during the last week of the financial reporting period" (p. 629).

A program can easily fail because of lack of management commitment. Senior managers often appoint someone to head the program. Slogans and meetings whip up enthusiasm, but nothing really happens. Half-hearted starts can be worse than doing nothing. Niccolò Machiavelli and Li Ch'uan actually cited this as a technique for demoralizing an enemy army. The idea is to get the enemy soldiers to prepare for battle and then not fight.

> *If an enemy offers you battle early in the morning, you ought not to draw out your army to fight him immediately; rather, let his men wait under arms for some hours until their ardor is abated. (Machiavelli 1965, 123)*

The commentator Li Ch'uan cited the following story to clarify a principle in Sun Tzu's *The Art of War.* Duke Chuang commanded the Lu Army against the Ch'i. When he heard the Ch'i beat their drums he wanted to attack. His advisor Ts'ao Kuei advised him to wait. Only when the Ch'i drums rolled for the third time did he suggest an assault. The Duke followed this advice and won a victory. Afterward, Ts'ao Kuei explained what had happened. "In battle, a courageous spirit is everything. Now the first roll of the drum tends to create this spirit, but with the second it is already on the wane, and after the third it is gone altogether. I attacked when their spirit was gone and ours was at its height" (Clavell 1983, 33–34).

In many companies, upper management beats the drums to announce a new quality and productivity campaign. Without action, this is a superb way to destroy the enthusiasm of one's own organization. Feigenbaum (1991, 193) writes, "after an initial fanfare in introducing the quality program, top management may . . . give it the lukewarm support which may be the kiss of death to the quality-control program." The management team that does this is actually using the art and science of war against itself.

We also can remember the lesson of the boy who cried wolf. Eventually, no one paid attention to him. We also can look at Rudyard Kipling's "Road Song of the Bandar-Log." The Bandar-Log (Monkey People) sing about all the wonderful deeds they are going to do someday. They never do what they talk about. No one in the jungle respects them. When instituting a new program, don't be like the Bandar-Log.

From, "Road-Song of the Bandar-Log"
(or, "How Not to Run Your Quality Program")
(© 1940, Elsie Kipling Bambridge)

Here we sit in a branchy row,
Thinking of beautiful things we know;
Dreaming of deeds that we mean to do,
All complete, in a minute or two—
Something noble and grand and good,
Won by merely wishing we could.
    Now we're going to—never mind,
    Brother, thy tail hangs down behind!

All the talk we ever have heard
Uttered by bat or beast or bird—
Hide or fin or scale or feather—
Jabber it quickly and all together!

Excellent! Wonderful! Once again!
Now we are talking just like men.
     Let's pretend we are—never mind!
     Brother, thy tail hangs down behind!
     This is the way of the Monkey-kind!

Then join our leaping lines that scumfish through the pines,
That rocket by where, light and high, the wild grape swings.
By the rubbish in our wake, and the noble noise we make,
Be sure—be sure, we're going to do some splendid things!

Hayes, Wheelwright, and Clark (1988) cite three obstacles to success. The first one is lack of confidence in the program. If previous programs have come and gone, this problem becomes worse. "Down at the factory level, however, both managers and workers usually respond with the attitude that 'just like the other programs, this will pass and a different one will take its place next year. So we'll just wait it out'" (pp. 344–345). Short-term pressure to meet delivery schedules and lack of training are the other two obstacles.

The program must become part of the corporate culture. Hradesky (1988) makes this point very clear in discussing productivity and quality efforts. This means the program must become part of the organizational psyche, or "the way we operate here." The corporate culture is a set of attitudes, values, and beliefs the organizational members share (Schermerhorn, Hunt, and Osborn 1985). Something that becomes part of the corporate culture becomes a solid part of the business process.

PERFORMANCE MEASUREMENT

The performance measurement system is management's tool for evoking behavior. Management *always* gets what it asks. Be careful what you wish for. You may get it. Performance measurements must promote the desired behavior.

Did not God/Sometimes withhold in mercy what we ask
We should be ruined at our own request

—Hannah More (1745–1809)
Moses in the Bullrushes

In comparing organizations, Sun Tzu (1963, chap. 1) asks, "Which administers rewards and punishments in a more enlightened manner?" Machiavelli (1965, 164) wrote this about the Romans. "It is no wonder, then, that a people who were so exact in rewarding merit and punishing offenders should extend their empire to such a degree as they did; they are certainly highly worthy of imitation in these respects."

Today we recognize that punishment is not effective in promoting desirable behavior. We reserve it to deter illegal or otherwise undesirable actions. We may replace punishment with absence of reward. The idea is to reward merit and not mediocrity. Organizations often get into real trouble when they define merit. The performance measurement system interacts with the reward system. It determines who gets promotions, raises, and bonuses. The performance measurement system is management's magic lamp. Subordinates are the genies or djinns that grant the masters' wishes.

There is an ancient proverb that says, "Be careful what you wish. You might get it." Various folk tales and horror stories use this theme. The entity granting the wish always fulfills the wish's exact wording. The genie or magical item, however, perverts the request so the result is harmful. In *The Monkey's Paw*, a family receives a withered monkey paw that can grant three requests. The husband and wife ask for money. The malevolent magic kills their son in an accident so they can collect the insurance. In another story, a dragon grants a woman three wishes. She is not greedy, and merely asks that her family's farm always produce enough food. The dragon nods and flies off. It returns shortly and says, "I've eaten your family. Now, even if their farm produces nothing, it will always be enough for them."

These are just folk tales and horror stories. Business and industrial monkey's paws are always more subtle, and often more destructive. Also, business managers rarely have a second and third wish with which to fix the results of the first. Unlike the evil magic in the stories, employees are not malevolent. They won't pervert directives merely to hurt the company; however, they do respond to the performance measurement system. If the system is bad, management will get dysfunctional results. The organization ends up serving the measurement system, instead of the system serving the organization.

Figures 3.1 and 3.2 provide simple examples of dysfunctional performance measurements in football. Suppose the coach rates the players solely on statistics. These include interceptions by defenders and offensive rushing yards. In Figure 3.1, Team X is ahead in the last quarter.

Figure 3.1

Fourth down for Team O. Should defender X intercept the ball?

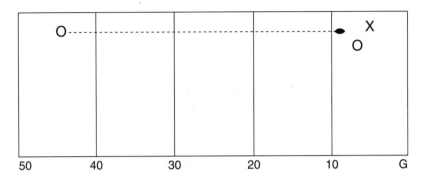

Team O's quarterback throws a "Hail, Mary" pass on fourth down. The defender is in a better position to catch the ball than the receiver. The receiver, however, is close enough to tackle the defender. The defender can't return the ball more than a few yards. What should he do? Catching the ball will put an interception on his record, however, his team will get the ball on its 5- or 10-yard line. If the pass is incomplete, the defense will get the ball on the 45-yard line. From an individual standpoint, the

Figure 3.2

Team X wants to run the clock out. Which way should the ball carrier go?

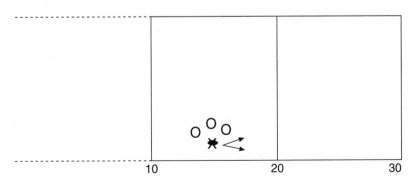

defender should catch the ball. From a team standpoint, he should knock the pass aside to make sure it is incomplete.

In Figure 3.2, Team X is ahead in the last quarter. It wants to run the clock out. What should the ball carrier do? Assume there is no chance of making a first down. If he runs as far as he can, he can gain 4–7 yards. The defenders, however, will force him out of bounds and stop the clock. If he turns toward the defenders, they will have to tackle him in bounds. The clock will keep running, but he'll get only a couple of yards. Again, the performance measurement system asks for behavior that hurts the organization. Now we'll go to some business examples.

Overhead as a Misleading Measurement

> The cost accounting system can greatly distort corporate decision processes.

Tom Peters provides this example. Suppose the accounting system assigns $10 of overhead to every dollar of direct labor. Suppose a job requires $2000 of direct labor, and a subcontractor will do the job for $5000. The plant manager hires the subcontractor. Under the performance measurement system, the plant manager did a great job. He or she has reduced the job cost from $22,000 to $5000 on paper; however, this decision actually raises the job's cost from $2000 to $5000. Reducing the direct labor doesn't make the overhead go away (except on paper). The company must still pay for utilities, indirect labor and staff, insurance, floor space, and so on. "You can't shut the heat off around one idle machine." Management got exactly what it requested—a $3000 loss (Peters 1987, 587–588).

The performance measurement system was at fault. It defined keeping the work in house as poor performance. The plant manager's punishment for saving the company money might have been loss of a promotion or bonus. The system defined giving the work to the subcontractor as a meritorious act. The manager's reward for losing $3000 is a bonus or good performance rating.

Promotion of Cheating

Cheating on standardized tests is a public sector example. Students' test scores affect the reputation of public schools. School reputations affect property values in a community. High scores also win state funding bonuses for schools. Test scores affect educator salaries. These factors promote cheating by administrators and teachers. "Teachers are under the gun to hike test scores in order to 'protect themselves'. . . . In a national survey of educators in 1990, 1 in 11 teachers reported pressure from administrators to cheat on standardized tests" (Toch and Wagner 1992, 66). One superintendent posted California Achievement Test scores in the school conference room for his county's 171 schools. His predecessor had displayed student art. This gave teachers a clear message about the superintendent's priorities. Another superintendent sent letters of praise to teachers whose students scored well. Toch and Wagner quoted a former director of testing in the San Francisco school system. "The message from superintendents is 'perform, perform, perform on standardized tests.' It puts the fear of God in principals" (p. 68).

Some teachers gave test answers to students ahead of time. Others corrected wrong answers before turning in the answer sheets. A less-flagrant approach emphasized the test subjects in class. This was not cheating, but it subordinated education to test performance. "Critics also charge that test-based teaching drives down the level of instruction in the nation's schools because the tests themselves focus on low-level skills" (p. 70). Other schools gave the tests only to their best students. These schools abused a law that exempts special-education students from state tests. They manipulated the rules to exempt two-thirds of their students from the exams.

The key problem is that the system rewards dysfunctional behaviors. School superintendents benefit because high scores lead to higher administrator salaries. Administrators reward teachers whose students produce the high scores. The community doesn't complain because high scores raise property values. Prestigious schools are a selling point for real estate. Test publishers also benefit from cheating. If students do well on the publishers' tests, the school will continue to buy them. This is a disincentive for publishers to make their exam materials secure.

Does the System Promote Teamwork or Rivalry?
There is a college legend that premedical students sabotage each other's academic work. They supposedly hide library reference books, sabotage lab experiments, and so on. This legend's origin has nothing to do with the kind of students who want to be doctors. It comes from the performance measurement system of grading on the curve. This means the professor ranks the students against each other to assign grades. There may be a quota like 10 percent As, 20 percent Bs, 40 percent Cs,

20 percent Ds, and 10 percent Fs. In theory, the lowest 10 of 100 students would fail no matter what their performance was. Since premedical students are under pressure to get good grades, they will do just about anything.

These legends may be tall tales, but the performance measurement does not promote teamwork. Students who are competing for grades are not going to help each other. Cooperation would promote the college's ostensible goal of education. The students would learn more. All the college's students would perform better against an objective standard. Grading on the curve, however, discourages this. Corporate performance measurement systems that rank employees against each other have the same drawback.

They don't promote maximum performance either. There was a story about some hunters on safari. A lion surprised them in camp, and they couldn't get to their rifles. One man began putting on a pair of running shoes. Another said, "Are you crazy? You can't outrun a lion."

The man said, "I don't have to. I just have to outrun at least one of you."

He can "pass" as long as someone else is a weaker performer. Mediocre performers in a ranking-type environment can survive while others are weaker. The strong performers all want to be first. They will not help each other if they can avoid it. Ranking creates *polarity*, or a win-lose situation. If you win, others must lose. This is suitable for promoting performance in an *individual* activity like a race. It is not a good system for promoting teamwork. Deming criticized performance appraisals *in general* (Graber, Breisch, and Breisch 1992, 59, 61).

> *Employees are rewarded for promoting themselves for their own good; the organization is the loser. . . . Making someone else look good is a dual liability because it takes time away from one's own concerns while strengthening someone else's case for scarce promotions. . . . Performance appraisals should be criterion-based. People should be evaluated against standards and expectations, not against each other. Forced distributions of ratings are competitive and terribly destructive to morale. All employees should have the opportunity to receive an outstanding rating.*

Fechter (1993) cites dysfunctional effects of ranking in service industries. Suppose a travel agency ranks agents by the number of customers they serve each hour. "Travel agents soon learn that meeting customers' needs has less influence on performance evaluation than maintaining a high customers-per-hour average" (p. 88).

Carroll (1993) cites dysfunctional effects of performance appraisal systems at IBM. "The IBM system mainly measured how many lines of [software] code someone wrote, which actually encouraged programmers to write inefficient software" (p. 101). A Microsoft software developer rewrote a 33,000-character (byte) piece of IBM code in 200 characters. Later, introduction of a ranking system in the research department actually lead to a *drop* in the number of IBM patent applications. It was easier to get a good ranking by writing technical papers.

In summary, the organization must set uniform standards and rate everyone against those standards. Teamwork and cooperation should be among the criteria. If everyone performs well, everyone should get an A. If no one performs well, no one should get an A. This system promotes cooperation and maximum performance.

Performance Measurement in Sales

Macke Business Products ties its sales representatives' commissions to collection of receivables. The sale is not complete until the customer pays. This discourages sales representatives from giving credit to customers who can't pay. If the customer doesn't pay, the sales representative tries to collect. Delinquents often find a call from their salesperson less offensive than a call from the company's credit department (Noble 1991). This author recalls that W. T. Grant measured its sales force on sales alone. The sales representative also had the authority to issue credit cards! This measurement system encouraged the indiscriminate distribution of credit cards. The measurement system also encouraged the sales force to urge customers to use the credit cards. A credit sale was still a sale, however, many of them produced bad debts.

The ROI Trap

> A return on investment performance criterion can hurt a company's long-term competitiveness.

The return on investment (ROI) measurement is a classic problem. Upper management measures the plant manager on ROI. Here are the plant manager's choices.

Don't buy new equipment   or   Buy new equipment

$$ROI = \frac{Income}{Assets} \qquad\qquad ROI = \frac{Income - Depreciation}{Assets + New\ capital}$$

The factory's old equipment may have no book value because of depreciation. Suppose the plant manager buys new equipment. This increases the divisor of the performance measurement. Since the new equipment depreciates, this decision also reduces the numerator. By keeping the old equipment, the plant manager does an outstanding job. He or she may even earn a promotion. Meanwhile, competitors may be investing in new equipment to gain a long-term competitive advantage (Hayes, Wheelwright, and Clark 1988).

Performance Measurements in Hotel Management

To maximize profit, Mississippi Management measures its hotel managers' gross profit per available room. Suppose the company tracked gross margin instead of gross profit. Restaurant sales are low margin. Room rents are high margin. This performance measurement system encourages managers to focus on selling rooms. It discourages them from trying to make more restaurant sales. "So if you want maximum profit, not maximum margins, give managers a performance measure that doesn't penalize them for picking up those extra profit dollars in low-margin sales" (Noble 1991, 100).

In summary, we must use appropriate performance measurements. Deficient measurements produce dysfunctional results. Does the performance measurement system serve the organization, or does the organization serve the system?

THE WORKFORCE

> Training and education empower workers and increase their flexibility. They instill confidence and pride. They increase the organization's agility and competitiveness.

For a city consists in its men, and not in its walls nor ships empty of men.
—Nicias (470–413 B.C.E.), *speech to the defeated Athenian army at Syracuse, 413 B.C.E.*

Quality of the Workforce

An organization's technology is a good indicator of the quality of its workforce. Technology includes the physical and behavioral means of production (Klein and Ritti 1984). It includes organizational and psychological factors as well as science and engineering. Does the organization rely on rules and operating procedures, or does it look to workers for skills and initiative? Are the jobs monotonous assembly-line tasks, or are they craft jobs? The structure of the work says a lot about the quality of the workforce. The quality of the workforce defines the company's ability to respond to dynamic market conditions.

Structure Must Compensate for Low-Quality People

> Unskilled workers depend on mechanistic organizational structures for effectiveness; however, mechanistic organizations are not agile or adaptable. This limits their competitiveness.

Throughout history, countries have used two classes of soldiers. One is the individual warrior, whose success depends on his or her personal skill at arms. The individual warrior may follow orders and fight in a unit; however, he or she must use skill and initiative to succeed. The other is the team-component soldier, whose success depends on the organizational structure. Some examples are shown in Tables 3.1 and 3.2.

Note the empty space in Table 3.2. Organizational structure must make up for low-quality personnel. Guerrillas and partisans are the only troops with little formal training or organization. These troops usually have a special advantage like extensive knowledge of the local terrain. Even if the invader's soldiers have better training, they do not know the theater as well. Without this special advantage, the partisans lose their value. World War II French Resistance fighters would have been ineffective against the Soviets in Afghanistan. Afghan guerrillas would have done poorly in occupied France. Partisans are not effective against an enemy in the open field. They must raid enemy supplies or isolated outposts, and disperse when heavier forces show up.

"The Masses" and Their Tools

> A worker's tools say a lot about his or her skills.

It didn't take much skill to be an infantryman in the eighteenth and nineteenth centuries. One needed courage to face enemy fire and endurance to

Table 3.1

Types of soldiers.

Personal skill at arms	Individual combatants (Low organizational structure)	Team-component soldiers (High structure)
High, developed over a lifetime of training	Medieval knight Samurai Medieval longbowman	Spartan phalanx
Medium, extensive training upon entering service	Fighter pilot Eighteenth/nineteenth century light infantry (jaegers, chausseurs) Eighteenth/nineteenth century light cavalry (hussars) Modern light infantry (marines, rangers, special forces)	Roman legion Swiss pikemen Eighteenth/nineteenth century elite infantry (guards, grenadiers) Eighteenth/nineteenth century heavy cavalry (lancers, cuirassiers)
Low, rudimentary training upon entering service	Guerrillas/partisans (but they have special advantages such as knowledge of the local theater of operations)	Medieval crossbowmen Eighteenth/nineteenth century infantry (lower quality)

march long distances. Marksmanship was not a requirement. The soldier pointed his musket in the enemy's general direction and awaited the command to fire. Aiming was futile at more than 100 or so yards. (Held 1957).

Firearm expert Jeff Cooper (1990) has a similar criticism of the M-16 carbine. The weapon's theoretical effective range is 500–600 yards; however, "troops armed with the standard 5.56 [.223 caliber] cartridge of the Western World pose very slight hazard to individual, indistinct, intermittently visible human targets at 300 meters—under battlefield conditions" (p. 184). Rifles are for elite troops who learn to shoot properly. The 1898 Mauser and its relatives the 1903 Springfield and 1905 Lee-Enfield are

Table 3.2

Sources of strength in combat units.

	Organizational structure has little or moderate value.	Organizational structure is important.
Individual skill has little value.		Low-grade infantry
Individual skill is moderately important.	Light infantry/ cavalry Guerrillas/partisans (skill is knowledge of the local theater)	Swiss Pike Roman Legion Elite Infantry (guards, grenadiers) Heavy cavalry (cuirassiers, lancers, dragoons)
Individual skill is very important.	Fighter pilot Knight, samurai (could fight alone or in formations)	Spartan phalanx Knight, samurai (could fight alone or in formations)

deadly at 1000 yards with good riflemen behind them. Cooper cites a Marine officer (who later became corps commandant) who said he would "rather attack ten machineguns working together than one platoon of riflemen who could shoot" (p. 174). Cooper derisively calls automatic carbines, like the M-16, weapons for "the masses" (p. 176).

The masses, however, did win battles. The British won dozens of engagements with Brown Bess (the smoothbore Tower musket). Rudyard Kipling even wrote a poem praising the weapon. The British success secret was *mass production.* "If you cannot shoot well, shoot a lot" (Cooper 1990, 175).

This philosophy has persisted. Even during the Civil War, many soldiers used smoothbore muskets. They loaded the guns with a musket ball plus buckshot. "Buck and ball" inflicted horrific casualties at Antietam (1862) (Bilby 1993). Georg Luger patented a multiple-bullet cartridge in 1910. Even in the 1950s, the U.S. Army investigated multiple-bullet cartridges. The army's interest came from "investigations into marksmanship and the lack of it among soldiers." The army even introduced a "Duplex" 7.92 mm NATO round in 1960 (Hogg 1979, 178–179).

Loading drill was an early product of ergonomics and time-motion studies. There was a precise series of steps the infantryman followed to load and fire as quickly as possible (Held 1957). These loading drills pre-dated Frederick Winslow Taylor by hundreds of years. Volley fire won the Battle of Nagashino (1573) for Oda Nobunaga. The Swedes under Gustavus Adolphus (1594–1632) helped introduce volley fire to Europe. The infantry regiment was the eighteenth and nineteenth century version of the assembly line.

Systematic volley fire allowed a British regiment to fire 10,000 rounds a minute. The system was effective, but it required total reliance on the organization. The soldiers had to stay in a formation and fire in volleys. If the formation broke, they were almost helpless.

The Elite

> Craftspeople can use complex tools to achieve outstanding results.

Light infantry of the eighteenth and nineteenth centuries was very different from regular infantry. Light troops used rifles, and they did not need a formation to be effective. They were frequently professional hunters or woodsmen before becoming soldiers. They could operate in forests without becoming lost or dispersed. While musket volleys were almost harmless at 200 yards, a rifleman could hit at 300 or more yards. Light infantry could harass line infantry, and disperse into a forest if the line infantry chased it.

The cavalryman had to command a horse while maneuvering in formation with his comrades. The sabre and lance required considerable skill. One test of skill was "tent-pegging." The lancer tried to skewer a tent peg while charging at full gallop. Hussars under Frederick the Great had to meet the following requirements: "A trooper was trained to snatch a small object from the ground at full gallop; he had to be able 'to wheel and turn on the space of a thaler [coin]'" (Asprey 1986, 284). Good cavalrymen could fire a pistol or carbine from horseback and expect to hit with it. The Japanese samurai could achieve the same results in his role of mounted archer. Cavalry always enjoyed more prestige and status than line infantry.

The army sometimes refers to armor units as "cavalry;" however, the team dynamics in a tank are more like those in a chariot. A chariot crew included a driver and one or more archers and spearmen (gunners). An elephant crew was similar. Tanks, chariots, and war elephants are similar in that the team members must cooperate smoothly and efficiently to succeed. This requires extensive training and practice.

Why do we attach so much romance and admiration to the fighter pilot? From the Red Baron to *Top Gun,* we have always admired the knight of the air. Aerial combat is one of the few places in modern war where the personal skill of the combatant is still decisive.

Parallels in Modern Industry

Now we come to modern industry. The assembly line is the tool of the masses. Time-motion studies and detailed operating procedures are for the masses. In contrast, the craft worker or machinist is an elite worker. The outcome of the task rests on his or her personal skill. The drill press, lathe, or mill is not for the unskilled worker. American industry needs to fear and respect this, since we still rely on the assembly line. Countries like Germany have maintained their craft traditions (Peters 1987). Typical blue-collar Germans are not just pairs of hands. They have probably gone through a three- or four-year craft apprenticeship program. They do not need detailed operating procedures and directions. Give them a piece of metal and a diagram, and they'll make the part. We've looked at sources of strength in military units. Now consider industrial work situations as shown in Table 3.3.

Qualitative Versus Numerical Superiority

Admiral John Jervis commanded 15 English ships of the line at Cape St. Vincent (1797). The lookout sighted the enemy, and soon counted 27 sails. Jervis finally said, "I don't care how many there are. We are going through them." You can say this when you know your officers and men are better than the enemy's. The battle was a decisive English victory.

Sun Tzu wrote that numbers alone are not an advantage. He warned against relying on numerical superiority to win. The quality of the workforce is a critical competitive factor. This author does not agree with Ries and Trout (1986) that numerical superiority is decisive. Yes, "a good big man can beat a good little man." The heavyweight champion can beat the featherweight champion; however, the advantage of size or numbers assumes equal skill or quality. A lightweight professional boxer can make short work of a 200-pound slob. In analyzing organizations, Sun Tzu specifically asks which side has the better-trained officers and men.

Table 3.3

Sources of strength in work units.

	Organizational structure has little or moderate value.	Organizational structure is important.
Extensive training (skilled craftsperson or master) or substantial training (journeyman)	Auto mechanic Machinist (job shop) Skilled tool operator Plumber Electrician Carpenter	Machinist (mass production) Welder (mass production) Construction plumber Construction electrician Construction carpenter Construction mason
Low training (unskilled)		Unskilled assembly worker Unskilled tool operator

Concentration of Force at the Decisive Point

> Concentration of force is a decisive factor in war and business.

What is concentration of force at the decisive point? The edge of a sword or axe concentrates the force of a blow along a line. A mace's spike focuses it on a point. An armor-piercing shape charge directs the entire force of an explosive charge at a small portion of the enemy's defense. This is how a bazooka, or TOW missile, works. *The idea is to meet a small part of the enemy's strength with an overwhelming force.* Even if the enemy force is bigger and stronger overall, we can overpower it at the point of contact.

Overall numerical superiority does not guarantee superiority at the point of contact. "Consequently, the forces available must be employed with such skill that even in the absence of absolute superiority, relative superiority is attained at the decisive point" (Clausewitz 1976, Book 3, chap. 8). Naval commanders did this by crossing the enemy T. This meant placing one's own ship broadside to the enemy's bow or stern. Most of a ship's guns fired to the sides. Suppose an English 74-gun ship crossed the T of a Spanish 130-gun ship. The British now had a 37-gun broadside against a couple of bow or stern chasers. The enemy's advantage in guns did not matter because the enemy could not use them.

The enemy was not stupid and knew about this maneuver. Achieving it was a matter of management and training. The captain had to take advantage of wind and position. Special techniques included getting between the wind and the opponent. This was the possible origin of the phrase, "taking the wind out of his sails." The captain had to outsail the opponent, and he needed a good crew to do it. Maneuvering involved far more than turning the wheel. It required taking in or letting out sail at the proper times. British officers and crews were usually better than their opponents. They knew the ropes better than the opposing sailors. (Sailors used ropes to control the sails.) *Training and management are critical factors in achieving concentration of force at the decisive point.*

Trafalgar and Tsushima were two of history's most decisive naval battles. In both cases, the numerically weaker force conducted an almost one-sided massacre. Concentration of force was the decisive factor. The British broke through the French line at Trafalgar, and crossed the T. The Japanese defeated the Russians in detail at Tsushima. The Russians had more guns, but had made an exhausting trip halfway around the world. The Japanese crews were better, and their ships were a little faster.

Defeating the Enemy in Detail

Defeating the enemy in detail means defeating its forces a portion at a time. "The goal of the tactician is to ensure that the fight, when and where joined, is never 'fair.' It is his business to bring overwhelming force to bear on a particular subdivision of his adversary's array and to dispose of it. . . . He can [then] engage an enemy reduced in strength by the amount he has just destroyed" (Cooper 1990, 43). Sun Tzu discusses methods for making the enemy divide its forces. Then one can attack each piece separately.

Defeat in detail is an extension of the concentration-of-force principle. This is really how the Japanese won the Battle of Tsushima. They used their superior speed to fight only a portion of the Russian line at a time.

Most of us have watched movies that show a lone hero disposing of several bad guys with fist or sword. The choreography is predictable. The bad guys attack one at a time. The hero downs the first villain. The next villain takes his turn, and so on. (This was especially true in the Batman and Robin TV series.) This is an example of *defeat in detail*. We tell ourselves the bad guys would never be so stupid in real life. They'd all attack together; *however, skilled fighters can maneuver so they face only one opponent at a time.* Unless the attackers know how to work together, they may even get in each others' way.

Miyamoto Musashi introduces the concept of "there are many enemies." The idea is to drive the enemy together, "as if tying a line of fishes," so they get in each others' way. This looks like the technique he used in his fight with the Yoshioka Kendo School. Even Musashi could not fight several swordsmen at once. He maneuvered so he was never actually in contact with more than one or two. It was almost like a movie. While the Yoshiokas had overwhelming numerical superiority, Musashi had superiority at the point of contact. He killed many of the Yoshioka swordsmen, including a couple of the leaders, and then escaped (Yoshikawa 1961, 521). This brings us back to the value of training. Miyamoto Musashi, the best swordsman in Japan, could make this work. An average, or merely good, man would have died.

Tom Peters has a laminated business card with the ratio 3750/126 printed on it. It commemorates a 1983 visit with Kelly Johnson of Lockheed Corporation. Lockheed and a competitor were working on Air Force projects of almost equal size. The competitor was "years behind and hundreds of percent over budget," with 3750 people. Johnson was "on schedule and under budget," with 126 people (Peters and Austin 1985). Therefore, we contend that qualitative superiority in people, leadership, and equipment can be decisive.

Training and Organizational Effectiveness

An organization with skilled workers enjoys the following competitive advantages.

1. Line workers can participate in problem-solving and process improvement activities.
2. Line workers feel ownership for the quality of the work. This is a source of *intrinsic motivation* (Schermerhorn, Hunt, and Osborn 1985).
3. The factory can be more flexible in responding to changing business needs. Workers can easily learn new tasks. Making part B

instead of part A may be routine to a skilled machinist, but not to an unskilled laborer.

4. Training promotes commitment and loyalty. Tom Peters (1987) cites examples of lower absenteeism (GM) and less turnover (Amdahl). Stew Leonard's groceries can hire the best employees from the market.

Clausewitz discounted the competitive value of training and equipment. This was because training standards were similar in all European armies of his day. He pointed out that technological advantages are temporary, because opponents promptly copy them.

Clausewitz's argument about technology applies to modern business. The same technology is available to everybody, unless someone owns a patent. The competitor can buy a computer-controlled multiaxis machining station as easily as we can. The same training also is available to everybody. Not everybody, however, chooses to exploit it. The standards of training for modern workforces are *not* equal. Therefore, training can confer a decisive advantage. Ross Perot once said, "Brains and wits will beat capital spending ten times out of ten" (Peters 1987, 388).

Clausewitz shows the importance of human resources in difficult or complex competitive situations. In complex environments, each frontline service provider is often on his or her own. In these situations, "the courage, skill, and spirit of the individual will be the decisive factor. Only in cases in which the two armies are of equal quality, or where their special virtues cancel each other out, can the talent and insight of the supreme commander again become paramount" (Clauswitz 1976, Book 5, chap. 17). What happens when training and commitment are not adequate?

The more these characteristics and circumstances are missing in one army, and the more pronounced they are on the other side, the more this army will fear fragmentation and the more it will tend to avoid rough country. But this is seldom a matter of choice: one cannot choose a theater of operations by trying it out as if it were merchandise. Hence troops that are by nature at an advantage when fighting as a concentrated mass, will exert their efforts to the utmost in order to use this system as far as it is at all possible, in spite of the nature of the terrain. They will thereby be exposed to other disadvantages, such as difficulties of supply and poor billets; and in action they will be exposed to frequent flank attacks. But they would pay an even greater penalty if they were to give up their own special advantages.

Suppose we treat "rough country" as a complex, dynamic business environment. A company whose workers lack skill, enthusiasm, and commitment would prefer not to compete in this environment; however, it might not have a choice. Nonetheless, the company will have to rely on mechanistic, close-control management methods. It cannot trust the workers' judgment, initiative, and loyalty. This is not the workers' fault. It is management's fault, for not having the foresight to train the workers and foster commitment. This company will suffer from marketing flank attacks by agile opponents with organic management systems.

These opponents can rely on small, entrepreneurial groups of employees to act independently. They can work to meet the needs of individual customers or small market segments. They can open new market segments or niches, or seize existing ones. This is especially true when the people who make the products also talk to the customers. A large organization that must rely on close management control cannot respond to each threat.

Craft Apprenticeships in Germany and Japan

> The other two big players in the world economy, Germany and Japan, value and promote craftsmanship.

Germany and Japan have long traditions of craft apprenticeship programs. The blue-collar worker is far more than a pair of hands. His or her training is similar to that of the old apprentice/journeyman/master guild system. "Major German companies . . . typically sponsor apprenticeship programs, in which workers spend up to two years learning both the theory and practice of a trade before they actually make a product to be sold to a customer" (Hayes, Wheelwright, and Clark 1988, 256).

Wilfried Prewo, the chief executive of the Chamber of Industry and Commerce in Hanover, cites the skill of the German workforce. "Seventy percent of young Germans sign up for apprenticeships—and, usually, guaranteed jobs. Contrast this with the aimless wandering from low-wage job to low-wage job of many U.S. high school grads." German high school graduates serve two- to three-year apprenticeships. They become craft workers, machinists, and lab assistants. Apprentices earn $500–$800 a month or $6000–$9600/year. These would be poverty wages in the United States. Their pay, however, quadruples after they earn certificates in their trades. (Under the old guild system, they would be "journeymen.") This means they earn $24,000 to $38,400 annually.

About 10 percent of these workers sign up for more training, usually in their late 20s. They become supervisors ("masters" in the guild system). "The cream of the alumni crop then trains the apprentices in the workplace." The German economy is very competitive despite high income taxes, and labor costs that are 60 percent higher than ours. (W. Prewo, "The Sorcery of Apprenticeship," *Wall Street Journal*, 12 February 1993).

Workstation Ownership at IBM

Several years ago, IBM introduced its Workstation Ownership (WSO) program. The program empowers manufacturing employees to take ownership of their workstations. Traditionally, the manufacturing operator merely ran the workstation. If it needed maintenance or repair, he or she had to call the maintenance department. The WSO program also makes the operators responsible for product quality. Traditionally, the quality control (QC) department had this job. QC sometimes performed inspections that duplicated in-line manufacturing inspections. Finally, the WSO program encourages operators to participate in problem-solving and process improvement efforts.

How empowered can a person with just a high school diploma be in a high-technology environment? IBM addresses this issue with the Manufacturing Technology Training School (MTTS). The company pays for operators to take math and science courses from a local community college. The manufacturing personnel learn math, physics, chemistry, electronics, and statistical process control (SPC). When they finish, they are a few courses short of a two-year (associate) technical degree. If the employees want to finish this degree on their own time, the company pays for the courses.

Empowering Workers at Harley-Davidson

Before the 1980s, Harley-Davidson treated workers as extensions of the machinery. It called manufacturing operators "machine hands." However, "labor problems forced management to begin treating manufacturing employees as rational human beings who could handle statistics." This helped Harley-Davidson introduce SPC into its operations. Harley-Davidson calls SPC statistical operator control (SOC). SOC allows operators to shut down out-of-control machines. It also provides a common language for operators, engineers, and maintenance workers. The company also introduced just-in-time (JIT) manufacturing. Harley-Davidson's version is materials as needed, or MAN—"because Harley is a macho company" (Page 1991, 7–8).

Training and Morale

Training raises the morale and confidence of workers, managers, and professionals. Training and experience improve the morale of the workforce.

"Inexperience is the mother of cowardice, and compulsion makes men mutinous and discontented; but both experience and courage are acquired by arming, exercising, and disciplining men properly" (Machiavelli 1965, 29). Clausewitz stressed the importance of experience. Long times of peace can weaken an army. He suggested that a country that has been at peace hire foreign officers who have distinguished themselves in war. Tu Yu, a commentator on Sun Tzu's *The Art of War,* wrote, "Therefore Master Wang said: 'if officers are unaccustomed to rigorous drilling they will be worried and hesitant in battle; if generals are not thoroughly trained they will inwardly quail when they face the enemy.'" (Sun Tzu 1963, 66). Training is thus important at all levels of the organization.

Skill-Based Pay Programs
Consultant Towers Perrin studied 27 companies that have skill-based pay programs. These companies pay workers for learning new job skills. Seventy to 88 percent of the companies reported higher job satisfaction, product quality, or productivity. Seventy to 75 percent reported lower operating costs or lower employee turnover. Workers with more skills are more versatile too. It is easier to schedule vacations because several employees can perform each job. Corning Glass has skill-based pay at nine plants. At one factory, workers can increase their wages from $9.50/hour to $13.50/hour by learning new skills. Workers at American Steel & Wire can raise their annual salaries by up to $12,480 by learning extra skills ("Skill-Based Pay Boosts Worker Productivity," *Wall Street Journal,* 23 June 1992).

Good training and equipment make workers confident. Chang Yu wrote, "Chariots strong, horses fast, troops valiant, weapons sharp—so that when they hear the drums beat the attack they are happy, and when they hear the gongs sound the retirement they are enraged. He who is like this is strong" (Sun Tzu 1963, 65–66). We may summarize by heeding Tom Peters' advice—train, and retrain!

MOTIVATION AND PRODUCTIVITY

> Intrinsic motivation promotes sustained intensity of effort. Job design, training, and empowerment are factors in intrinsic motivation.

Productivity means *sustained intensity of effort despite fatigue and distractions* (Miller 1985–1986). Pay and bonuses alone cannot evoke these efforts. To get them, the job itself must provide the motivation. Management must consider this in designing jobs.

Intrinsic and Extrinsic Motivation

Die Tat ist alles, nicht der Ruhm
The deed is all, and not the glory
—Johann Wolfgang von Goethe (1749–1832)

Intrinsic motivation is a vital contributor to productivity. It means the worker receives satisfaction and enjoyment from performing the task. It comes from the relationship between the worker and the task. It promotes sustained intensity of effort despite fatigue and distractions (Miller 1985–1986). Extrinsic motivators merely affect the employee's decision to participate. Extrinsic motivators like pay and good working conditions help the company hire and keep workers. They also reduce absenteeism. The workers feel that the company is taking care of them and that they owe the company a full day's work. Extrinsic motivators, however, do little to sustain persistent concentration on a dull, repetitious task. Bored workers become careless and make mistakes. Therefore, intrinsic motivation is critical. The opportunity to apply skills and training promotes it. When the workforce has a high skill level, workers can take more responsibility for the work.

The following factors foster intrinsic motivation (Miller 1985–1986).

- Skill variety. The job exercises a variety of the workers' skills.
- Identification with the work. Workers can see and understand the outcome of their tasks. The workpiece is not just a widget or meaningless subassembly.

- Task significance. Workers believe the outcome of the task is important to the organization.
- Autonomy. Workers have responsibility for, and control over, the work.
- Feedback. Workers receive meaningful and timely feedback. For example, workers inspect their own work. This provides immediate feedback on its quality. "Virtually all inspection should be self-inspection" (Peters 1987, 476).

Intrinsic Motivation and Video Games

> A video game is an excellent example of an intrinsically motivating activity (albeit without a productive outcome).

Why are video games so addictive, especially to teenagers? The games require the intense concentration we'd like workers to give their jobs. Educators would like students to give this effort to their studies. Video game players get instant feedback from their actions. Players identify with the work and instantly see the results. Video games are an ideal model for intrinsic motivation. Meanwhile, the score is an extrinsic motivator. How many players pay attention to the score until the game is over?

Some educators have taken advantage of this to write educational computer games. These games can be more effective than lectures since they are participative. "Where in Time Is Carmen Sandiego?" has players take the role of a time-traveling detective. The settings are authentic elements of world history. By playing this game, teenagers can learn this subject. There also is a Math Blaster game for children.

Training and Intrinsic Motivation

> Training is a cornerstone of intrinsic motivation.

Training is critical in promoting intrinsic motivation. Untrained workers cannot take responsibility for work, so they have no autonomy. Untrained workers cannot successfully inspect their own work. Workers must understand the overall process to answer the question, "Where does my job fit into the organization?" This is a prerequisite for task significance and identification with the work. Finally, workers cannot exercise a variety of skills they don't have.

Worker Autonomy at Johnsonville Sausage

Tom Peters (1987, 1989) discusses worker autonomy at Johnsonville Sausage of Sheboygan Falls, Wisconsin. Johnsonville Sausage raised its market share from 7 percent in 1978 to 50 percent by 1987. Employee empowerment played a major role. Teams of hourly wage sausage workers could recruit, appraise, or dismiss their own members. Members learned new skills as needed. The teams performed the following jobs.

- Developed and tracked annual budgets
- Proposed capital investments
- Took full responsibility for quality control
- Developed new products and packaging
- Monitored and improved productivity and quality

President Ralph Stayer explained his approach. "Workers felt here's where I get my money and I have fun elsewhere. [This is extrinsic motivation.] In the final analysis, a person's work determines what they are in life. . . . What I decided to do, if I take my business and turn it this way and that, I can bring out the greatness in people. . . . I listened to people more, asked them how they do things. . . . I wanted to help people become the instrument of their own destiny" (Peters 1987, 345).

Stayer found that workers were unfamiliar with autonomy and empowerment. They had taken direction for so long that they didn't know how to exercise judgment and initiative. Eventually, though, Stayer's approach succeeded.

Frontline Workers in Customer Relationships

> Frontline manufacturing workers can participate in customer-supplier relationships.

Harris Semiconductor and Ford showed that manufacturing operators can play major roles in total quality management (TQM). Harris supplies parts to Ford. Although the parts met Ford's specifications, Ford's manufacturing people did not like them. We'd normally expect managers and engineers from the two companies to settle the issue. This is not what happened. Harris and Ford operators met face to face. "Harris operators explained the dos and don'ts on how to handle wafers, and the Ford employees identified some of the real problems they faced."

"Rather than losing business, the Mountaintop (Harris) plant captured more business because of the focus and subsequent results they were able to achieve. It took everyone's involvement, understanding, and dedication to the customer to turn the situation around" ("Harris video dedicated to Mountaintop" 1993).

Pride in Workmanship

Pride in workmanship is a vital factor in intrinsic motivation. How can companies help employees recognize the importance of their work?

In ancient times, even rank-and-file soldiers were aware of their role in organizational success. Even the lowest ranking foot soldier was a member of the military social class. Before engaging an enemy, he would declare his name and ancestry. In the *Mahabharata*, Kripa, the Kaurava's archery teacher, speaks to his nephew Aswatthaman "We are masters of all weapons; what should we fear in the morning when we tell our names and crush the enemy?" (Buck 1973, 323). At the Battle of Kurukshetra, the patriarch Bhishma fought from his chariot. "There was Bhishma, in white robes and armor, first calling the names of those he killed, his white bow drawn in a circle, burning like smokeless fire" (p. 265). The Japanese followed similar customs. At the Battle of the Anegawa in 1570, a samurai volunteered to cover the retreat of the Asakuras. "'I am a person called Makara Jurozaemon,' he shouted in a loud voice. 'If anyone forgets it, I shall show who I am by gaining my customary victory!'" (Turnbull 1987, 63). Homer's *Iliad* recites the lineage and nationality of each combatant. The warrior wanted to glorify his personal and family name in battle. War was his work product, and he put his name on it.

Civilian artisans took similar pride in their work. Products were not anonymous goods. Craft workers stamped their names or trademarks on their products. This was a form of advertising and a guarantee of quality. Manufacturers who put their names on junk wouldn't stay in business long.

Eriez Magnetics realizes production workers often feel anonymous and unimportant. Therefore, it puts 4" x 30" nameplates in work areas.

Each employee has a nameplate at his or her workstation. The nameplate says, "Sales/welding" or "Sales/machine shop." This reminds the employees that the quality of their work affects sales. Each of Cleveland-based Original Copy Center's 94 employees has his or her own business card (Noble 1991). The employees are proud to give these cards out. This is also free advertising for the company.

Quality Improvement Teams

> The quality improvement team relies on frontline workers' participation.

The quality improvement team (QIT) is another organizational tool for empowering workers. It is an interdisciplinary activity that crosses organizational boundaries. QITs involve professional and hourly workers. They follow Tom Peters' (1989) advice that the person closest to the job knows the most about it. This means using the experience and insight of frontline workers to improve productivity and quality. W. Edwards Deming said, "The greatest waste in America is failure to use the abilities of people" (Covey 1991, 264). Recall that workers' skills and insights are resources, or competitive weapons. Musashi (1974, Ground Book) wrote that a warrior must make fullest use of his or her resources. "It is false not to do so, and to die with a weapon yet undrawn."

General Patton emphasized the importance of talking with frontline workers. During maneuvers, a sergeant complained that army truck transmissions could not take desert heat. Patton ordered a report sent to Washington and the truck manufacturer. Since Patton later fought in North Africa, this may have had significant results (Williamson 1979).

It took an outside consultant to get one company to listen to its frontline workers. There was a quality problem with an aluminum weld. A cross-functional team was trying to solve it. The vice president of finance, manufacturing manager, and quality manager on the team wouldn't listen to the welder. The welder wanted to discuss the problem with welders at other companies that used the same alloy. The managers wanted to hire an expert metallurgist and do a costly study. The consultant persuaded them to take the welder's advice. "It's an ideal benchmarking situation. Let him find five other companies welding these same materials, describe your problem exactly, and find out how they would handle it" (Sprow 193, 62).

QITs and Cause-and-Effect Diagrams

Frontline workers can use problem-solving and problem-preventing tools like the cause-and-effect diagram.

The QIT plays a vital role in using tools like the cause-and-effect diagram and corrective and preventive (CP) action matrix. The cause-and-effect diagram is an analytical tool for systematic problem solving (Contino 1987; Hradesky 1988). Figure 3.3 follows Contino's cause definitions.

The term *fishbone diagram* comes from the figure's similarity to a fish skeleton. The problem definition is at the fish's head. This diagram is an excellent tool for QITs. Team members use it to identify potential problem sources. They must then indict or exonerate the suspect sources through investigation or experimentation.

The cause-and-effect diagram is a natural feeder to the CP action matrix (Hradesky 1988). (Harris Semiconductor calls this an out-of-control action procedure, or OCAP.) The CP action matrix identifies a problem's causes and the proper corrective and preventive responses. The CP matrix also assigns responsibility for the causes. Therefore, it is useful to select main causes (the main branches on the fishbone diagram) by departmental responsibility. Then other causes can be considered as appropriate.

- Machines: Equipment engineering and maintenance
- Materials: Material quality assurance; suppliers

Figure 3.3

Cause-and-effect diagram.

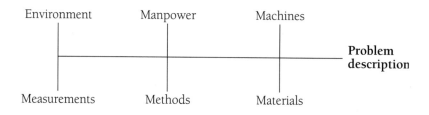

- Measurements: Inspection/measurement departments
- Methods: Manufacturing engineering; process development
- Manpower (human resources): Manufacturing
- Product design: Product development
- Environment: Contamination engineering; facilities department

This list suggests possible task force or QIT participants. The key point is that a QIT is an interdepartmental and interdisciplinary effort. Tom Peters and W. Edwards Deming urge breaking down interdepartmental barriers. The QIT follows this advice.

Developing Immunity to Manufacturing Problems

> The CP action matrix is a manufacturing line's immune system.

Suppose we treat defect causes as diseases. The human body gains immunity to diseases through experience. Having certain diseases like chicken pox or smallpox confers immunity. After fighting off the disease, the body recognizes the bacteria or viruses that caused it. If they appear again, the immune system destroys them instantly. Foresight and prevention also can provide immunity. A vaccine introduces the disease in a harmless form. It teaches the immune system what the bacteria or viruses look like.

Having a CP action matrix is like being immune. After the work team finds and fixes a problem, its description and corrective action go in the matrix. The team can foresee problems and record them in the matrix (vaccinate). Now the manufacturing process has an immunity system. A person who gets a disease on his or her immune system's "list" rarely feels sick. Similarly, a problem in the CP action matrix rarely makes a manufacturing process "sick." In contrast, some manufacturing processes do not use this system. They react to problems instead of anticipating them. They do not learn from experience. They get the same diseases repeatedly. Sometimes, they go out of business. This would be the fate of an animal species that could not develop immunity to diseases.

Figure 3.4 shows the interaction of the cause-and-effect diagram, CP action matrix, and QIT in a *process management system*. Together, they play critical roles in feedback process control. This includes statistical

Figure 3.4

Process management control loop.

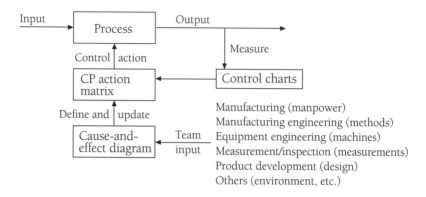

process control (SPC). The control chart shows when the process is out of control. The CP action matrix tells what to do when the process is out of control. The cause-and-effect diagram helps identify the problem sources. The QIT uses the cause-and-effect diagram and updates the CP action matrix. *Frontline workers are vital contributors to the QIT. They can play major roles in process management for better productivity and quality.*

EFFECT OF ORGANIZATIONAL STRUCTURE

Organizational structure can help or impede performance. The table of organization and the decision-making process affect performance. Organic systems are far more flexible and responsive than mechanistic ones.

We have looked at the quality of the individual worker as a factor in organizational performance. Organizational structure must make up for poor training. Whether the workers are strong or weak, they must perform in the framework of this structure. The structure affects organizational performance. Does it aid or impede it?

Sparta and Switzerland: Victims of Structure

> Sparta and Switzerland had the best soldiers in the world; however, they became victims of their own organizational systems.

The Spartans relied on the phalanx for success in battle. They lined up shoulder to shoulder so their shields overlapped. The spears of several ranks projected in front of the formation. The phalanx could run over enemy infantry, unless the enemy also used a phalanx. Other Greek city-states did use this combat tactic.

A phalanx's front was a terrifying instrument of mass destruction; however, it could not turn quickly to fend off flank attacks. If the enemy hit it in the sides or rear, it was easy to destroy. The agile Roman maniple did this to the Macedonians.

If men with swords and bucklers (small shields) got past the pike heads, the pikemen were almost helpless. Rome's Spanish auxiliaries used this technique. The Swiss hero Arnold Winkelreid (d. 1386) took a more cold-blooded approach when facing an Austrian pike formation. He grabbed several pikes. Their owners ran him through, but his comrades rushed into the gap and overthrew the phalanx. (James Montgomery describes Winkelreid's deed in his poem, "The Patriot's Password.") *This is a key problem with mechanistic systems. They can't handle problems their rules don't cover.*

Although the individual Spartan was stronger, tougher, and better trained, his own organization made him an easy victim. More than 1500 years later, Switzerland's famous pikemen learned the same lesson from Spanish sword-and-buckler troops (Regan 1987). There is a clear lesson here. You may have the best workforce in the world. You may have the workers' commitment, and their morale may be good. Poor or inappropriate organizational structure and management, however, can make workers ineffective.

Mechanistic and Organic Systems

Like a phalanx, or a line-infantry formation, a *mechanistic* organization relies on rules and procedures. Decisions and judgments are unnecessary. There is a rule to cover everything. The viability of a mechanistic system *assumes the absence of change and uncertainty* (Miller 1985–1986). This is a very bad assumption today.

An *organic* system is adaptive. Participants apply *judgment and initiative* to their work. Judgment means reaching a decision without a rule. Initiative means using judgment to respond to a new situation (Miller 1985–1986).

Note the contrast between the assumptions of the mechanistic system and a dynamic competitive environment. Mechanistic organizations cannot survive this environment. Carl von Clausewitz recognized this long ago. "A standard order of battle or system of advance guards and outposts are methods by which a general may be fettering not only his subordinates, but, in certain cases, also himself. . . . Any method by which strategic plans are turned out ready-made, as if from some machine, must be totally rejected" (Clausewitz 1976, Book 2, chap. 4).

Benefits of Small Units— Agility and Responsiveness

Small business units can respond quickly to changing situations and customer needs.

> *In short, it is difficult for large numbers of men to change position, so their movements can be easily predicted. An individual can easily change his mind, so his movements are difficult to predict.*
>
> —Musashi, *A Book of Five Rings*

> *He who understands how to use both large and small forces will be victorious.*
>
> —Sun Tzu, *The Art of War*

Big is not always better. Small, entrepreneurial business units are often superior to large organizations. Recall Clausewitz's discussion of concentration of force at the decisive point. A small unit can often outmaneuver a larger one. Then the small unit can gain superiority at the point of contact or contention. The enemy's superior numbers do not help because most of them cannot fight.

Small units can act and reorganize faster than large ones. "Further, the smaller the total force, the sooner will the victor master the crisis and recover his former effectiveness. A cavalry picket chasing the enemy posthaste can regain its proper order in a few minutes, and that is the extent of the whole crisis. A whole cavalry regiment will need more time" (Clausewitz 1976, Book 4, chap. 7). Suppose a small group of Hussars or Jaegers attacks a regiment of line infantry. The infantry must deploy into a square or line to repel the raid. Once it deploys into an effective formation, the light unit must retreat, but it will take a long time for the infantry to reorganize. Meanwhile, the light unit can reorganize quickly and go about its business. Even if there are no casualties, the larger force uses much more energy. A minor effort by the light unit causes its less agile opponent a major inconvenience. In practice, light cavalry accompanied infantry to deal with these annoyances.

Agility at Gateway 2000

The Gateway 2000 personal computer company made this point in a recent ad. The staff dressed as characters from the recent *Robin Hood* film. (The costumes are good, but the bows are obviously modern composites.) The ad refers to the "PC Titans," or large PC manufacturers. "The Titans, having grown to lumbering proportions, are no match for the swift, lean woodsmen." Swift, lean woodsmen are Jaegers, Chasseurs, or Rangers. Lumbering titans are huge line infantry formations. Gateway 2000 recognizes the value of agility and responsiveness to market needs.

The Maniple: Rome's Small Business Unit

The Romans showed how a large organization (legion) can use small-unit tactics.

The Romans are objects of comedy in the French comic book *Asterix the Gaul.* Asterix is a pint-size but immensely strong barbarian. The comic sometimes shows him felling a dozen Roman soldiers with one punch. The Romans line up in a tightly packed order. Asterix hits the first, who falls into the second. They go down like bowling pins or dominoes. Their helmets fly off, and Asterix's companion collects them.

The Romans didn't conquer most of Europe by fighting this way. A corporation cannot conquer the market by doing business this way. The Roman military organization was actually very flexible. A legion (the basic large unit) consisted of 30 maniples of 120 soldiers. The maniples normally fought in a checkerboard formation, however, they could disperse and fight independently. "Again and again, enemy forces would break when confronted with a few spare maniples coming at them from an unexpected direction" (O'Connell 1988, 39). At Cynoscephalae (198 B.C.E.), Roman maniples outmaneuvered and chewed up Macedonian phalanxes. The Macedonians did fight like Asterix's fictional enemies. Their fate was similar. The same goes for modern corporations that rely on clumsy, mechanistic structures. An intelligent corporation will think like the Romans.

We will later discuss the merits of light troops in more detail. For now, we can recognize that light units are not the exclusive province of small companies. Miyamoto Musashi (1974) wrote, "From olden times it has been said, 'Great and small go together'" (Wind Book). Large organizations can use small business units (SBUs). These are independent, entrepreneurial entities. They can play a combined arms role with the big organization's economy of scale and automation. SBUs have the agility of light units in responding to market needs. They can call upon the large organization's resources to meet these needs. This can give the large organization an advantage.

The Decision Process

A committee is a form of life with six or more legs and no brain.

—Robert A. Heinlein

Hiero, or "sacred," is the Greek root of *hierarchy.* Hierarchy originally meant rule by priests, who were privy to the sacred mysteries. Hiero is also the root of *hierophant,* or "interpreter of sacred mysteries." Hieroglyphics were sacred writings. Today *hieroglyphics* is a synonym for illegible or mysterious writing, or *poor communications.* Poor communications are among the most frequent causes of organizational problems and bad decisions (Schermerhorn, Hunt, and Osborn 1985).

Reduce the Layers of Management
Peters and Waterman (1982) call for flatter organizations. This means less staff, fewer layers of management, and less bureaucracy. A flat organization can respond to changing circumstances faster than a pyramidal hierarchy can. General Clausewitz (1976) told us this 163 years ago.

> *First, an order progressively loses in speed, vigor, and precision the longer the chain of command it has to travel. . . . Every additional link in the chain of command reduces the effect of an order in two ways: by*

the process of being transferred, and by the additional time needed to pass it on. It follows that the number of subdivisions with equal status should be as large as possible, and the chain of command as short as possible. (Book 5, chap. 5)

Armand Feigenbaum (1991, 182) echoes this principle. "Keep layers of supervision to a minimum so lines of communication can be kept as short as possible."

Clausewitz's quotation shows downward filtering of information. The order loses its effectiveness and meaning as it passes down the hierarchy. Upward filtering of information also can occur. In upward filtering, subordinates may remove information they think superiors don't want to see.

The Catholic Church is an example of a flat organization. This worldwide organization has only five levels in its hierarchy. These are priest, bishop, archbishop, cardinal, and pope. Part of the reason is the lack of specialization. All churches or parishes perform the same function. There is little need to coordinate their activities, for each is self-sufficient. Another reason is avoidance of top-down management. Subordinate clergymen obey Church policy, but they rarely receive specific directives. The pope can set a policy that all bishops must follow, but he cannot give a command to a particular bishop (Klein and Ritti 1984). Can a flat structure work for organizations with specialized subunits that must coordinate activities?

Tom Peters (1989) cites Wal-Mart as a positive example. He compares Wal-Mart's organization chart to its three-story headquarters. In contrast, Sears' hierarchy is like its tower (or an Egyptian pyramid, which is doubtless full of hieroglyphics). Wal-Mart "cleaned Sears' clock," and Sears had to sell its tower. Nucor Corporation, with $755 million in sales, has four layers of management. So does Chaparral Steel. Lincoln Electric, with $500 million in sales, has one supervisor for every 100 employees (Peters 1987). Peters does not see a need for more than five levels of management at any organization. He cites a study by A. T. Kearny. "Winners had 3.9 fewer layers of management than losers (7.2 versus 11.1) and 500 fewer central staff specialists per $1 billion in sales" (p. 432).

Decisions should happen at the lowest possible level in the organization. The person closest to the situation knows the most about it. It is usually a mistake to refer judgment to upper management or committees. This causes what Professor Lawrence Carr of Babson College calls, "paralysis by analysis."

Bureaupathology and White Mutinies

> Punishing mistakes and rewarding compliance with rules is a formula for a do-it-yourself white mutiny.

A committee is often a tool for avoiding responsibility. A committee disperses accountability for decisions. Asking upper management to decide is another way of avoiding responsibility. If the choice is poor, the subordinate can say, "I was just following orders." The dysfunction of bureaupathology is an unwillingness to exercise judgment, initiative, or discretion. (Klein and Ritti 1984). A culture that punishes mistakes and rewards compliance to mechanistic rules promotes bureaupathology.

Bureaupathologic behavior is like a white mutiny. Regular mutiny includes refusing to obey orders and trying to overthrow superiors. Since mutiny is a serious military crime, people developed the white mutiny. A white mutiny means *only* obeying orders. The subordinates refuse to exercise judgment, initiative, or discretion. They do what their superior says to do and nothing else. It is a good way to sabotage a superior without breaking any rules. It relies on compliance with rules and orders! Obviously, a culture that promotes or forces such behavior is deficient. We can call this a do-it-(to)-yourself white mutiny. (Recall the discussion of performance measurements. Management always gets what it asks.)

Defer Decisions to Line Management

> The person responsible for the job should decide how to do it. Upper management and headquarters staff should not interfere.

Sometimes subordinates want to take responsibility, but the organizational structure won't let them. Upper managers or owners may insist on deciding or involving a committee. Sun Tzu warned of interference by upper management or owners. He specifically warned against the sovereign's interfering in military affairs.

Commentators on *The Art of War* criticized the use of army supervisors, commissars, or political officers. The army supervisor is like those staff fellows from headquarters. Ho Yen-Hsi warned against making the general wait for the sovereign's approval before acting. He compared it to waiting for approval to put out a fire. By the time you get it, the ashes are cold. Consulting the army supervisor was like building a house and taking advice from passersby. You will never finish the job (Sun Tzu 1963, chap. 3).

We have already discussed the role of commissars in the French Army after the Revolution. The radical Minister of War, Bouchotte, ruined the French Army with these political officers. Two commissars, Billaud and Ronsin, arrested 10 generals and 17 staff officers. Most of them died on the guillotine. Soon, no one wanted to assume command (Koch 1982).

This principle changed the results of several modern wars. Tsar Nicholas II could have won the Russo-Japanese War. The Kaiser could have won the First World War. The Allies were *very* lucky that Hitler did not read and understand *The Art of War.* President Bush's failure to defer to Norman Schwarzkopf's judgment may have long-term consequences in the Persian Gulf.

Let's begin with the Russo-Japanese War. The Tsar's government helped "manage" the Baltic Fleet on its way to the Pacific in 1904–1905. "[Admiral] Rozhestvensky's enemy Klado had decided that reinforcements should be sent to join the Admiral. Anything would do, however unfit and derelict it might be" (Regan 1987, 36). This "archaeological collection of naval architecture" (to use Rozhestvensky's terms) kept the Russians from maneuvering at full speed at Tsushima.

Political interference caused both sides to lose the battle of Verdun during the First World War. Politics made the French government insist on defending this militarily worthless position. German artillery caused hundreds of thousands of French and British casualties. Then the Kaiser insisted on capturing Verdun. The Germans lost hundreds of thousands of soldiers to the defenders' machine guns. French stupidity handed the Germans the war on a silver platter. The Kaiser's pride and arrogance handed it back.

The German commander at Stalingrad wanted to retreat before the Russians could surround him. Adolf Hitler declared that German supermen did not retreat from racially inferior Slavs. Germany lost half a million men.

Recently, political considerations forced General Norman Schwarzkopf to stop short of a decisive victory in Iraq ("Hollow victory" 1992). Another day or so would have allowed American and British forces to surround the Republican Guard. The Republican Guards escaped with most of their equipment. Saddam Hussein later used them to crush Shiite and Kurdish rebels. We have yet to learn how much mischief will come from letting Hussein escape total defeat.

Summary—Organizational Structure

This section has several major lessons for business managers.

1. Management systems must be organic to survive in a turbulent and chaotic environment. Mechanistic systems can handicap their own members.
2. Large companies often need to deploy independent small business units. Success depends on successful use of both large and small forces.
3. Make the organization as flat as possible.
4. Defer decisions to the lowest possible level. Do not hamstring line managers and employees with committees. Owners and upper managers must avoid micromanaging line operations. They need to define goals, but delegate responsibility for achieving them to the front line.

MANAGING CHANGE

> Organizational survival in a dynamic competitive environment requires change. The organization must recognize when change is necessary. Using the proper techniques helps overcome resistance to change.

Managing change is among the most difficult parts of leadership. The dynamic, turbulent, competitive environment makes organizational change more important than ever. Many factors, however, combine to resist change. Armand Feigenbaum (1991, 193) cites "the natural resistance by members of the organization to change of any sort." Niccolò Machiavelli said the following about managing change (1965, 33).

We must bear in mind, then, that there is nothing more difficult and dangerous, or more doubtful of success, than an attempt to introduce a new order of things in any state. For the innovator has for enemies all those who derived advantages from the old order of things while those who expect to be benefited by the new institutions will be but lukewarm defenders.

Factors that resist change include the following (Miller 1985–1986).

1. Social norms and expectations
2. Group cohesiveness
3. Fear of the unknown
4. Vested interests in the status quo
5. Status uncertainty; perception of threats to one's current skills, status, and autonomy
6. Networks of alliances
7. Ingrained habits
8. Perception of a threat to people's careers

The following forces support change (Klein and Ritti 1984, fig. 19.2).

1. Magnitude of the problem that creates a need for change
2. Significance of the problem
3. Importance of the people who perceive the problem
4. Number of people perceiving the problem
5. Credibility of data identifying the problem

Recognizing the Need for Change

> Most people and organizations need a crisis to show them the need for change. Foresight can prevent the crisis.

General Patton replied to people who said never to get in a "professional" contest with a skunk. His detractors said, "See no evil, hear no evil, speak no evil." (If it ain't broke, don't fix it.) You must kill the first skunk that shows up. Otherwise it will get under the house. More skunks will follow. Then you will have to burn the house to get rid of them. "We let the skunks get under our front porch, and so we had to burn at Pearl Harbor" (Williamson 1979, 98). Patton meant we have to forestall trouble as soon as we recognize it. We can't wait and hope it will go away.

People must recognize there is a problem before they will accept change. For example, alcoholics must realize they have a problem before they will change their behavior. ("I don't have a drinking problem. I drink, I get drunk, I fall down, I sleep it off. No problem.") Some drug and rehabilitation experts say substance abusers must hit bottom. Only then do they realize they have a problem. The same is true of many companies.

There is an adage that if you put a frog in boiling water, it will jump out. The frog instantly realizes that it has a problem. The appearance of Commodore Perry's Black Ships off Edo (Tokyo) had this effect on the Japanese. The Japanese responded with supposedly impossible changes in their society. The Pearl Harbor attack similarly shocked America out of its isolationist attitudes.

The tower is one of the Major Arcana in the Tarot deck. The card has a picture of lightning striking a tower. It means, "unforeseen catastrophe, disruption of one's style of life or way of thinking which may be followed by enlightenment" (Aquarian Tarot 1975). This is the splash of boiling water that brings recognition of the need for change.

If you put the frog in warm water and heat it slowly, it will cook. The frog never notices a need for change. This was the fate of England and France as they watched Hitler take over Europe one country at a time. First he marched into the Rhineland. This wasn't too bad because the Rhineland was part of Germany. Next he wanted the Sudetenland. This wasn't too bad because many ethnic Germans lived there. The Anschluss (annexation) of Austria was acceptable too. Then he took the rest of Czechoslovakia. This was acceptable because it was his last demand. Then he invaded Poland. This was unacceptable, however, England and France could no longer stop him. This is an example of the water heating gradually. By the time the frog notices, it is someone's dinner.

Many major companies suffer the latter fate. They let the problems creep up on them. They don't cure the disease in its infancy. They let the skunks get under the house. Tom Peters warns that you must always worry about the competitor. If you have less than 100 percent of the market, *someone* likes the competitor's product better than yours. The competitor's 1 percent may become 2 percent, and then 3 percent. An overall loss of 0.25 percent might be a 20 percent loss in an important market niche. That's the water heating around you (Peters 1987).

Former *Wall Street Journal* reporter Paul Carroll (1993, 3) says IBM suffered the frog's fate. In *Big Blues—The Unmaking of IBM* he writes, "IBM's executives actually saw most of their problems coming, both in PC's and the rest of the business. They . . . forecasted the changes in the market that would cripple IBM, but IBMers couldn't quite bring themselves to do anything about those cataclysmic changes."

Proactivity and Foresight

An excellent company will recognize the need for change before events force change. Niccolò Machiavelli (1965) said, "No one should ever submit to an evil for the sake of avoiding a war. For a war is never avoided, but is only deferred to one's own disadvantage" (p. 23). It's too bad that Neville Chamberlain didn't read this. Recall the three Chinese doctors in the introduction. The famous doctor cured serious illnesses. His obscure brother stopped them in their infancy. Machiavelli (p. 20) also uses the analogy of prevention versus cure.

> *As the doctors say of consumption [tuberculosis], that in the early stages it is easy to cure, but difficult to recognize; while in the course of time, the disease not having been recognized and cured in the beginning, it becomes easy to know, but difficult to cure. And thus it is in the affairs of state; for when the evils that arise in it are seen far ahead, which is given only to a wise prince to do, then they are easily remedied; but when in consequence of not having been foreseen, these evils are allowed to grow and assume such proportions that they become manifest to every one, then they can no longer be remedied.*

Cannibalize Your Market Share

Deliberate market cannibalization is an example of such foresight. Cannibalization means your new product takes sales away from your old one. It may even make your old product obsolete. The common wisdom is that cannibalization is bad. Cannibalization is often good, and even mandatory. Tom Peters makes this clear in *Thriving on Chaos* (1987). If you don't do it, your competitor will. The new product helps keep and expand your market share.

Carroll (1993, 246) says IBM underdesigned its Bluegrass, or PS/1, personal computer to avoid cannibalizing the PS/2. The PS/1 "had been designed to be difficult to upgrade, lest someone actually decide to buy the Bluegrass machines instead of PS/2s for their office." This strategy ignores the customer's obvious alternative: a competitor's machine.

Obstacles to Change

People resist change that threatens comfortable and familiar conditions.

We will look at three case studies. One is fictional, one historical, and one industrial.

The Connecticut Yankee

Mark Twain's *A Connecticut Yankee in King Arthur's Court* is a fictional but excellent parable. Hank Morgan, a nineteenth century American foundry superintendent, finds himself in King Arthur's sixth century Britain. He gives the people the benefits of nineteenth century technology: telegraphs, printing presses, electricity, and locomotives. He sets up schools to teach the illiterate people to read and write.

The wizard Merlin opposes Morgan's efforts. Until the end of the story, Merlin is a quack, or a medicine show proprietor. Morgan's efforts also threaten the privileges of the nobility and the church. Merlin and the church represent the vested interests in the existing conditions. After King Arthur's death, the church turns the people against the Yankee. The forces of medieval superstition triumph over modern technology.

The Shah of Iran

Twain's story repeated itself in Iran many years later. The Shah was an authoritative but progressive monarch. He wanted to give the benefits of modern society to his country. Iran's oil revenues funded a public education system. Many Iranians came to the United States for college educations.

Much of what the Shah did to westernize his country, however, went against traditional Islamic values. Ayatollah Khomeini overthrew the Shah by appealing to religious beliefs. The people supported Khomeini, although they gave up some benefits of Western society.

In these two examples, the societies did not perceive a problem. The Connecticut Yankee and the Shah had educations and knew of superior ways of life. They perceived that illiteracy and lack of modern technology were problems. The people, however, were content with their lives. They had never experienced anything better. Therefore, the forces for change were weak. There also were people with strong stakes in the existing structure. In both cases, the prevailing social norms made the people side with the traditional institutions. Vested interests were therefore a very strong factor against change. Fear of the unknown, including fear of societal changes, also played a role.

The Luddites

The third example took place during the Industrial Revolution. Between 1811 and 1816, the Luddites destroyed textile manufacturing machinery. The Luddites were English workmen who thought the machines would take their jobs away. In this case, the vested interest in the status quo was obvious.

Strategies for Change

There are three processes for causing change (Schermerhorn, Hunt, and Osborn 1985). The *change agent* is the person or group that wants to make the change.

Force-Coercion

The *force-coercion* approach uses authority, punishments, and rewards to compel change. People respond out of fear of punishment or desire for reward. This approach is poor, because it cannot achieve lasting change. It works only when the change agent is visible and can exercise its power. Force-coercion can antagonize people who might otherwise accept the change.

Empirical-Rational

The *empirical-rational* approach uses persuasion and the power of expertise. The change agent convinces people the change is good for them. For example, explaining to Luddites that machines take over dull and repetitive tasks would be an empirical-rational approach. The machines allow workers to exercise skills and initiative. Higher productivity through machinery means higher wages. With the advantage of hindsight, we know this is true. Many companies export unskilled labor jobs to low-wage countries. Mechanized jobs that require skilled workers remain in the United States.

This approach assumes people are rational. This means they act in what they perceive to be their own best interests. It takes longer than the force-coercion approach; however, it can achieve long-lasting, internalized change. Internalized change means the people accept the change because they think it is good.

Normative-Reeducative

The normative-reeducative approach seeks to change attitudes and values. It addresses group norms, personal values, and common goals. This approach also can achieve long-lasting, internalized changes. The empirical-rational and normative-reeducative approaches can change an organization's "true name," or culture. The organization internalizes the change. It becomes part of "the way we do business here." This is clearly better than imposing change through authority and coercion. When the change becomes part of the culture, social forces and group dynamics support it. When the change results from coercion, these forces may oppose or sabotage it.

Accommodate Existing Structures

> A change has a better chance to succeed if it accords with existing structures, attitudes, values, and norms. Let the organizational culture supply the framework for change.

Machiavelli (1965, 17) raises an important point about introducing change. "Hence, in order to retain a newly acquired state, regard must be had to two things: one, that the line of the ancient sovereign be entirely extinguished; and the other, that the laws be not changed, nor the taxes increased, so that the new may, in the least possible time, be thoroughly incorporated with the ancient state."

This has obvious implications in corporate takeovers. The new owner must be wary of making unnecessary changes in the organization's culture. The concept also applies to a new manager taking over a department. He or she should not rush to change the way subordinates do their jobs. Finally, the concept applies to organizational change.

Modern management texts echo this principle. Klein and Ritti (1984, 571) offer the following advice. Note especially the first two items. These accord with Machiavelli's advice.

1. Accommodate the existing system structure.
2. Accommodate existing attitudes, norms, and values.
3. Give those affected a stake in the outcome.
4. Address potential consequences of the change.

The critical point is that we must avoid changing the norms, customs, and culture unnecessarily. The British followed this policy and were successful colonialists. They made Christianity available to the pagan natives, but did not impose it. They did not suppress local customs or practices, unless they involved murder or human sacrifice. (These included Thuggee, or ritual murder by worshippers of Kali, and suttee, or widow burning. Indiana Jones' enemies in the Temple of Doom were Thugs.) The British enjoyed relatively good relations with their colonial subjects.

Another important tactic is to give the supporters of the existing structure a stake in the change. Show them how the change helps them. Klein and Ritti (1984, 572) ask an important question. "Are the incentives such that those affected will be induced to 'buy in' rather than to resist or subvert the proposed changes?"

What happens to those who don't respect the existing structures and norms? "Business history is full of CEOs who have tried to impose new cultures on existing corporations only to find the old cultures the victors and themselves the victims" (Deal and Kennedy 1982, 175).

Christianization of the Aztecs

> These strategies for change sold Christianity to unlikely prospects— the Aztecs.

We have seen how missionaries superimposed Christianity on pagan cultures. It is hard to see bloodthirsty Aztecs becoming Christians. They worshipped many gods and performed human sacrifices. Many Aztecs, however, converted voluntarily. The Aztecs ate human flesh as part of their religion. Many cannibals believed that eating someone gave them the person's virtues. For example, eating a mighty warrior made one brave and skilled in battle. The Spaniards superimposed the Mass, with the wafer symbolizing the body of Christ. By eating the consecrated wafer, Aztecs could gain Jesus' virtues. The Aztec god Quetzalcoatl rose from death after overcoming the forces of hell. The Spaniards quickly superimposed Jesus' death and resurrection. The Aztecs viewed the deity Tonantzin as "the mother of our flesh." The Spaniards superimposed the Virgin Mary (Cavendish 1989).

Motion Efficiency at Bethlehem Steel (Taylor)

> Frederick Winslow Taylor used these techniques to institute motion efficiency at Bethlehem Steel.

Frederick Winslow Taylor had more respect for workers than Taylorism ("Leave your brains at the door.") suggests. In 1898, Bethlehem steelworkers earned $1.15 a day for loading pig iron onto a freight car. The average daily load was 12.5 long tons, in 92-pound pigs. Taylor thought he could more than triple that, "without bringing on a strike among the men and . . . to see that the men were happier and better contented," despite the higher rate. He noticed that workers wasted energy by holding the loads without moving. Just holding the 92-pound pig was almost as tiring as carrying it. Taylor decided a worker should carry a load 43 percent of the time and rest 57 percent of the time. He should never stand still while under load.

Taylor singled out a worker and asked if he wanted to earn $1.85 a day. The worker showed interest. Taylor introduced his assistant to the worker. He told the worker, "You will do exactly as this man tells you tomorrow, from morning till night. When he tells you to pick up a pig and walk, you pick it up and walk, and when he tells you to sit down and rest, you sit down." Taylor got the worker's cooperation by giving him a stake in the change. Cooperating earned the man a 61 percent wage increase. The experiment worked, and the man loaded 47.5 long tons in a day. Taylor extended the method to the other workers. They became more productive without working harder. Their pay went up. The company got more useful work for its money. The workers got more money for the same effort. Everyone was happy (Gies 1991).

The Shah and the Connecticut Yankee, Continued

The Shah could have tried to buy off or co-opt the Iranian clergy. He could have made concessions to their institution. He could have given the mullahs important (or important-looking) government offices. Giving the old order a stake in the desired change can get its cooperation, or at least acquiescence.

In Mark Twain's story, Hank Morgan had to defeat Merlin to secure his own position. He did this by blowing up Merlin's tower with modern explosives. Having done this, he could have given Merlin a stake in the new order. Morgan's only safe paths were to befriend Merlin or kill him. (Recall that Merlin symbolizes the old order and resistance to change.) Instead, Morgan continued to humiliate Merlin. Merlin bided his time, and took revenge at the end of the story.

Summary—Managing Change

Being a change agent can be a difficult and sometimes dangerous task. The following guidelines are useful.

1. Use data to prove the need for change. The organization must *recognize the need for the change.*
2. Recognize the common barriers to change.
3. The normative-reeducative and empirical-rational approaches can achieve long-lasting change. The force-coercive approach cannot.
4. Work within existing structures, norms, cultures, and customs as much as possible.
5. Give those with vested interests in existing conditions a stake in the change. Show how the change benefits them.
6. Let the people the change affects *participate* in implementing it. The change should be something they do, not something you do to them.

EVALUATING CULTURE AND MORALE

Chapter 1 discussed organizational culture and its importance. How can we learn our opponents' true name? How can we learn our own organization's true name?

Industrial espionage deals with technical and financial secrets. It's illegal. There is an equally valuable, but legal, intelligence activity. Sun Tzu (1963) gave examples of this kind of organizational assessment. Spies don't have to steal the battle plans from the enemy's headquarters. You can learn a lot by watching the enemy's behavior. It is very hard for the enemy to hide or distort these signs and clues.

Failure of the enemy to exploit an advantage is evidence of fatigue. Do employees exercise initiative and judgment? If they see a better way of doing a job, do they pursue it? Suppose they are apathetic and indifferent. The competitor may have the physical resources to attack or defend, however, its workforce may lack the will. Remember Clausewitz's statement that morale can be more important than physical power. Now suppose the workers show the former characteristics. Even if the competitor's balance sheet is not great, it could still put up a tough fight.

Soldiers whispering in small groups show their lack of confidence in the general. Informal discussions reveal a lot about morale. Do they focus on problem solving? Do they center on complaints and gripes? The former points to good morale. The latter shows poor morale and possibly loss of commitment.

The general should not have to use rewards or punishments to get performance. Remember that intrinsic motivation is more effective than extrinsic motivation in promoting productivity. If management has to use rewards and bonuses to get extra efforts, there is a problem. A rise in punishments or firings also shows a problem. Coercion is not effective in getting long-term results.

This form of research may not do any good against an excellent competitor. In-depth knowledge of the culture of the Special Forces would not help an enemy much. (It could make the enemy think twice before taking them on.) The same applies to the cultures of Procter & Gamble, Delta, and the other companies on Tom Peters' excellence list. We can try, however, to assimilate features of their cultures into our own organization. We can use them as role models. We don't have to send someone to research these companies' cultures. They are happy to talk about them.

Assessing Internal Culture

Remember Sun Tzu's advice to know the enemy and yourself. Knowing ourselves means knowing our own culture. Periodic opinion surveys are useful tools, however, other tools can be more effective.

Staying in Touch with the People

> An excellent leader will have good rapport with his or her followers. The people will be comfortable in talking with the leader.

Management by wandering around (MBWA) is among the best tools (Peters 1985, 1987). This means talking with the frontline employees. Robert Gallant, Louisiana division manager of Dow Chemical, says to listen to employees even (or especially) when they complain. "There's nothing wrong with complainers if they'll tell you face to face what they say during bull sessions on the midnight shift" (Gallant 1987, 70). General

Patton said, "Always talk with the troops! They know more about the war than anybody. Make them tell you all their gripes. . . . Always remember in talking to the troops the most important thing to do is to listen!" (Willaimson 1979, 102).

General Patton also said, "Get up front! . . . You will never know what is going on unless you can hear the bullets. You must lead the men. It is easier to lead than to push" (p. 113). So MBWA goes back at least to the 1940s. We can trace it back much further.

King Frederick William I of Prussia practiced MBWA. "He ruled the country in a fatherly German way, supervising it like a private estate, prowling the streets of Berlin in an old seedy uniform, and disciplining negligent citizens with blows of his walking stick" (Palmer and Colton 1971, 243). By contemporary standards, Frederick William was an eccentric, uncouth boor. Unlike the other monarchs of Europe, he despised ostentation and the arts. He was actually one of Europe's better kings. The others built Baroque structures with their subjects' taxes. Frederick William cut out waste in his government and lowered the taxes. We can compare him to Louis XVI and Marie Antoinette. They were completely out of touch with their people. It is hard to imagine Louis XVI daring to walk the streets of Paris by himself, let alone chastising negligent citizens.

If workers won't say to a manager what they say to each other, the organization is already in deep trouble. In such a case, one could consider planting an organizational psychologist in one's own workforce. No one likes to have someone spy on them. The psychologist should report morale and culture only, not names. If morale is poor, imagine the effect of discovering a spy reporting alleged troublemakers!

There are many legends and stories about kings and even gods disguising themselves as commoners and mingling with the people. This is the theme of *The Prince and the Pauper*. King Arthur and Hank Morgan do this in *A Connecticut Yankee in King Arthur's Court*. This lets them learn what the people really think. Suppose the king goes up to a peasant and asks, "What do you think of the kingdom?" The king will hear what he wants to hear. He will hear that the kingdom is wonderful. He will hear that he is an excellent king. This is especially true if he has a reputation for punishing those who bring him bad news. Even if the Sans-Culottes are oiling the guillotine, he will still hear what he wants. The word for this is *filtering*. The same is true in a company with an atmosphere of fear. One of Deming's 14 points is, "Eliminate fear. Encourage two way communication."

Filtering and Detroit's Potemkin Village

> The management team that sees and hears only what it wants creates its own Potemkin Village.

Filtering is not new. In the late eighteenth century, Catherine the Great was Empress of Russia. She invited Emperor Joseph II of Austria to tour Russia with her. One of her ministers preceded the tour and constructed special villages. He filled them with prosperous, happy peasants. The Potemkin Village has gone down in history as an example of showing the king what you want him to see. Tom Peters (1987, 514) says, "That meticulously planned state visit by the chief of the 16- or 16,000-person unit or firm will be fashioned by subordinates to ensure the views they've espoused to the boss before won't be distorted by, say, an irate customer." The subordinates will show the CEO the Potemkin Village!

Tom Peters and Nancy Austin (1985) show how General Motors' executives made Detroit their own Potemkin Village. The company virtually required its employees and suppliers to buy American cars. GM executives in Detroit saw mostly American cars on the roads. They assumed that foreign competition was not a problem. Also, company mechanics made special efforts to make the company cars run well. The executives driving these cars thought quality was good. Had they visited California, they would have seen plenty of Hondas, Toyotas, and Nissans.

Role Models in Mythology

> Mythological gods, who were role models for mortal leaders, practiced management by wandering around (MBWA).

In India, the gods Indra, Shiva, and Yama often disguised themselves as beggars. The Greek/Roman myth of Baucis and Philemon involves Jupiter and Mercury disguising themselves as travelers. They wanted to test the hospitality of the local people. A modern equivalent would be a CEO pretending to be a customer. We can imagine how the CEO might react to receiving poor service! Recall that Ray Kroc allegedly revoked the franchise of a McDonald's because he found a fly in the restaurant. The overall goal, however, should be constructive and not punitive. Tom Peters and Nancy Austin (1985) suggest contacting your company, and competitors, and asking for service or information. Is the organization responsive to customers? This alone is useful information.

Odin, the ruler of the Scandinavian gods, did a lot of wandering. From the high seat of Hlidskjalf in Asgard, he could see everything that happened in the nine worlds. Hlidskjalf was his own management information system, however, he frequently wandered the earth as a common traveler. He dressed in a blue cloak and wore a wide-brimmed hat that hid his face. He used his spear Gungnir as a staff. He was always seeking knowledge, and would talk to anyone. As the Germanic Wotan, he was the Wanderer in Richard Wagner's *Siegfried*. Tolkien's wizard Gandalf, "The Grey Wanderer," was essentially Wagner's Wotan. Odin was the patron god of the Jarls, or Scandinavian nobles. He was a role model for kings and rulers. The ruler or god who wanders around learns more about his or her domain.

We can summarize this section as follows:

1. Look for signs and symptoms that reveal organizational culture.
2. Look at your company from the customer's viewpoint.
3. Talk to the frontline employees. Good leaders shouldn't have to disguise themselves to get honest feedback.

COMMUNICATIONS

Clear communications are essential for harmonious and effective working relationships

Mistaking my instructions which within my brain did gyrate
I took and bound this promising boy apprentice to a pirate.
> —Gilbert and Sullivan, *The Pirates of Penzance*

If words of command are not clear and distinct, if orders are not thoroughly understood, then the general is to blame.
> —*The Art of War* (Clavell 1983)

Communications are a vital part of any business operation. Poor communications are a major cause of poor decisions. Poor communications are a frequent cause of internal and external disputes and conflicts. Much contract litigation comes from misunderstanding instead of bad faith. If contracts are ambiguous, lawyers and courts may spend years interpreting them. Ambiguity is especially dangerous when one party (like an insurance company) drafts a contract. Courts usually resolve such ambiguities *against* the drafting party. Courts choose the interpretation that favors the party that did not write the contract (Anderson, Fox, and Twomey 1988).

The section on marketing topography will show that advertising effectiveness depends on the cultural and linguistic context. Literal translation of advertising from English to a foreign language is often inadequate. The results are often ineffective or embarrassing.

Quality improvement teams (QITs) and design for manufacture (DFM) require cross-functional communication. Manufacturing, manufacturing engineering, R&D, marketing, and other groups must exchange information. We will later see that DFM is important in getting new products to the marketplace first. Communications are important in internal operations and in relations with the public and customers.

Unclear instructions can frustrate employees and customers. Vague directives can cause disastrous actions. "Many armies have been thrown into great confusion when the general's orders have been either not heard or mistaken" (Machiavelli 1965, 138). Here are some examples.

Charge for the Guns! Which Guns?

> Poor communications caused the disastrous Charge of the Light Brigade. Poor communications caused the British to miss opportunities or lose ships in three sea battles.

Alfred Tennyson immortalized the "noble six hundred" and their deed during the Crimean War. Let's examine the "reason why" a light cavalry brigade charged an intact artillery battery. The Russians had captured some British guns and were dragging them away. Lord Raglan sent an order to "advance rapidly to the front—follow the enemy and try to prevent the enemy carrying away the guns." His aide-de-camp Captain

Nolan took this order to Lord Lucan. As Nolan left, Raglan shouted, "Tell Lord Lucan the cavalry is to attack immediately." Lucan read the order, but considered an attack useless. Nolan then gave him Raglan's verbal order to "attack immediately." Lucan could not see the guns Raglan wanted. The only guns he could see to his "front" were the Russian battery. (When Raglan gave the order, he and Lucan were facing different fronts.) Amazingly, the Light Brigade actually reached the guns and inflicted some damage, however, it lost two-thirds of its men (Regan 1987, 67–69).

More Examples of Unclear Directives

During the First World War, Admiral Sir David Beatty had an inept flag-lieutenant (officer in charge of signaling). Beatty himself said of Ralph Seymour, "He lost three battles for me." The man was not even a signal officer, but Beatty kept him anyway. During the Scarborough Raid (1914), Seymour's signaling allowed the German cruisers to escape. Seymour's unclear signals allowed the escape of three German battle cruisers at Dogger Bank (1915). At Jutland (1916), unclear signals helped lose the battle cruiser *Indefatigable* with almost all hands (Regan 1987).

In 1992, an American aircraft carrier fired a Sparrow missile into a Turkish destroyer. This happened during a "live" drill. The crew who fired the missile actually believed it was to fire a live weapon. The crew probably didn't aim at the Turkish ship, but the Sparrow looks for radar reflections.

Modern military organizations have special procedures to make sure communications are clear. For example, they use words to designate letters such as

A = alpha	P = Peru
B = bravo	R = Romeo
C = Charlie	S = sierra
D = delta	T = tango
E = echo	U = uniform

D and T sound similar, but one cannot mistake *delta* for *tango*. Similarly, B and P sound alike, but *bravo* and *Peru* are clearly different. This is a simple tool to prevent errors in communication.

Commanders have long recognized the need for clear communications. Sun Tzu wrote of the use of drums, bells, gongs, and flags to control troops. Takeda Shingen had a special messenger corps. Samurai considered appointment to a messenger corps an honor.

Centipede banner of Takeda Messenger Corps.

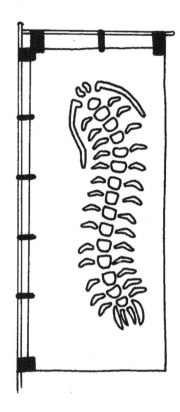

Purpose and Effectiveness of Communication

Effective communications are vital in leadership, persuasion, and advertising.

Military organizations have always valued clear and rapid communications. Communications are equally important in business. Communications serve the following purposes (Miller 1985–1986).

1. Persuade
2. Change
3. Activate/motivate

4. Complain
5. Develop status
6. Inform

Persuasion is vital in advertising, promotion, and politics. We want to convince someone to do something—accept an idea, buy a product, or vote. Our message must appeal to the target audience. During a campaign speech in 1964, Barry Goldwater supposedly said "thermonuclear holocaust" several times. He was probably talking about avoiding one, but he linked himself to the idea of nuclear war. He did not think about how his audience would react to the words *thermonuclear holocaust.* The Democrats helped with the famous "Daisy Girl" commercial. It showed a girl counting the petals on a daisy. Then the commercial switched to a countdown and a nuclear fireball. Then the words, "Think before you vote," appeared. As the 1988 GOP made Willie Horton Mike Dukakis' running mate, the 1964 Democrats made the hydrogen bomb Goldwater's running mate.

Mark Antony's eulogy for Julius Caesar described the assassins Brutus and Cassius as "honorable men." The context of his words turned the audience against the assassins. Antony never called Brutus and Cassius murderers and betrayers of their friend. The context of honorable men implied it, however. "I fear I wrong the honorable men whose daggers have stabbed Caesar; I do fear it." This brings us to Shakespeare's works as examples of effective communication.

William Shakespeare's mastery of the English language lay in his ability to create a picture with words. His skill was so great that we enjoy his works almost 400 years later. Even in Elizabethan English, Shakespeare's works keep their beauty and elegance. Quotes from his plays live on in everyday conversation, and in book and movie titles. Joe Haldeman's science fiction title, *All My Sins Remembered,* is from *Hamlet.* The Star Trek movie title, *The Undiscovered Country,* is from Hamlet's soliloquy. (The show featured a Shakespeare-quoting Klingon.) *Something Wicked This Way Comes* is from the cauldron scene in *Macbeth. Fatal Visions* also is from *Macbeth. Brave New World* is from *The Tempest.*

"Method in the madness," was originally, "Though this be madness, yet there is method in it" (*Hamlet*). "Cry havoc, and let slip the dogs of war," is from *Julius Caesar.* "A rose by any other name," comes from *Romeo and Juliet.* "The wheel has come full circle," is from *King Lear.* A full eighth (12.5 percent) of *The Oxford Dictionary of Quotations* (3rd edition) is from Shakespeare.

Franklin Roosevelt used his fireside chats to communicate with the American people. His skill at imparting ideas made him a more effective president. Recently, Ronald Reagan earned recognition as "The Great Communicator." *Effective communications are a critical part of leadership.*

Factors in Effective Communications

Elements of communication include the following (Miller 1985–1986).

1. Source
2. Message
3. Receiver
4. Social content
5. Feedback

How credible is the source? This depends on the source's authoritativeness or competence. It also depends on the source's trustworthiness, status, and position. Recall that the halo effect can give a source more credibility than it deserves. We will now look at other factors that affect communications.

Perceived Urgency and Importance

A communication's media (form, mode of delivery) say a lot about the message's importance and urgency.

The effectiveness of a message depends on several factors. Does the sender deliver the message in person? Does it come by letter, telephone, fax, or electronic mail? How important does the message appear? This author sometimes sends letters by certified mail to get extra attention for them. I give little attention to letters that come by bulk mail, even if the envelopes say "URGENT." (How urgent can it be if it came by bulk mail?) Those that come without business reply postage go in the wastebasket. This includes market research surveys. Asking people to take their time to fill out a survey is asking a favor. Asking them to supply return postage is presumptuous.

Some companies try to make customers pay postage for surveys by putting them on warranty registration cards. The customer must return the card to get warranty protection for the product, however, nothing forces the customer to fill out the survey. Other companies include return postage. An interesting statistical experiment would compare the return percentages for surveys that come with and without postage.

Clarity of the Message

> Effective communications are clear and easy to understand.

The message itself must be clear. Poor writing can keep the audience from understanding the message. Most of us know the difference between good and poor teachers. Good teachers hold the students' interest. Good teachers generate enthusiasm for the subject. Poor teachers lecture into the blackboard or use esoteric language no one understands. Unclear instructions for using or assembling equipment are very frustrating to users. Unclear instructions for operating industrial equipment can cause poor quality or even unsafe working conditions. It helps to repeat the message through several channels. This reduces opportunities for misunderstanding. Some people respond better to written media than to verbal media. Others prefer verbal communications. Using both methods makes sure that more people will understand the message. Pictures are especially powerful media, especially in politics.

Importance of Getting Feedback

> Feedback tells us whether our audience understands our message. It is vital to effective communications.

Receivers will project their expectations into the message. People often hear what they expect or want to hear. People often shut out messages they don't agree with or don't like. Recall the discussion in chapter 2 on perceptual distortions and prejudices. Leveling means screening out details, such as qualifiers. Condensation means memorizing what the receivers think are the important parts of the message (Miller 1985–1986). The message the receivers hear is not always the one we send. *Feedback* helps us make sure the receivers did get the right message.

Feedback is very important. At the simplest level, feedback means reading back an address or account number over the telephone. At higher levels, the person who receives the message asks questions or restates the message to the sender.

Avoid Newspeak, Doublespeak, and Euphemisms

Misleading euphemisms and doublespeak make the audience unreceptive.

Few people appreciate misleading euphemisms. Some "politically correct" folks want to use "differently abled" to describe handicapped people. This insulting euphemism implies handicapped people have compensating, and superhuman, abilities. The fictional comic book hero Daredevil is "differently abled." His superhuman hearing makes up for his blindness. Unfortunately, abilities that offset handicaps exist only in comic books and science fiction. Some politically correct terms have become jokes, in this author's opinion. For example, people who wear glasses are "visually challenged." Senior citizens are "chronologically gifted." Criminals have "ethical disadvantages." Companies in Chapter 11 face "financial challenges."

In George Orwell's *1984*, misleading euphemisms went even further. The government propagated newspeak (or doublespeak). When the government made someone disappear, he became an "unperson." The Ministry of Plenty "increased" rations from 10 kilos to 9 kilos, and so on. The Ministry of Plenty was in charge of rationing. The Ministry of Love performed brainwashing and interrogations. The Ministry of Peace directed military operations. The Ministry of Truth distributed propaganda. The Soviet news organ, *Pravda,* also means "truth." Before the reforms, it told whatever stories the rulers wanted it to tell.

Corporate ministries of truth refer to "downsizing" (layoffs). Government talks about "revenue enhancements" (tax hikes). (The RightWriter spelling and style checker flags "downsizing" and "revenue enhancements" as misleading euphemisms. It does the same for "economic slowdown," a synonym for "depression.") The explosion of the space shuttle *Challenger* was a "major malfunction." No one respects doublespeak, newspeak, or misleading euphemisms.

W. Edwards Deming had little use for slogans. "Eliminate the use of numerical goals, slogans, and posters for the workforce." As we saw earlier, slogans are meaningless without management commitment. Slogans and posters can, however, reinforce policies that have wholehearted organizational support. During the Second World War, posters urged workers to help win through productivity. No one doubted that the government and people were behind the war effort. These slogans and posters were probably effective. Slogans and posters are effective if there is real commitment behind what they represent. If not, they are useless or offensive, like misleading euphemisms.

Telemarketing

> Telemarketing is invasive and offensive to many people; however, it sometimes works.

Junk mail isn't intrusive, as one can throw it away. An unsolicited and unwelcome phone call is invasive. "You don't know me, and I don't know you. Who asked you to call me?" There is always the chance of getting someone in the shower, at dinner, watching television, and so on. This author has disposed of brokerage cold calls as follows. "You have a plan involving your brains and my money? That makes us even. I don't have any money." (Actually, "I don't have any money," is effective by itself.) Receiving a message from a tape recorder is even more offensive. Some states have outlawed these. The automatic dialers call police, doctors, and fire stations. Hanging up does not disconnect the dialers, and they tie up emergency phone lines. It is very tempting to report such a call as harassment if one cannot hang up on it.

Telemarketing must work, however, or people wouldn't spend money on it. There was a story about a man who stood on a street corner proposing indecencies to every attractive woman who walked by. They slapped him or coldly ignored him. A bystander finally asked, "Why are you doing this? All you're getting is rejection and abuse."

The man replied, "I score on about one in every hundred." Telemarketing may thus be effective, as long as we don't have to worry about generating a negative image. We don't want *our company name* interrupting someone's dinner or other activity.

Pictures and Symbols

> Pictures and symbols are very effective methods of communication. A picture or symbol can deliver an entire idea or message instantly.

"A picture is worth a thousand words," is a well-worn adage. *Pictures are very powerful psychologically. A picture or symbol can represent an entire idea.* We might need several sentences to express the same idea. A picture gives the idea immediate impact. This is why political cartoons are so powerful. A picture of a politician or government agency as a pig eating tax money from a trough is powerful. It conveys the idea far more quickly than an editorial describing waste and fraud. Cartoons were war propaganda during both world wars. Cartoons helped start the Spanish-American War. A famous cartoon of that era showed a Spanish soldier as a semihuman beast with a bloody knife. Later cartoons showed bestial spike-helmeted Huns and Japanese with exaggerated Oriental features. German cartoons portrayed French men as lechers and Germans as heroic supermen. These conveyed ideas far more quickly than detailed accounts of enemy atrocities. Cartoons were weapons against the political corruption of Tammany Hall. They led Boss Tweed to exclaim, "Those damned pictures!"

A good advertisement for wearing seat belts shows a used automotive crash test dummy. The caption says, "You can learn a lot from a dummy. Wear your seat belt." Another shows the dummy with a tire around his neck. The caption says wearing seat belts will keep you from getting "ring around the collar." Again, this is more effective than statistics about prevention of injury by seat belts.

Computer programs use icons to make themselves more user-friendly. Icons are symbols that represent a function. For example, a wastebasket represents erasure of a file. To select a function, the user moves the cursor to the icon.

Symbols in the Japanese and Chinese Languages

The Japanese and Chinese languages use ideographs or symbols. Each symbol represents an entire idea. *Kanji,* or Chinese characters, appear as works of art (calligraphy) in Japan and China. Caravan International sells greeting cards with kanji motifs.

The ideographs developed from actual pictures of objects. For example, the character for "tree" looks like a tree. The character for "forest" is two "tree" characters. Western languages do not promote the ability to appreciate the power of symbols for expressing ideas. The Japanese and Chinese languages may even facilitate thought processes that are not possible with a Western language.

Protest signs, advertising, and political slogans must deliver their messages in a few words. Those of us who are not fluent in Japanese can only imagine the impact of a few symbols that convey entire ideas.

Implications for Advertising

> In advertising, we often have only a couple of seconds to get our message across. This is a good application for pictures and symbols.

Advertising is expensive. Television, radio, and newspapers cost money. Advertisers must generate maximum impact with their messages. They may have only a couple of seconds to do so. Pictures and symbols can play a critical role here.

Newspaper readers read the ads that interest them. They are often looking for a particular item. If they don't want what we're selling, they'll ignore us. If they do, they'll read the ad. The main problem is letting them know our ad is there. A picture or large letters can draw attention to it.

The TV remote control has changed the effectiveness of television advertising. (This is an example of the impact of changing technology on business.) We must seriously consider buying only ad slots that immediately follow or precede the program. Our ad must be either first or last in the series. The first slot is probably better. We assume no one is watching the ones in between. When the first ad appears, viewers reach for the remote control. When they think the program is ready to return, they switch back. They are likely to see part of the last ad, but we can't count on this. The message, "Our show will return in a few minutes" is the kiss of death for the next ad. ZAP! goes the remote control.

We have a couple of seconds from when the program stops to when viewers push the button. Get the brand name on the screen immediately. Now, even if they zap it, we at least have name recognition. Make the first few seconds interesting and fun, and they may watch the rest. We want no more than 15 seconds unless we're sure viewers will watch the whole ad.

Many companies include their products *in* movies. The appearance of Reese's Pieces candy in *ET* was a major coup for this product. This form of advertising relies on pictorial and symbolic recognition, instead of long-winded pitches no one listens to. Some parents complain that children's cartoons are 30-minute ads for toys. All controversy aside, incorporating the product in the show is effective.

Summary—Communications

Clear and unambiguous communications are critical to success in business, politics, war, and statecraft. Communications must be credible, believable, and easy to understand. They affect external relationships that depend on advertising or persuasion. They affect internal relationships that depend on information and instruction.

Using several communication media and getting audience feedback are helpful. We must account for the audience's educational, social, and political background. Pictures and symbols are particularly effective. Spoken or written words could take much longer and might not hold attention. A picture can deliver the message in seconds.

4

Types of Work Organizations

COMPARISON TO MILITARY UNITS

Many business units and employees are roughly similar to military units. Their roles in economic competition are similar to the military units' roles in battle.

We have compared employees to troops. We have examined their training and organizational structures. Now consider their use in competitive environments. We will examine four types of regular troops and three types of irregular troops.

Basic Characteristics of Competitive Units
1. Light troops are flexible and agile. They have high skill and extensive training. They can work independently of organizational structure and heavy equipment.
2. Elite heavy troops have skill and extensive training. Heavy troops do rely on organizational structure and equipment.
3. Unskilled workers (conscripts, levies) must work in a mechanistic organizational structure. They are of little value. We can upgrade them through training and education.

4. Artillery is automation. It intensifies productivity, but it is not flex-ible. We pay its fixed costs whether we use it or not.
5. Militia are part-time workers. We can call them up when we need them. They may have little or extensive training and skill.
6. Auxiliaries are mercenaries and allies. They include consultants, subcontractors, and joint venture allies.
7. Partisans and guerrillas are familiar with a specific theater of operations.

Light Troops (Small, Entrepreneurial Business Units)

Light military units include Jaegers, Chasseurs, Hussars, Special Forces, Rangers, Marines, Paratroopers, and Velites. The Roman maniple could detach from its legion and fight independently. Light business units include Milliken's customer action teams.

Skilled employees in small, agile units are very responsive to cus-tomer needs. Small, flexible, entrepreneurial business teams can pene-trate market-entry barriers. We will discuss these barriers in detail later. For now, a market-entry barrier is like a geographical barrier in war. It can be natural, like a river or forest. The defenders may create it, as they would a fortress or palisade. The barrier defends our position (or market share) by impeding the competitor's approach; however, excessive reliance on such barriers is very dangerous. In 1940, the French assumed that German armor could not go through the Ardennes Forest. They thought the Maginot line would protect them. General Heinz Guderian quickly showed the French their errors. Those who rely on static defenses are fair prey for corporate Guderians.

Clausewitz discussed the role of light troops in penetrating forests. "No forest is so impassable that small units cannot infiltrate it in hun-dreds of places. In a defensive chain, these are like the first few drops of water leaking through a dam: a general breakthrough is sure to follow" (Clausewitz 1976, Book 6, chap. 21). A forest is no barrier to hunters and woodsmen. A complex, multisegment marketplace is no obstacle to entrepreneurial small business units.

Small units can do what large ones can't. Small units can address individual customers' needs and wants. They can customize products and services to meet the needs of each customer. A large organization that has to mass-produce identical units can't do this. This allows the small units to capture market share a customer at a time.

If the small business units have the backing of a flexible factory, they gain an even greater advantage. The factory gives them economy of scale for price competitiveness. The factory's flexibility allows customization of the products. The small units become the factory's eyes and ears. They pinpoint market niches, segments, or targets for the plant's output. Together, they form a combined-arms team of light troops and the industrial equivalent of mobile artillery.

Milliken's Maniples: Customer Action Teams

The textile maker Milliken & Company has more than 1000 customer action teams (CATs). Each works with one of Milliken's customers to discover new market opportunities. The customer also must supply team members to work with Milliken's representatives. The Milliken team includes people from manufacturing, sales, finance, and marketing. The CATs' goals are to find better ways to serve existing markets, and to create new ones (Peters 1987). The CATs are Milliken's Jaegers and Chasseurs.

Elite Heavy Troops (Skilled Workers)

Elite troops include Guards, Grenadiers, Cuirassiers, armor, and mechanized infantry. Elite troops have extensive training, however, they rely on organizational structure and equipment for effectiveness. Skilled employees can operate complex equipment and help improve the process. Their skill gives them confidence and raises their morale. Like elite troops, they get pride and satisfaction from their jobs. They can benefit from intrinsic motivation if we design their jobs properly. They can participate in problem-solving efforts and quality improvement teams (QITs).

Importance in New, Complex Ventures

> Use elite employees to spearhead new, complex ventures.

Elite units with excellent training and high morale are essential to any new business venture. Suppose we must introduce a complex manufacturing process to make a new product. Maybe we want to introduce a process management technique like statistical process control. How can we give the whole organization confidence in the venture? How can we get everyone moving in the right direction?

Sun Tzu said to use shock troops to lead an attack. The commentator Chang Yu added that we must use elite troops as the vanguard. This strengthens our side's determination and blunts the enemy's edge (Sun Tzu 1963).

Suppose we don't do this. Our weaker employees fail to achieve the goal. This affects the morale and confidence of everyone else. The vanguard's retreat does not inspire confidence in the rank and file. Our only hope lies in having some strong, confident employees who think they can do better. "Now *we'll* show you how to do it!" In Kipling's "Drums of the Fore and Aft," elite Gurkha troops watch Afghans rout some raw British recruits. "They run! The white men run! Colonel Sahib, may *we* also do a little running?" (The Gurkhas want to run toward the enemy.) In the story, the new regiment rallies and beats the enemy. It is best, however, to win the first time.

Statistical Process Control at IBM

IBM used elite employees to implement statistical process control (SPC) at its East Fishkill site. Each manufacturing department selected a tool operator as SPC driver. The basis for selection was enthusiasm about SPC and quality improvement, plus some training. Some SPC drivers took a college course in SPC. The SPC driver led the department's efforts. Thus, manufacturing played a decisive role in adding SPC to the corporate culture.

Low-Skill Troops (Unskilled Workers)

Low-skill troops include peasants, conscripts, and levies. Arthur Wellesley, the Duke of Wellington, once called British troops "the scum of the earth." The typical recruit probably was the scum of the earth. He usually enlisted because he could not find civilian work. He was the "idle vagabond" kings could "lay their hands on" to use in war (Clausewitz 1976). Even naval press gangs were selective about whom they took. They often shanghaied merchant sailors from waterfront taverns. They only took landsmen when they couldn't get anyone else.

Unskilled workers are pairs of hands. They rely on organizational structure and mechanistic rules. They lack the training to function independently. Their morale is often poor because their job is merely a source of pay. It does not give them pride or a sense of accomplishment. Unskilled workers are cheaper than skilled workers; however, there is not much we can do with the unskilled workers. With advancing technology, their jobs will go to low-wage countries. This has been the fate of manual wire-bonding operations in the semiconductor industry. Wire bonding means attaching a computer chip to an electronic substrate with tiny wires. It is a dull, repetitive job. Many of these jobs are now in Mexico and Indonesia.

Cypress Semiconductor recently transferred 200 computer chip assembly jobs to Asia. Cypress' president said, "All our competitors already assemble offshore." The jobs include assembly, testing, marking, and shipping ("Cypress Semiconductor moving assembly offshore" 1992, 15–16).

Enlightened commanders upgrade low-skill troops through training and exercise. Discipline and training made Wellington's "scum of the earth" equal to any soldier in Europe. Discipline and training instilled him with skill, pride, and confidence. An enlightened employer can upgrade even high school dropouts. Remember the exemplary performance of Johnsonville Sausage's hourly workers.

Human Wave Tactics Don't Work

> Numerical superiority does not guarantee success in war or in business.

Here are some lessons for managers who prefer quantity over quality. Russia and China tried to fight wars with untrained and underequipped soldiers. They outnumbered their enemies by millions. The German eastern front plans for World War I were defensive. The Germans planned to defeat France first. This plan failed, but they knocked Russia out of the war. The Soviet Union suffered horrific losses in the Second World War. Only Hitler's incompetence and interference with his generals saved the Soviets. Chinese numerical superiority was never enough to stop the Japanese.

Hordes of low-quality troops just aren't that useful in modern war. We have to transport them, feed them, and supply them. Suppose an elite soldier earns three times as much as a poor one. On paper, we can hire 300 unskilled troops instead of 100 good ones. We'll need, however, three times as many trucks or rail cars to move them. We have to use three times as much fuel and provide three times as much food. This *overhead* makes them no bargain.

Business overhead includes benefits, employment taxes, and work space. We have to supply more supervision, because unskilled workers must wait for instructions. We don't really get three times as much labor for the same money. Unskilled workers have zero assets in education and training. Three times nothing is nothing. Skilled workers bring intellectual assets to the job. They can help solve problems and improve the process. We are better off paying for skilled employees, training, and education.

Job Skills and Macroeconomics

> A high standard of living depends on a skilled workforce.

A nation's wealth depends on its manufacturing capability. Wealthy nations turn raw materials into products. Third World nations sell raw materials and cheap labor. Manufacturing helped England rule half the world for a century. Loss of manufacturing ruined Spain and Portugal.

In a free trade environment, manufacturing superiority means supplying the best value, which includes low cost, high quality, and good service. The superior manufacturer's goods displace the factories of the inferior manufacturers. Japan has done this to the United States. Japan's exports have displaced thousands of U.S. autoworkers and other skilled workers. The Japanese made better cars. They gave American consumers the best combination of price and value. Japan's gain in sales supported more jobs for its workers. Detroit's loss in sales cost American jobs.

To supply the best value, good people must use the right tools. The organizational structure must help them perform. We've discussed organizational structures and tools. Let's look at our people versus their people. Their people have the equivalent of an associate degree when they finish high school. This is true in many European countries too. In Finland and Germany, high school seniors can learn differential equations. This is a sophomore college course in the United States. Japanese high school students can take mechanical engineering courses. The Japanese school year is 240 days, versus 180 in the United States. Their school day is longer, and students even attend "cram" schools during their spare time. Japanese students bow and address their teacher as *sensei*. Teachers have a very high status in Japan. There are several applicants for each teaching position. Fewer than 10 percent of Japanese students drop out of high school; 99 percent of all Japanese are literate.

One American in four is functionally illiterate. Even many college graduates lack a good command of the English language. Some American high schools offer a "lifestyles" course. It teaches students how to prepare meals and balance checkbooks. (Anyone for Remedial Introductory Basket Weaving?) Only 10 percent of our students study calculus in high school. Our educational system produces graduates (and dropouts) who can be little more than pairs of hands.

This is why skilled manufacturing jobs are going to Japan and Germany. Meanwhile, Russians and Eastern Europeans aren't stupid. They're poor. Their educational systems are probably better than ours. Their students may not have computers, but they learn math. Their economies are victims of socialism (a hamstringing organizational system). Without the chains of socialism, these people will start playing major roles in the world economy. The cheap/unskilled labor approach will make us an economic colony of our betters. Do we really want to be the cheap labor source of the twenty-first century?

Douglas Booth, president of the Society of Manufacturing Engineers, stresses the need for a well-educated workforce. "The search for the 90s is not for a lower wage workforce but for a better-educated, more value-adding workforce" (Booth 1992, 4). The skilled workers, wherever they are, will get the good jobs. Employers' and governments' attitudes toward education must change. This will do more for our country than any number of "Buy American" bumper stickers.

Artillery (Automation)

Artillery is mechanization or equipment. On the battlefield, artillery is the most effective means of destruction. In the factory, automation is the most efficient means of production. Artillery and automation, however, are not very agile. The assets cannot quickly change direction to new targets or product lines. Also, both represent fixed costs. We pay for them whether we use them or not.

Equipment and automation represent capital investment and fixed costs. If fixed costs are high, we say the company has high *leverage*. A traditional breakeven chart shows the effect of leverage. We can make a big profit if demand for the product is high. If demand slips, the fixed costs bleed us to death. "Because fixed costs are high, costs are highly dependent on utilization of capacity" (Heizer and Render 1991, table 7.1). In the nineteenth century, artillery was a fixed cost for an army on the march. Horses pulled the artillery carriages. The army had to feed the horses whether it used the guns or not. Today it's interest on debt, or other capital costs, instead of hay and oats. General Clausewitz warned against too much leverage. "This is one of the reasons why too much cavalry and artillery can be a real burden, and an actual source of weakness to an army" (Clausewitz 1976, Book 5, chap. 14).

"Artillery intensifies firepower; it is the most destructive of the arms. Where it is absent, the total power of the army is significantly weakened. On the other hand, it is the least mobile, and so makes an army less flexible" (Book 5, chap. 4). Equipment and automation intensify productivity. They reduce variable costs. A company must have automation to compete in high product volume environments.

Effect of leverage.

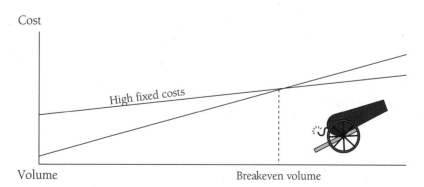

Cost

High fixed costs

Volume

Breakeven volume

Automation Must Be Flexible

Inflexible mass-production equipment is a strategic liability. Progressive manufacturers are developing or using flexible automation.

Equipment must be adaptable. It was difficult to turn a large cannon to face a new threat. The Prussians under Frederick the Great recognized this. They developed a mobile three-pound cannon to accompany infantry battalions (Asprey 1986). It is similarly hard to retool a continuous process to make a new product. Job shop equipment is more flexible. The general-purpose tools can make many products. A job shop requires a higher skill level than a continuous process or assembly line. Job shops make about 75 percent of the products in the United States (Heizer and Render 1991, 292, table 7.1).

The semiconductor industry has learned this lesson. "Here's a secret some [computer] chip packagers have found out too late: too much automation on the assembly line is as bad, maybe worse, than too little. . . . Flexibility also argues against extreme levels of automation. Where equipment tooling must be changed one or more times a shift, current wisdom avoids excessive automation" (Iscoff 1992, 86–87).

Computer numerical control (CNC) increases the flexibility of modern production equipment. This means a computer tells the machine what to do. Changing products is as simple as changing the program. The concept is almost 200 years old. In 1804, Joseph Jacquard invented a system that used punched cards to control automatic looms. (This was the origin of the computer punch card.) To change the fabric design, one merely changed the cards. Today, a computer can control a lathe, drill press, or other machine tool. To change the setup, one merely changes the program.

Flexible Equipment for Semiconductor Manufacturing

The semiconductor industry uses two methods to make computer chips. Photolithography means using light to create a wiring pattern. The silicon wafer has a photosensitive coating. During the process, it plays the role of camera film. A wiring pattern on a lithographic mask is the subject of the photograph. The single-pattern masks are expensive. Photolithography is useful for mass production.

Electron beam lithography writes the wiring pattern with a beam of electrons. The tool is similar to a television set. A TV has an electron gun that draws pictures on the screen in response to the signal. It draws 30 or so pictures a second. (The human eye interprets this as a continuous moving picture.) The industrial electron beam responds to computer instructions instead of a TV signal. It draws an image on each computer chip. To change the wiring pattern, the manufacturer just changes the program. Photolithography can make more chips per hour, so people use it for high-volume jobs. The electron beam is useful for low-volume specialized jobs. It is a form of flexible automation.

Flexible Automation at Federal-Mogul

Federal-Mogul's experience shows the need for flexible automation. The auto part maker thought it could cut costs through extensive automation. According to Amal Naj, in the *Wall Street Journal* (7 May 1991) article entitled, "Some Manufacturers Drop Efforts to Adopt Japanese Techniques," "Before long, Federal-Mogul found that although the plant turned out parts much faster than before, it couldn't shift gears quickly. . . . The plant couldn't respond quickly to customer needs." Federal-Mogul corrected this deficiency through flexible automation. "Now, when a production line is switched . . . workers simply wheel away sections of the assembly line and replace them with those geared for the next product." The new setup supports just-in-time (JIT) manufacturing. Federal-Mogul no longer has to make long production runs and store the inventory. Instead, it makes only what customers order.

Competitors Can Buy Automation

> Purchase of a factory, with its equipment and employees, is a quick way to enter a market. It creates a sudden strategic threat.

Competitors can buy machines and entire factories. "Artillery is the only one of the three arms [the others were infantry and cavalry] whose main equipment—guns and carriages—can be promptly used by the enemy *against* its original owner" (Clausewitz 1976, Book 5, chap. 4). At Breitenfeld (1631), Gustavus Adolphus of Sweden captured the Empire's artillery and turned it on the Imperial troops. This warning applies to automation and equipment, with an addition. A competitor doesn't have to capture our production equipment. It can buy the equipment from someone else. Therefore, we cannot blindly rely on high-tech automation for competitive advantage.

Tom Peters criticizes aimless takeovers and mergers. He quotes an economist at the Securities Exchange Commission. "You don't put two turkeys together and make an eagle" (Peters 1987, 9). Strategic takeovers and buyouts are another matter. Suppose our competitor, Brand X, is in financial trouble. Brand X is a turkey that can't compete with our product. Suddenly, Gustavus Adolphus Corporation (GAC) *buys* Brand X's factory and equipment. It's not an aimless merger, but a strategic move. It fits GAC's existing line of business. Now we face a competent opponent who just bought the means of production. It probably kept the key workers and engineers on the payroll. This means it has not only the guns but the gun crews. This creates a *sudden* threat to our market share. If our competitor had to build a plant and hire workers, we'd have time to see it coming.

This is not a hypothetical question. Who is going to buy those plants General Motors is closing? "Toyota said Tuesday it is considering several options to build its new midsize pickups in the United States, and one option is using a closed GM plant" ("Flint Workers Worry about Future," *Poughkeepsie Journal*, 25 December 1992). Detroit may find itself looking down the muzzles of its own artillery. The movie *Gung Ho* was very entertaining, like Gilbert and Sullivan's *Mikado*. Detroit may not find the real-life Gentlemen of Japan so amusing. Even "Buy American" slogans won't be a defense. American autoworkers will make the "rice burners." They'll make good ones too. Honda's plant in Marysville, Ohio is the most efficient automobile factory in the world (Brown 1987). Nissan has a very successful operation in Smyrna, Tennessee.

Only a Luddite would discount the advantages of modern automation in business competition; however, blind reliance on mass-production technology is dangerous. A competitor can get the same machines or can buy an entire factory. In the latter case, the competitor also can get the workers and engineers (gun crews).

Militia and Reservists (Part-Time Workers)

Don't you see—you are using no energy until it is needed; your lightning is there, and ready, like the load in a gun; but it isn't costing you a cent till you touch it off.

—Mark Twain, *A Connecticut Yankee in King Arthur's Court*

Militia have military training, but are not on active duty. The U.S. National Guard is a form of militia. Militia troops hold civilian jobs, but are available for military service. Nineteenth century Prussia relied on militia for offense as well as home defense (Clausewitz 1976, Book 6).

Part-time employees may have training, and we can call them up when we need them. Companies often hire unskilled part-time or temporary workers. These workers are like levies or conscripts. They have little strategic importance. A pool of *skilled* part-timers, like retirees, can be strategically significant. Their key advantage is their independence of the organization for a living. We don't have to pay them unless we use them.

Aggregate Planning

> Part-time workers are useful in handling cyclic demand.

Companies face dilemmas in aggregate planning. Product demand may be cyclic or irregular. The company may vary workforce levels by hiring and discharging workers as necessary. This has several disadvantages. Expanding the workforce always carries hiring and recruitment costs. New workers need training. If the company discharges them, it loses this investment. If the workers cannot rely on steady employment, the company may be unable to get good workers. Alternatives include making and storing inventory during low-demand periods, but it is expensive to carry inventory (Heizer and Render 1991).

Another alternative is to use part-time workers. IBM used temporary and supplemental workers. When the workload was high, the company hired temporary workers. When it dropped, it let existing contracts expire and did not replace the temporaries. Supplemental employees were often retirees who were willing to work up to 1000 hours a year. Some of them were professionals with considerable technical expertise.

Traditional disadvantages of part-time workers include poor training and high turnover. Many companies use them to fill low-skill jobs. This helps if it frees regular employees for better jobs. In warfare, a general might use militia for missions that require little skill. These could include static defense, garrisoning a fortress, holding a safe position, and so on. This frees regular and elite troops for demanding missions.

Use of Retirees as Reservists

> Consider using retirees as skilled, veteran reservists.

The reserve system was a factor in prolonging the First World War and swelling the casualties. Most European nations made every able-bodied man serve in their armies. After a couple of years, a man could leave full-time service if he wished; however, he had to go into the reserves. Now we are no longer talking about citizens or minutemen who formed ranks when danger threatened. These were soldiers with regular army experience. They maintained their skills with refresher exercises. The size of the regular army might have been a million on paper. The country could readily call up two or three million more on short notice. The reserve system produced enormous casualties by increasing the number of combatants. A country without a reserve system, however, would not have lasted even a few months. Its opponents would have crushed it.

How could this work in industry? A company could offer its retirees reserve status. It now has a pool of reservists, *each of whom has a lifetime of experience.* Such reservists would be superior even to younger regulars. If the company needed a major production effort, it could mobilize these reserves. The lightning is available and ready for use. Suppose new technology becomes available. Who will have an easier time learning it—a new hire or a skilled worker with a lifetime of experience?

Why would a retiree want to be available for part-time work? Many people retire because they don't want the pressure of a 40-hour work week. With a pension and Social Security, they don't have to work. Retirement, however, can be boring or worse. Many people get satisfaction from work, and stopping completely can be stressful. University of Alabama's football coach Bear Bryant died six months after retiring. IBM's Thomas Watson, Sr., died shortly after giving up the helm. Many retirees enjoy working part-time. If we don't need an all-out effort, we can have them train new employees.

Now suppose a new market opportunity opens. We have 200 regular employees and 200 reservists willing to work half-time. (The Social Security penalty for wages over a certain level may affect this for workers between ages 62 and 70.) Our competitors think we have 200 employees. They think we can't invade the new market. The usual procedure is to hire new workers and train them.

Within one or two weeks the competitors discover that we really have 300 employees. We have our regular 200, plus 200 at half-time. Not only that, the extras are not new hires. They're veterans who are ready to produce. Our reserve employees are the potential of a thunderhead, or the energy in a cocked crossbow. When we need them, we squeeze the trigger and release the thunderbolt.

Auxiliaries and Mercenaries (External Dependencies)

Auxiliaries are the troops of allies. Their business counterparts would be employees of a joint venture ally. *Mercenaries* are independent troops who fight for pay. These include contract workers and consultants. This section emphasizes the hazards of depending on them excessively.

Joint Ventures and Alliances

> The modern joint venture is like a military alliance.

The joint venture is a method of entering a market and capturing market share. Long ago, countries used joint ventures to grab territory or achieve political goals. General von Clausewitz saw military alliances as "business deals" where each ally "invests" soldiers. How much commitment do our allies have toward the joint goal? In an alliance, "the affair is more often like a business deal. In the light of the risks he expects and the dividend he hopes for, each will invest about 30,000 to 40,000 men, and behave as if that were all he stood to lose" (Clausewitz 1976, Book 8, chap. 6). A successful joint venture requires the commitment of all participants. The partners must agree on control of the venture. Each must agree to a certain share of the effort. A military alliance faces the same considerations.

Do Not Rely on Outsiders for Technology

> We must avoid hiring outsiders to handle our key technologies. We must do this ourselves.

Machiavelli saw several dangers in using mercenaries and auxiliaries. Their commanders could turn them against you. "Turn the guest into the host," is one of feudal Japan's *Thirty-six Strategies*. "This is when a business is taken over by one of its own clients or consultants" (Cleary 1991, 91). This problem is not very likely in modern business; however, Hayes, Wheelwright, and Clark (1988) point out a real danger in excessive reliance on outsiders.

Some managers assume they can buy technology and expertise. They don't want to maintain it in house. They hire outsiders to design and build equipment. They hire consultants to set up and run quality systems. But "world-class Stage IV companies dislike being dependent on outside organizations for expertise. They want to grow their own people, equipment, and systems, but they also respect the capabilities of others" (Hayes, Wheelwright, and Clark 1988, 24–25).

Reliance on outsiders for military security ruined Rome. The Romans hired Goths (Germans) to protect them. "The valor of which the Romans divested themselves was thus transferred to the Goths" (Machiavelli 1965, 71). A company that depends on external technical expertise soon loses its own technical vitality. We have seen this on a national scale in the semiconductor industry. American computer chip makers must depend on the Japanese for photolithographic and other manufacturing equipment.

Cooperative technological ventures are viable. The difference is that we hire outsiders to work *with* us, not *for* us. The virtù of the English Army did not suffer from hiring Gurkhas and Sikhs. The English hired these troops to fight *alongside* Englishmen, not for them. The Romans lost their virtù by hiring Goths to do what Roman citizens should have done. The Romans put off their harness and laid down their swords. They grew fat and indolent while outsiders practiced the profession of arms. Modern corporations must avoid this.

Dangers of Losing Your Manufacturing Capability

> The owner of the gold doesn't make the rules. The owner of the means of production makes the rules. Competitive strength comes from the ability to create or add value.

Here is another lesson on excessive reliance on outsiders for manufacturing capability. Captain Alfred Thayer Mahan (1840–1914) described how too much money can actually ruin a nation. The reason is the *decline in manufacturing capability*. Mahan's (1980) discussion centers on issues of economy and trade. What applies to nations also applies to businesses. A business that loses its ability to provide goods and services cannot prosper. Like an addictive drug, gold from the Americas made Spain and

Portugal ecstatic with wealth. The "high" the gold provided ruined them in the end. Similarly, the United States became a credit junkie in the 1980s. This degraded our manufacturing capability.

Too many managers denigrate manufacturing. Hayes, Wheelwright, and Clark (1988) interviewed such a manager. He actually said, "Oh, business would be fine if only we didn't have to make the stuff" (p. 15). What would the gentleman sell if no one "made the stuff?" Does he want to be at the economic mercy of those who do make the stuff? The Socialists' main priority wasn't the finance offices, brokerages, or banks. They wanted to control *the means of production*. (They couldn't run it when they got it. Look at where the Soviet "Dis-Union" is today. The former West Germany made Mercedes and BMWs. The former East Germany made Tribants. The Tribant has two exhaust pipes. According to one joke, this makes it useful as a wheelbarrow.)

England dominated the world for a long time because of its extensive industry and merchant marine. Why was the United States so prosperous after the Second World War? In the 1950s and early 1960s, we were clearly the richest nation in the world. Everyone expected to own a house and two cars, on one income. In 1945, Germany's and Japan's industrial bases were in rubble. England, France, and Russia weren't in good shape either. The bombers' goal was to blow up the other side's factories—not banks, brokerages, or marketing firms. The United States was the only player with an intact postwar means of production. Perhaps this made us too complacent.

How Gold Ruined Spain and Portugal

> The discovery of gold in the New World undermined the manufacturing capability of Spain and Portugal.

The Spanish and Portugese led the explorations of the fifteenth and sixteenth centuries. The discovery of gold in the New World destroyed the maritime vitality of these nations. Gold allowed Spain to buy what it needed from Holland. Spain produced few goods besides wool, fruit, and iron. Its industries declined, and eventually Spain depended on Holland for manufactured goods. Dutch merchants usually took money abroad to buy commodities, however, they brought money home from Spain, in exchange for Dutch goods.

Spain's shipping declined because it took only a few ships to bring gold from the New World. English and Dutch shipping expanded because their bulkier goods needed more merchant tonnage. By 1648, Spain's merchant marine was in such contemptible condition that Spain had to hire Dutch ships to sail the Indies. This was despite Spain's desire to keep foreigners away from these possessions (Mahan 1980). The Dutch were not just foreigners, but Protestants. To Spain's religious institutions (the Inquisition), they were agents of the Devil. Spain had to hire heretics to provide shipping!

Spain's wealth was vulnerable because capture of one treasure ship represented a huge loss. When England and Spain were at war, English captains had a special fondness for the treasure fleet. (Errol Flynn starred in *The Sea Hawks,* a movie about Elizabethan privateers and raids on Spanish shipping. His fictional character emulated Sir Francis Drake, who looted Spanish colonies and galleons.) Loss of an English merchant ship was inconvenient but not devastating. Mahan said there is a correlation between a country's merchant marine and its navy. He pointed out that the Spanish Navy has not done anything noteworthy since Lepanto (1571). The Spanish Navy has *lost* some big battles since then. Its performances at Gravelines (the Armada), Cape St. Vincent, and Trafalgar (with the French) were pathetic.

Similarly, "the mines of Brazil were the ruin of Portugal, as those of Mexico and Peru had been of Spain; all manufactures fell into insane contempt" (Mahan 1980, 46). Eventually, Great Britain supplied Portugal with everything. England had a mercantile tradition of importing raw materials and exporting manufactured goods. Portugal depended on England even for commodities. The British earned enough Brazilian gold from Portugal to buy Portugese land. During 50 years, the Portugese extracted $500 million in gold from Brazil. This was enormous wealth in the sixteenth century. Fifty years later, Portugal had $25 million left. It paid 95 percent of its gold to foreign countries for luxuries and necessities.

Manufacturing and Economic Colonialism

Let's speculate on the use of the money and the goods. Spain got the gold from its American colonies. Spain paid only transportation costs. Since one galleon could carry a lot of gold, this cost was minor. Spain bought goods from Holland. Some of these were presumably durable, but others were consumable. Spain's wealth was *ephemeral.* Spain held a *consumption party* that did nothing to enrich the nation. The Dutch invested the gold they earned in manufacturing capability and ships. A ship or factory is *permanent* wealth because it can carry or make something. Maybe the Dutch (or English) bought Spanish wool. They made the wool into garments for domestic sale and export. This was economic colonialism or imperialism, with *Spain* as the colony. The colonialist buys raw materials from the colony and sells back manufactured goods. The colonialist power enriches itself by *adding value* to the raw materials.

This should sound alarm bells for the United States. Japan is buying American timber while selling us manufactured goods. Japan is an island nation like England. Both must earn their livelihoods by manufacturing goods. Japan has few natural resources, and must import them. The only way to pay for them is by exporting manufactured goods. Our trade balance with Japan in raw materials is positive. Our trade balance in manufactured goods is negative. This is an early symptom of economic colonialism. Japan could accomplish with economics what its armies and fleets could not do 50 years ago. This is not a Japanese conspiracy. We made the problem for ourselves. We let our manufacturing capability deteriorate.

How Easy Credit Can Ruin Us

> Access to easy credit undermines the United States' manufacturing capability. It lets us consume without producing, while leaving us in debt.

Here is another warning for the United States. Excess gold ruined Spain and Portugal, although these countries' explorers found the gold. (Actually, the Indians found the gold. The Conquistadors robbed the Indians. The key point is the absence of an offsetting liability. Spain and Portugal owed nothing to creditors or stockholders.) During the 1980s, the United States borrowed money from abroad and held a consumption party. Now we have debt without offsetting durable wealth. As the English did in Portugal, the Japanese bought capital assets and land in the United States. Meanwhile, our manufacturing sector lost hundreds of thousands of jobs. This is dangerous to our economic and military strength. "The tendency to trade, *involving of necessity the production of something to trade with*, [author's emphasis] is the national characteristic most important to the development of sea power" (Mahan 1980, 46).

The 1993 Postwar Depression

> The current economic slowdown is, at least partially, a postwar depression.

The Cold War *was* a war, although we never met the Soviets on a battle-field. The war was an endurance trial between economic systems. Ours was stronger. Our arms buildup in the 1980s gave the Soviets a challenge they could not match. They could not make the ante and had to fold. Their economic system collapsed under the strain. The competition hurt us too, but we survived. The world is now much safer. The former Warsaw Pact is free, as are the Russian people. Many people don't realize that *we fought and won a third world war.* No one signed a surrender in a railroad car or on a battleship deck. No one wants *revanche,* as the French did after 1871. This improves the prospects for future peace because there are no bitter losers. Serbia is at it again, but (probably) can't start a world war like it did in 1914. This is the good news.

Here is the bad news. The Cold War forced us to make military equipment and keep a large army. The Cold War was economically indis-tinguishable from a shooting war. Now we are demobilizing soldiers while reducing armament manufactures. There are more job seekers and fewer manufacturing jobs. We can welcome the end of the Cold War and the defeat of communism; however, this has created a *postwar depression.* We don't have pent-up consumer demand like we had after the Second World War. We do have overseas competitors we didn't have in 1945. Rebuilding a competitive civilian economy is a major challenge.

Hire Reliable Suppliers

> Machiavelli said the major problem with mercenaries was their cow-ardice and bad faith. In industry, we can replace these deficiencies with poor service and incompetence.

This author has experienced the following examples of excessive depen-dence on suppliers. In the first case, a company bought a computer-con-trolled piece of manufacturing equipment. The vendor's representatives had to make any program changes. They charged more than $150 an hour, with a half-day minimum. In the second case, automatic inspection equipment had excessive downtime. Again, the customer had to rely on the vendor's good will and competence to fix the problems. The vendor missed several target dates for corrections. In a third case, a vendor supplied equipment that handles two dangerous chemicals. The equipment leaked repeatedly. When the customer called the vendor, the vendor sent an obviously untrained representative. He said, "The chemistry attacks the seals." (We needed him to tell us that?) This problem also went uncorrected.

This does not mean we cannot rely on reputable suppliers and other outsiders. Tom Peters supports the modern trend of strong customer-supplier partnerships. The danger lies in abandoning our own technical capabilities and assuming we can buy them from outsiders. In summary, we can use consultants, contractors, vendors, and other outsiders, however, we must not depend on them completely. We must always be able to fall back on our own capabilities if outsiders fail us.

Partisans and Guerrillas

The primary strength of partisans and guerrillas is familiarity with a specific theater of operations.

We are the Little Folk—we! Too little to love or to hate.
Leave us alone and you'll see
How we can drag down the State!
. . .
Mistletoe killing an oak—
Rats gnawing cables in two—
Moths making holes in a cloak—
How they must love what they do!

—Rudyard Kipling, "A Pict Song "

Clausewitz (1976) wrote the following about partisans and guerrillas. "The element of resistance will exist everywhere and nowhere. . . . They are not supposed to pulverize the core but to nibble at the shell and around the edges" (Book 6, chap. 26). In actual war, partisans act like Kipling's picts. The enemy finds dead sentries in the morning. Warehouses, magazines, and supply wagons catch fire. Marching troops find bridges out. Trains stop at broken rails. There are no major defeats. There is a series of minor annoyances that add to the friction of war. Enough friction can stop a war machine. This is guerrilla warfare (Clausewitz 1976, Book 1).

In business, the competitor does not lose sentries. It loses a customer here and an account there. Business partisans don't want to hurt the competitor. They just want the business for themselves.

The primary strength of partisans is their familiarity with the theater of operations. This can be a location or a market niche. This advantage can give partisans an edge over larger and stronger opponents.

Tupperware's Partisans

Tupperware uses partisans very effectively. Military partisans rarely have formal military training. The people take up arms after an enemy invades their country. Their government, or allies, might send them supplies. The regular army might try to coordinate activities with them. This is about as much formal support they can expect. Here's what Tom Peters and Nancy Austin (1985) says about Tupperware.

> The creative party giving of the autonomous Tupperware salesperson becomes "magic" only because she is "overtrained" in the Tupperware Way before ever being allowed to conduct her first house party. That is, Tupperware ensures beyond a reasonable doubt that the first independent try will indeed result in a small win. . . . Substantial autonomy without prior training "overkill" is sure prescription for disaster. (pp. 366–367)

Tupperware has combined the extensive training of a Jaeger, Chasseur, or Ranger with the home-ground advantage of a guerrilla. The Tupperware representative enjoys the advantages of personal contacts with customers *and* formal training.

IBM's Partisans

IBM's 300,000 employees may soon become partisans in the OS/2 versus Windows 3.1 market share battle. IBM's OS/2 and Microsoft's Windows are competing computer operating systems. "The company will grant awards such as medals, IBM software and hardware, and cash to the employees who do the most for [OS/2], the *Wall Street Journal* reported Friday. IBM is asking them to spread the word among their friends, neighbors, and anyone else. IBM will arm its workers with brochures and other information about the system" ("IBM Wants Employees to Push OS/2 System," *Poughkeepsie Journal,* 28 March 1992).

Three hundred thousand employees have many friends, neighbors, and associates. Even without IBM's famous professional sales training, personal contacts make the employees a formidable sales force. Microsoft cannot match this strategy because it does not have 300,000 employees. "The Mighty Jed [Chieftain] of Goolie" is a comic relief chapter in Edgar Rice Burroughs' (1967) *Synthetic Men of Mars.* The Goolians claim to have the best warriors and strategists on Mars. What is their secret? The Goolians never fight unless they outnumber the enemy 10 to 1. They consider a fair fight to be poor strategy.

5

The Competitive Environment

IMPORTANCE OF THE ENVIRONMENT

> The business environment includes customer needs, technology, language, customs, infrastructure, and raw materials. We must know this environment and use it to help us.

The environment is one of Sun Tzu's five critical factors for success in competition. Dozens of military and business disasters have resulted from failure to understand and exploit the environment. If we study and examine it, we can use it to help us.

The Art of War says, "Know the enemy, know yourself; your victory will never be endangered. Know the ground, know the weather; your victory will then be total" (Sun Tzu 1963, chap. 10). Ground, or terrain, means geography. The ground may be easy or difficult to cross. It may expose troops to danger, protect them, or pose a barrier to the enemy. (We will later examine *barriers to entry* in marketing.) Topography is static. Mountains, rivers, and roads do not move or change. In contrast, weather is dynamic. Some weather follows seasonal cycles that we can predict. We expect July to be hot and January to be cold. Demands for some products follow predictable seasonal cycles.

Some forms of weather are harder to predict. A storm at sea can scatter or sink a fleet. A "Divine Wind," or *kamikaze,* saved Japan from invasion by scattering a Mongol fleet. English warships shot up the Spanish Armada, but ran out of ammunition before finishing the job. Then a storm rose and sank many of the Spanish warships before they could make safe harbors. On land, rain can mire a road and keep troops from marching. Adverse conditions can make life hard or even dangerous. Severe Russian winters destroyed Napoleon's and Hitler's armies. Generals "January and February" played major roles in the Russian victories.

Sun Tzu, Miyamoto Musashi, Carl von Clausewitz, and Niccolò Machiavelli stressed the importance of the environment. Sun Tzu said,

> *We are not fit to lead an army on the march unless we are familiar with the face of the country—its mountains and forests, its pitfalls and precipices, its marshes and swamps. We shall be unable to turn natural advantages to account unless we make use of local guides.* (Clavell 1983, 68)

A *local guide* is a resident or inhabitant of the theater of operations. He or she can be immensely valuable. Recall that a guerrilla or partisan's major advantage is knowledge of the environment. The local guide has the same advantage. There is a lawyer who hires a taxi driver to help him pick jurors. The lawyer tells the driver the juror's address. The cabbie uses his extensive knowledge of the city's neighborhoods to estimate the person's socioeconomic status and political attitudes ("Taxi Driver Helps Choose Juries," *Poughkeepsie Journal,* 14 June 1987).

Machiavelli (1965) advises a general who is invading a country to do the following. The general can get maps if they are available. He should hire local inhabitants as guides and use cavalry for reconnaissance. Machiavelli also said a prince's duty includes learning the character of the country. He must know the mountains, valleys, rivers, and swamps. This helps him in strategic and tactical operations. Musashi (1974) also advised his readers to know the environment and use it to gain an advantage.

Clausewitz (1976) defined the nature of the terrain to include "the country and people of the entire theatre of war" (Book 2, chap. 2). In business, the theater is the market or market segment. Customers are the inhabitants. Clausewitz (Book 5) says that geography has three effects on tactical operations.

1. It can serve as an obstacle to the approach.
2. It can impede visibility.
3. It can provide cover from fire.

In marketing, the first item is a barrier to market entry. Barriers alone, however, do not protect market share.

Cultural and Linguistic Obstacles

> Advertising, and other communications, must account for the local language and culture. Idioms, and other aspects of a language, can trip even fluent non-natives.

Countless marketing disasters have resulted from failure to account for the environment. Usually, the sellers did not take the time to understand the local customs or language. Some examples are very entertaining.

Esso was once a famous gasoline brand name in the United States. The syllables "es-so" mean "stalled car" in Japanese. Pet Milk would have a similar problem in France. There, "pet" can mean flatulence (Cateora 1987). The automobile name Nova sounds like the French and Spanish words for "doesn't go."

Asians misinterpreted the slogan "Coke Adds Life." They thought it meant, "Coke Brings You Back from the Dead." (Schermerhorn, Hunt, and Osborn 1985, 508). The company tried to introduce its product in the People's Republic of China. Translators came up with characters that sounded like "Coca-Cola." Unfortunately, they meant "bite the wax tadpole" to the Chinese (Cateora 1987). Another soft drink company developed phonetically correct Chinese characters for its brand. These characters meant, "female horse fattened with wax." Pepsi didn't do much better in Germany. The translation of "Come Alive with Pepsi" conveyed the idea of returning from the grave.

Europeans developed some fascinating English translations. A Copenhagen airline office "will take your bags and send them in all directions." A Paris shop advertises "dresses for street walking." A Roman doctor is a "specialist in women and other diseases." A Rhodes tailor suggests ordering summer suits early, "because in [the] big rush we will execute customers in strict rotation" (Goldsmith, "Look See! Anyone Do Read This and It Will Make You Laughable," *Wall Street Journal*, 19 November

1992). Cateora (1987) advises hiring someone who lives in the foreign country to develop slogans and brand names. This accords with Sun Tzu's advice on using local guides.

Douglas Harbrecht (1993) describes the effectiveness and special challenges of using animals in advertising. Dogs are popular in the West, but they can be offensive to Moslems who consider dogs unclean. In some other countries, dogs are merely food. Animals that Westerners find repugnant can be good marketing symbols abroad. Chinese regard bats as symbols of prosperity. Southeast Asians are friendly to snakes and pigeons. The Japanese believe that black cats, like all other cats, bring good luck.

In some countries, people take pictorial labels literally. Korean soldiers who didn't read English supposedly ate dog food because the cans had pictures of dogs on them. Many Koreans and Chinese consider dog a delicacy. (The American reservist who told this story says he didn't have the heart to disillusion the Koreans.) A baby food manufacturer had a similar experience in Africa. Consumers were aghast at seeing pictures of babies on the jars. They assumed the jars contained ground-up babies (Cateora 1987).

Raw Materials and Infrastructure

The environment includes raw materials and infrastructure. A military campaign can depend on access to supplies or transportation. A business venture may depend on access to raw materials, infrastructure, or distribution channels. For example, where is the best place to put an aluminum plant? Aluminum comes from the electrolytic reduction of bauxite ore (alumina). This requires 6–9 kilowatt-hours per pound. The aluminum plant must be near a source of cheap electricity (Shreve and Brink 1977). A country with a large supply of bauxite made the mistake of going into the aluminum business. The venture failed because the country did not have cheap electricity.

Similarly, one must locate a steel mill near a coal mine. Steelmaking uses several pounds of coal or coke per pound of iron ore. This is why Pennsylvania has so many steel mills. Pennsylvania is rich in coal. It would be a mistake to build the mill near the iron mine and ship coal to it.

Changing Customer Needs and Wants

> Competitors must focus on their customers' needs. It is a mistake to focus on a specific technology.

The environment includes customer needs and wants. A company succeeds by filling customer requirements. Technological change can affect these requirements. Companies must respond to changing technology to survive. Railroads were once the principal method of overland travel in the United States. Trains provided luxurious accommodations like Pullman sleeper cars and club cars. Unfortunately, the rail owners saw themselves in the train business and not the transportation business. When private automobiles became readily affordable, the passenger rail business suffered. Passenger planes did not help. A train trip might be preferable to driving a thousand miles, however, a plane with only a moderately higher fare was faster.

Passenger trains do better in Europe and Japan. European and Japanese trains go 150–200 miles an hour. Meanwhile, gasoline is more expensive in Japan and Europe. There are still a few American passenger routes, but most trains now haul freight. Trains are still cheaper than trucks for overland transportation of goods.

Airplanes also put the ocean liners out of business. Ocean liners were once the principal method of travel between Europe and America. The first-class passengers enjoyed luxurious accommodations. The few remaining ocean liners still perform this function as mobile luxury hotels. Today, no one takes a ship to get somewhere. A passenger plane is cheaper and faster than a ship for intercontinental travel.

Advances in Computer Technology

> Computer technology is advancing rapidly. Computers will change or displace many products and services.

The mainframe computer is the passenger train of data processing. The minicomputer is the automobile. If you wanted to use a computer 15 years ago, you had to use a mainframe. You might have submitted a deck of punched cards for processing. Writing and debugging the programs were arduous and time-consuming tasks.

Today a small business or individual can afford a minicomputer. The best ones cost $2500–3500 and use Intel's best chip, the 486-66. In late 1993, this became the Pentium. The first number refers to the technology level. In advancing order, these are the 8088, 80286, 80386, and 80486. The suffix refers to the processing speed in megahertz. Minicomputers come with 4–16 megabytes of random access memory (RAM). A byte is one character, and mega means million. These memories dwarf even those of the mainframes of the 1960s. The minicomputers can store 500 or more megabytes of information on their hard disks. This book is under a megabyte. It fits on one floppy disk. Computers can read optical disks that are like compact music disks. A set of optical disks can hold an entire encyclopedia, including illustrations. This has implications for book publishers too. Automobile cassette players created a market for books on tape. Now there is a market for reference books on disk.

Minicomputer technology has grown exponentially. In the early 1980s, the 8088 was the best chip. The industry still uses its speed for reference. An 8088 chip has a speed of one. Today there are minicomputers with speeds of 140 and higher. Minicomputers are 140 times as fast as they were 10 years ago. In 1980, a computer might come with 64 kilobytes (K) of RAM. The most a minicomputer could have was 640K. Today this is nothing. A top-line minicomputer can have 64 megabytes (M) of RAM. Lesser minicomputers are available for under $800. These meet the needs of many students, families, and small businesses.

A modern mainframe is still much faster than any minicomputer. Mainframe technology is also progressing exponentially; however, most customers' needs have not grown exponentially. Some large organizations and universities can use the newest mainframes' colossal power. Small businesses and individuals do not need it. This explains many of IBM's recent problems. Paul Carroll (1993, 150) writes, "some companies found PCs so inexpensive that they were even dumping some mainframes and replacing them with PCs." Mainframe manufacturers must recognize that the minicomputer is eating up part of their market. They must realize they are in the information processing business—not the mainframe business.

Computers can send electronic mail over a telephone line. We can ask how this affects overnight mail services. Overnight mail services charge at least $6–8. A letter by modem or facsimile machine costs less than a dollar. Delivery is not the next day, but the same minute. Junk fax mail has already become a problem. If the U.S. Postal Service keeps raising its first-class rates, the phone companies will become competitors. Many people already use electronic bulletin boards and E-Mail. A long distance call during off-peak hours already costs less than 29 cents per minute. A fast modem can easily send several pages in a minute. If postal rates rise faster than telephone rates, many people may switch to electronic mail.

In summary, the environment can be a friend or enemy. It depends on our ability to adapt and respond to it. This section has shown the effects of local languages and of changing technology. The next section will discuss environmental aspects in detail.

MARKETING TOPOGRAPHY: GROUND

The marketing environment includes static and dynamic factors. Static factors such as social cultures and languages change very slowly. We can treat them as topography. A river, forest, or mountain will affect our campaign, but it will not move. In contrast, currency exchange rates and interest rates are dynamic. They also affect our operations, and they can change quickly.

Corey (1983, 1) writes, "In business the 'terrain' is the marketplace, in particular, and the economic, political, social, legal, and technological environments in general." Here, terrain means the whole environment. We break the environment into its static and dynamic parts. We will treat the static aspects first.

Linguistic and Cultural Considerations

> Hire natives (local guides) to help with international marketing ventures.

We have seen some entertaining examples of the effect of language barriers on advertising and labeling. We cannot overemphasize the importance of using local guides in international marketing. The local guide is a native of the country who knows its languages and customs.

Suppose we are fluent in a country's language. Does this qualify us to write our own advertisements and product labels? The best advice is, don't. Sentence structure, style, and idioms can trip even a fluent nonnative.

C.S. Forester gives an excellent example in one of his "Horatio Hornblower" stories. The English have the services of a forger who can fake Napoleon's signature. They want to send phony orders to the French

Navy. Should a French-speaking Englishman write the phony orders? The forger advises against it. The English person might write grammatically correct, textbook French; however, the French will know that a foreigner wrote the letter. A foreign language student, no matter how good, does not write like a native. Should the English give a Frenchman a draft to translate? The French would be grammatically and idiomatically correct, however, the structure and flow of ideas would be English. The best procedure is to give the Frenchman a general idea of what the orders should say.

Countries Are Not Homogenous Markets

International marketers must subdivide nations into ethnic and cultural regions.

Consider markets like Germany, England, India, and China. Suppose we want to sell a product in Germany. Should we hire just any German as our local guide? Look at a map of medieval Germany. There are dozens of principalities and states, each with its own history and culture. There are Bavaria, Hanover, Saxony, Silesia, Prussia, and many others. If you want to sell in Bavaria, hire a Bavarian. Italy is not a homeogenous country either. There are Venetians, Florentines, Milanese, and so on. Italy and Germany were not even single nations until the late nineteenth century.

England is not a homogenous country. The British all sound alike to Americans, and vice versa. (We speak American, not English. The languages have had more than 200 years to diverge.) Great Britain includes distinct cultural regions like Wales and Scotland. Don't refer to the Scots as English. They may resent it. Belgium has two distinct cultures, Flemish and Walloon. The Walloons speak French, and the Flemings speak a West Germanic language. Canada has French and English roots. Each Canadian ethnic group is very proud of its origins.

Regional differences are becoming obvious in the former Soviet Union, Yugoslavia, and Czechoslovakia. Yugoslavia includes over half a dozen distinct peoples, many of whom hate each other. Czechoslovakia has peacefully divided into Czech and Slovakian portions. Ukrainians, Moldavians, and Lithuanians are not "Russians." Each former Soviet Republic is a separate country with its own history, customs, and language. India uses English and Hindi as common languages, but its regions have their own indigenous languages. Using the local languages shows the people you are thinking about *them*.

Take an outsider's view of the United States. There are several culturally distinct regions. The Pacific Coast, West, Midwest, South, Northeast, and New England have their own histories and cultures. Some immigrants keep cultural ties to their homelands. There are German, Asian Indian, and Ukrainian newspapers in New York City and its suburbs. Imagine the competitive advantage one gains by advertising in these newspapers in the Old Country's language! Remember to have a native or immigrant from that country write the ad.

Barriers to Entry

> Barriers to entry can help defend a market segment; however, a new entrant can overcome a passive defense. Defense must be active and not passive.

Geography and ground have the following effects in war (Clausewitz 1976, Book 5, chap. 17).

- They are obstacles to the enemy's approach.
- They impede visibility.
- They provide cover from fire.

To cross a river, an army must use boats or erect bridges. Mountains inhibit movement of troops and supplies. Forests and rough ground prevent cavalry and artillery from passing. The defender, however, cannot blindly rely on geographical obstacles. The enemy can cross a river if no one defends it. Enemy light infantry can penetrate forests. Enemy troops can bypass a fortress. A trench with barbed wire is an excellent defense until the enemy breaches it. The enemy doesn't have to defeat the entire trench, only a small part. Unless the defender has reserves that can quickly go to the breach, the attacker can roll up the entire trench. Defense must be active, not passive. An active defender can use the geographical obstacles as aids. Then the defender gains considerable power.

We can treat market barriers as active and passive. A passive barrier is like a geographical feature or immovable structure. It can be a normal feature of the competitive environment. This can include production technology. The competitor may create the barrier to protect its market share. A patent is an example. An active barrier is more mobile. It is usually a defensive artifact and not a natural feature.

Here are examples of market entry barriers (Porter 1980).

1. The product may require heavy capital investment to achieve the necessary *economy of scale.*
2. A famous brand name or good reputation can be like a fortress that protects the defender's market share. Brand name and reputation are facets of *product differentiation.*
3. The market entrant needs access to distribution channels. (In war, an invader had to consider the availability of roads, railroads, and so on.)
4. Patents may protect the technology of production or the product design.
5. Customers may face *switching costs* when they change to the market entrant's product.
6. Access to raw materials (supplies) or a favorable location may help the defender.
7. The defender may have experience that helps it make a low-cost, high-quality product. The *learning curve* can be a barrier to a new entrant.
8. The defender can retaliate by cutting prices.

Coca-Cola learned the value of the second item the hard way. For decades, Coke was "the Real Thing." The company jealously guarded the formula for its soft drink. The Coca-Cola brand name was a vital defensive asset. Then Coke changed its formula. Suddenly, Coke was no longer the Real Thing. Its competitors had a field day. Coke, however, recovered by reintroducing the old formula as Coke Classic.

Defense Must Be Active, Not Passive

> Passive defenses will merely delay an energetic, determined attacker.

We cannot overemphasize the importance of active defense. Barriers are not absolute defenses. An innovative, entrepreneurial attacker can breach or bypass them. Here is how a competitor might address some of the barriers.

Economy of scale

1. Develop new technology. The defender's economy of scale can even become a disadvantage if its plant and equipment are too inflexible.
2. Use higher-cost, but flexible, job shop technology to fill market niches. (See Elgin Corrugated Box in chapter 6.) Again, the opponent with the rigid mass-production setup cannot respond to threats in dozens of specialized niches.
3. Be innovative in meeting customers' needs. The technology revolution is helping to overcome the economy of scale barrier. Small firms are often very innovative. Innovation makes economy of scale less reliable as a defense (Peters 1987).

Brand name/product differentiation

1. Be proactive. Flowing water can erode stone if it has enough time. A persistent challenger can erode this defense. A brand name cannot hold off an attacker unless it has quality and value behind it. Without active support (continuous improvement in the product or service), the attacker will eventually win.
2. Educate the consumer. Brand X's sodium hypochlorite solution (household bleach) is exactly the same as the generic store brand's. The same applies to many brand name and generic mouthwashes. Just read the labels.

Lack of distribution channels

1. Find new distribution channels. For example, Timex sold watches through drugstores instead of jewelers.
2. Don't bother with distribution channels at all. Sell by mail order and cut the length of the supply line. (Chapter 6 will discuss this in detail.)
3. Use joint ventures as a way to get distribution channels in other countries. They also use the native partner's knowledge of the country and its people.

Patents

1. Wait for the patent to expire. When Polaroid's patents on instant photography ran out, Kodak entered the market.
2. Try to invalidate the patent in court.
3. Develop technology the patent does not cover. This bypasses the defense entirely and could be the best option.

Switching costs

1. Accounting for the customers' needs should go without saying. Design the product or service to reduce the switching costs. Make it compatible with the customers' existing setups.

2. IBM recently offered Microsoft Windows users an incentive to switch to O/S-2. IBM accepted Windows packages as trade-ins for credit for O/S-2.

Access to raw materials

Substitutes are sometimes available. Germany did quite well in the Second World War without oil. The Germans turned coal into synthetic fuels. When the war in the Pacific cut the United States' access to natural rubber, we developed synthetic rubber. Substitution may even force an organization to innovate. (This concept appears in Isaac Asimov's *Foundation* trilogy. Hari Seldon deliberately sited the Foundation on a resource-poor planet. "Necessity is the mother of invention.") Do not blindly rely on raw materials as a defensive barrier.

Experience/learning curve

1. Hire the defender's employees and use their experience. As long as they don't reveal trade secrets, this is legitimate.

2. Develop new production technology that bypasses the learning curve.

Price cuts (by the defender)

1. The attacker's product or service must offer advantages in quality or performance. In an ideal situation, the defender could not give its product away. Here are some extreme examples. How many commuters would want a free horse-drawn carriage? Who wants a precision German slide rule, except as a collector's item?

2. If the attacker's process is more efficient, the price cut becomes the attacker's weapon.

In summary, entry barriers are an important feature of the competitive environment, however, defense of a market is an active operation. An agile market entrant will overrun a passive defender who relies on barriers for protection.

Barriers to Exit

Beware of going into markets with exit barriers.

Sun Tzu (1963) warned of the dangers of *entrapping ground*. It is easy to leave entrapping ground, but difficult to return. If you leave the position to fight, you must win because you cannot return. This is the danger of a market with low entry barriers and high exit barriers. It is easy to invest a company's resources to enter the market. If the venture fails, it is hard to get the resources back.

An exit barrier is a disadvantage to leaving a market. Suppose good economic conditions entice many competitors into a market. Each company invests heavily in plant and equipment. Now market conditions deteriorate. Each competitor now has excess capacity (Porter 1980). Contribution pricing becomes the best available option. This means using as much capacity as possible to keep machines and workers active. A price that covers the direct costs (labor, materials, and direct utilities) becomes acceptable. This is an unprofitable situation, but you can't get out. Since there is excess capacity, no one will buy you out. Porter warns of the special dangers of low entry barriers and high exit barriers. Getting in is easy and attractive. Getting out is another matter.

Here is a list of exit barriers (Porter 1980, 259–265).

1. The company may have durable and specialized capital assets. If the market is declining, no one wants these assets. It might be hard to dismantle and transport the equipment. Porter cites an acetylene plant as an example.
2. Divestment may require labor settlements. This is especially true in countries like Italy.
3. The operation may be part of an overall business strategy. Divestment would undercut the strategy. It also could be part of a vertically integrated business. Divestment would affect the other portions.
4. Management may have an emotional stake in the business. Clausewitz (1976) mentions that pride often causes commanders to squander their reserves on unsalvageable situations. Waterloo was an example. Saving the reserves would have allowed the

French to recover. Per chapter 2, emotion and ego have no place in the Way of strategy. We must, however, recognize their existence.

5. Divestment may hurt relations with a community. The people may feel that the company has abandoned or betrayed them. This is especially true in one-company towns. The example of the mine running out is a classic example. The businesses that developed to serve the miners lost all their customers. The result was a ghost town.

In summary, exit barriers are part of the competitive environment. The best conclusion is—before going in, make sure you can get out! If we miscalculate, we must remember the sunk cost concept and not send good money after bad.

MARKETING ENVIRONMENT: WEATHER

Weather is dynamic, chaotic, and turbulent. It includes all factors that change rapidly. Some are predictable and some are not. Strategy and tactics must account for dynamic factors. Sun Tzu (1963) discussed how weather affects fire attacks. Hot weather helps attacks with fire. Strong winds blow when the moon is in certain constellations. This spreads fire. By knowing the time of year, one can *forecast* rising winds. He also warned against attacking from downwind of a fire.

Sun Tzu wrote about changing seasons and the waxing and waning of the moon. Seasons and the moon are predictable and *cyclical*, like many economic factors. Miyamoto Musashi's discussion of *timing* anticipates macroeconomics by hundreds of years. "Similarly, there is timing in the Way of the merchant, in the rise and fall of capital" (Musashi 1974, Ground Book). We will now consider some dynamic factors.

Currency Exchange Rates

Exchange rates are a simple example of a dynamic factor.

Exchange rates complicate international marketing. Prices are like the croquet wickets from *Alice in Wonderland*. We simply don't know how many marks, yen, or lira a dollar will buy tomorrow. A strong dollar hurts exports by making American products more expensive. A weak dollar helps exports by making American products easier to sell. It also makes imported raw materials or subassemblies more expensive.

Placing the factory in the customer's country avoids the effects of exchange rates on production costs and sales. We pay for labor and materials with the local currency. We sell the product for the local currency. The factory feels no effects from exchange rates. There is still the question of withdrawing the profits when exchange rates are favorable; however, this location strategy removes the production cost and pricing complications.

Some vendors protect themselves by insisting on writing contract prices in their home currency. This is safe, since they cannot lose or gain from changing exchange rates (Cateora 1987).

Interest Rates and Cost of Capital

> Interest rates affect customers' ability to finance purchases.

Long-term interest rates affect purchases of durable goods and capital assets. Mortgage rates affect house purchases. Mortgage rates thus affect the construction industry and its complementary industries. Loan rates affect car purchases, since some people borrow money to buy cars. Companies borrow money to buy plants and equipment. They usually finance capital assets through bonds, preferred stock, or common stock.

Interest rates primarily affect purchases of durable goods and capital. Credit card rates are moderately important. (Why do people pay 15 percent to 20 percent interest for anything in 1994? Many consumers actually carry credit card balances. Phineas T. Barnum was right. There is one born every minute.)

Low interest rates alone can't spur capital purchases. There must be business opportunities for the capital. If everyone in the industry has excess capacity, even interest-free loans won't convince them to buy more.

Legislation and Local Laws

> Legislation can alter the business environment. National laws affect international marketing.

Laws can increase costs or create opportunities. Environmental laws create compliance costs. They also create opportunities for sellers of pollution control equipment and environmental engineering services. The removal of lead from gasoline created markets for lead substitutes and octane boosters.

Laws and edicts can be particularly troublesome in international marketing. In 1982, General Electric lost a $175 million contract with the Soviet Union. The United States had imposed trade sanctions on the USSR because of the latter's repression of Poland (Cateora 1987). Sometimes U.S. antitrust laws conflict with foreign laws. These situations go beyond, "Anything not forbidden is compulsory" (p. 223). The host country's laws may *require* actions that are *illegal* under our laws. Our antitrust laws are extraterritorial. This impedes many international joint ventures by American firms.

Other countries have laws about advertising. If we say our product is better than a competitor's in Germany, we may have to prove it. The competitor can take us to court, where we must put up or shut up. In Canada, no competitor needs to challenge us. It is illegal to make false or misleading advertising statements. Canada uses the *credulous man standard*. This means, if a reasonable person *could* misunderstand the advertising, it is misleading (Cateora 1987).

Many countries' laws provide poor protection for intellectual property. As of 1985, Mexico and Thailand provided no patent protection for chemicals and pharmaceuticals. Taiwan and Korea provide inadequate patent protection for chemicals and pharmaceuticals. Music piracy is a problem in the Philippines. India's intellectual property laws are inadequate in all areas. Under Venezuelan law, one must "use or lose" a trademark within two years. McDonald's ran into this pitfall. There is now a "Mr. McDonald's" in Venezuela, complete with golden arches. There is no relation to Ray Kroc's McDonald's (Cateora 1987).

A company in Mexico or Thailand can pirate and sell a patented chemical product. Unless U.S. law blocks importation of such products, the company could even export it to the United States. (Presumably, the patent owner can sue a U.S. parent if its subsidiary pirates an invention.) Getting the U.S. patent requires disclosure of the invention. One cannot have both a patent and a trade secret. A simple literature search by the foreign company can get the production recipe.

This discussion suggests that trade secrets may be better protection than patents. Even trade secrets do not provide protection in some countries. Coca-Cola shut its Indian operations in 1977. India's government demanded that Coke reveal its secret formula or shut down by April

1978. The company left. The drink is no longer available anywhere in India (Cateora 1987).

Other examples include domestic content laws, and even nationalization and expropriation. Labor laws vary from country to country. In some countries, it is very difficult to discharge workers once we hire them. In others, companies may have to share profits with workers. (Per the discussion of commitment, we want to avoid layoffs. Profit sharing—the modern equivalent of prize money—is a good extrinsic motivator; however, we don't want a government or union telling us what we *have* to do.) The host country can change its tax laws, or impose price controls. Some countries use price controls to force companies to sell equity to local interests (Cateora 1987).

In summary, legislation and politics are sources of often unpredictable changes in the competitive environment. They are especially dangerous in international marketing.

Technological Change

Snowballing technological progress makes the organic organizational system more important than ever. The computer will play an expanding role in business competition.

Technological change is rapid, and the rate of change is rising. If we showed a graph of innovations versus time, the second derivative would be positive. The information explosion is largely responsible. Let's examine the history of information.

Before the invention of the Gutenberg press (1450), people had to reproduce books by hand. Priests and monks usually did this, since few others were literate. This made books enormously valuable. Each book was the product of hand labor by the equivalent of a college graduate. This arrangement gave the church a monopoly on education and learning for a long time. Modern graduation robes still symbolize clerical regalia.

The printing press allowed information to spread rapidly. Books and journals became widely available to scientists. Science began to displace superstition and magic in the 1600s. The scientific method established itself by the nineteenth century. Exchange of scientific information and ideas was primarily through the printing press and personal contacts.

Several inventions of the mid-to-late twentieth century accelerated technological growth. The mimeograph machine allowed mass copying of printed material. Xerography improved on and displaced the mimeograph.

Powerful mainframe computers became available in the 1950s and 1960s. These processed information and analyzed data on an unheard-of scale. Later, literature databases became available to scientists. A literature search was once a tedious affair. For example, one had to wade through volumes of *Chemical Abstracts* to find background information for a research project. Today, we can give some keywords to a computer and push a button. The computer searches through tens or hundreds of thousands of research articles. It picks those containing the keywords. This makes scientific research far more efficient than it was even 25 years ago.

The Role of the Computer

> Until recently, every tool was an extension of the human arm and hand. The computer is the first tool that extends the power of the human brain.

The minicomputer is a revolutionary invention that appeared about 15 years ago. Today, private citizens and small businesses can enjoy the computing power of a 1960s or even 1970s mainframe. Compact disks hold entire encyclopedias that we can search at the touch of a button. Networking systems allow computer owners to send electronic mail. Sophisticated programs perform work that would take unassisted humans weeks or months. Programs can even help engineers design and test products. Simulation lets engineers see how a product will work. Before this technology was available, they had to build and test prototypes. This was a slow and expensive process.

The minicomputer is among the most important inventions of the twentieth century. Before the computer, all tools were extensions of the human arm and hand. Weapons extended the arm's reach and force. Levers, gears, and pulleys multiplied the arm's strength. It is no surprise that *arm* is a word for tool (*armamenta*) and weapon.

The human arm serves the human intellect. The computer is the *first tool that is a direct extension of the human brain.* Computers do for the brain what the spear and lever did for the arm. The Greek engineer Archimedes said of the lever, "Give me a place to stand and I will move the world." The computer is the mind's lever. Everyone must learn to use this tool. A modern person without a computer is like a prehistoric cave dweller without tools or weapons. We have already seen how rapidly computer technology has progressed.

It took a million years to go from stone to copper. Thousands of years separated copper from bronze, and bronze from iron. Another few thousand years saw steam, our first mechanical servant. From there, it was less than 200 years to the internal combustion engine. Then it was 60 or 70 years to the atom. This is a quick history of our physical tools.

The first electronic computer appeared in 1944. From there, it was about a decade to the transistor. Another decade saw the transistor on a microchip (solid logic technology). By the early 1970s, we had the integrated circuit. The journey from vacuum tube to integrated circuit has taken less than a lifetime. During the 1950s, Isaac Asimov wrote a science fiction story, "A Feeling of Power." The setting is centuries in the future. People have forgotten their basic math because they have little boxes that add, subtract, multiply, and divide. Asimov lived to see those little boxes appear in the early 1970s. He even lived to see their successors surpass the power of the first vacuum tube computers. This is a quick history of the evolution of the electronic computer.

Now consider that innovative people like scientists and engineers are using computers to invent new technology. There is a snowball effect on technological growth. Science fiction is rapidly becoming reality.

Organizational Implications

> Mechanistic organizations cannot survive these turbulent changes. Organic systems can thrive on them.

This discussion should reinforce the statement that the mechanistic system is bankrupt. The mechanistic system assumes a *static* situation and a *stable* environment (Schermerhorn, Hunt, and Osborn 1985). It assumes absence of change and turbulence. Tom Peters has told us that today's environment is turbulent and chaotic. It will become even more so in the future. Only responsive, porous, and innovative organic organizations can thrive in today's environment.

In a mechanistic organization, information flows vertically. Subordinates pass information up, and wait for direction to come down.

This arrangement is suicidal today. An organic organization passes information horizontally. It breaks down interdepartmental barriers to help information flow freely. It is porous to customers and suppliers.

The organic organization relies on its employees' judgment, craftsmanship, and professionalism (Schermerhorn, Hunt, and Osborn 1985). To do this, it must have well-trained and well-educated personnel. We've already discussed the importance of training and continuing education. Rules cannot successfully govern their behavior. Corporate culture and *dharma* must do so. They create a framework that fosters cooperative relationships without inhibiting action. Each person knows what to expect from everyone else. This avoids anarchy and goal displacement. Unlike bureaucratic rules, culture and dharma do not hamstring performance.

The organic system is critical for success in an environment of technological change. It will become even more important in the future.

6

Marketing

In business, the marketplace is the battlefield. People often speak of marketing battles and price wars. Businesses capture market share instead of territory. Advertisements and articles talk about wars between products. There is glory in winning marketing wars, but profit in winning without fighting. General Wu Ch'i wrote the following.

One who gains five victories suffers calamity; one who gains four is exhausted; one who gains three becomes Lord Protector; one who gains two, a King; one who gains one, the Emperor. Thus he who by countless victories has gained an empire is unique, while those who have perished thereby are many. (Sun Tzu 1963, 152–153)

Anything worth having requires effort. How can we get what we want without fighting for it? This chapter discusses ways to gain market share without fighting. It also shows what to do when we must fight to capture or hold market share. *The Art of War* provides some very specific guidelines.

1. Get new products to the marketplace (battlefield) before competitors do.
2. Seize market segments and niches that competitors have overlooked.
3. Do not attack established products and services. This is like attacking an opponent who holds a fortified position. Bypass these positions unless you have a special, overwhelming advantage.

4. Avoid price wars, or "marketing Vietnams." Trying to gain market share in a mature market is like fighting a protracted war.

5. Shorten the distribution chain or supply line. Cut out unnecessary intermediaries.

BE FIRST ON THE BATTLEFIELD

The first market entrant gains a competitive advantage. Design for manufacture (DFM) and quality function deployment (QFD) are useful tools for rapid product introduction. Product quality begins in the design phase.

In King of the Hill, it helps to start at the top of the hill. We occupy the position without having to fight. Later arrivals must attack uphill. Sun Tzu wrote that the first side to get to the battlefield is at ease. The first company to introduce a product gains a huge advantage over potential competitors. Competitors can attack the first market entrant, but they are at a disadvantage. They don't have something new to offer customers. They have to show they have a better or less expensive product. The product life cycle shows the role of new or introductory products.

The Product Life Cycle

Most products go through the following life cycle. Table 6.1 shows the life cycle and the Boston Consulting Group (BCG) definitions (Rowe, Mason, and Dickel 1985, 194–195).

Ideally, a company uses income from cash cows to nurture introductory products into the growth phase. If introductory products are successful, they become stars. Stars mature into cash cows and nurture the next generation of products. Cash cows eventually decline and become dogs. We must use cash cows to support introductory and growing products. It is a poor strategy to use cash cows or stars to support dogs. Products in their declining phase have little future, so why spend money on them? A subsequent section will discuss this further. For now, we will focus on the introductory stage.

Table 6.1

The product life cycle.

Life cycle phase	BCG definition
1. Introduction	Question mark ? —High growth, low market share
	Star *
2. Growth	—High growth, high market share
	Cash cow $
3. Maturity	—Low growth, high market share
	Dog 0
4. Decline	—Low growth, low market share

Design for Manufacture

> Design for manufacture is a tool for getting products to the marketplace quickly.

We want to get to the marketplace first. Design for manufacture (DFM) is a tool for reaching this goal. Under the traditional system, research gets an idea from marketing. It does the basic research and hands the idea over to development. The product idea goes through process development and product design. The designers then hand it over to manufacturing. The problem with this approach is that it is *sequential*. It does not promote rapid product development and introduction. Sometimes there are other problems. Manufacturing may get a new product and find that the existing tooling can't make it.

Cross-Functional Teams

> DFM relies on cross-functional teams for success. This requires a porous organization.

DFM uses cross-functional teams to make sure the product is manufacturable. It adopts a *parallel* approach. The teams include representatives from R&D, design, manufacturing, field service, and marketing. Tom Peters says, "Use multifunction teams for all new-product/service development activities. . . . The single most important reason for delays in development activities is the absence of multifunction (and outsider) representation on development projects from the start" (Peters 1987, 257). It can greatly cut the product or service development cycle time. Peters says a 75 percent cut is achievable.

Peters cites Chaparral Steel as an example. Engineers and researchers work in the manufacturing shop with tool operators. They experiment in the mill itself. The successful Ford Taurus was another product of the DFM approach. Ford involved the design, engineering, marketing, manufacturing, and service functions from the beginning. The company also consulted insurance companies about accident damage. By doing this, Ford learned how to make a car cheaper to repair after a collision. Ford consulted auto dealers to learn what customers wanted. This happened during the design phase (Peters 1987).

DFM and Quality Function Deployment

> Improvements during the design phase have the biggest payoffs.

The DFM philosophy is part of quality function deployment (QFD). A study at Ricoh Copier showed that an improvement during the design phase has a 100:1 payoff. A process improvement has a 10:1 payoff. Correcting a manufacturing problem has a 1:1 payoff. Fixing a problem in the field has a fractional payoff, however, fixing field problems has high visibility and rewards. Design improvements have low visibility in most companies (Lorenzen 1992). *Engineering design has strong leverage on quality, cost, and cycle time. Quality starts in the design phase.* Inspecting quality into the product doesn't work.

Most American firms do not use the best design practices (Hoover 1991). Bruno Wenschel, president of Wenschel Engineering Company, reiterates this point. Japan and Germany emphasize DFM. In the United States, about two-thirds of product design emphasis is on design and one-third on manufacturability. In Japan and Germany, two-thirds of the emphasis is on manufacturability. Wenschel says, "Design quality into the product, instead of trying to inspect it into the product." Prevention is better than correction, and correction is better than field failures (Wenschel 1991).

Recall the story about the obscure Chinese doctor who cured diseases in their infancies. His brother was famous for treating seriously ill patients. Today we prefer vaccines over treatment for the illnesses they prevent. We must become equally wise in product development. DFM will assure our victory over competitors who cling to outmoded approaches. We will not have to fight them for market share. We will occupy the market while they are still mobilizing for the contest.

The next section treats a similar concept. Using it does not require a new product. We can win with existing products and services by delivering them where no one opposes us.

BE WHERE THE ENEMY ISN'T

> It is easy to capture market share where no competitors oppose us. Look for undefended market niches and segments.

Sun Tzu (1963) said you can always capture what the enemy does not protect. You can easily hold what the enemy does not attack. You can march without trouble by traveling where there is no enemy. The commentator Ts'ao Ts'ao said to go into emptiness and strike voids. Bypass the enemy's strong points. Hit the enemy where it does not expect you.

This approach sounds attractive and easy. If no competitor holds a market share, just walk in and take it! The concept is very simple, but it needs effort to make it work. General Clausewitz said everything is simple, but the simplest matter is difficult. To put the idea into practice, we must examine market segments and niches.

Niche Markets

> To capture a niche, satisfy the customer.

A *market segment* is a subgroup of customers who have specific needs. For example, consider the market for Florida vacation trips. College students who visit Florida during spring break are a segment of this market. Families who visit Florida during the winter are another (Holtje 1981). A *market niche* is similar. It is a set of special customer requirements that an organization can meet. A segment is a group of similar customers. A niche is a specialized set of customer requirements.

The underlying idea is very simple. Meet the customer's requirements. Don't be like Ford in its early days. Henry Ford told customers they could have any color car they wanted, as long as it was black. This works well when we have a monopoly. Today, like Burger King, we must tell customers, "Have it your way."

Adding Value at Elgin Corrugated Box

> We can even customize commodities to satisfy customers.

Dull, boring commodities can become profitable, value-added products. The Elgin Corrugated Box Company is expanding in a nominally declining marketplace. The traditional competitors have been fighting a price war because of excess capacity. Meanwhile, Elgin had to buy more capacity in 1987 to meet demand for its products. What are Elgin's success secrets?

1. Elgin makes a higher quality box. It uses a more expensive, but stronger, corrugation method. It uses better ink for labeling the boxes.
2. The company consistently ships orders on time.
3. The company is very responsive to customer needs. It will accept small orders its competitors won't touch (Peters 1987).

The last item shows another principle from *The Art of War.* We can avoid battle by drawing a line on the ground. This means taking a position it is inconvenient to attack. Attacking would divert the opponents from their priorities (Sun Tzu 1963). Elgin goes after small orders its competitors won't fill. Maybe the competitors could use their economies of scale to underprice Elgin, however, they'd have to disrupt their rigid mass-production systems to do it. This diverts them from doing what they want. They want to use their economy of scale to make many identical boxes very cheaply. They don't want to rearrange their factories and production schedules to meet specialized customer orders. The competitors' own setups are Elgin's best defense.

Niche Penetration/Infiltration Tactics

> Niche penetration is a way to infiltrate a market.

Massive frontal attacks are rarely effective in business or war. During the First World War, they produced high casualties for the attacker. Then the British developed infiltration tactics. These were more effective. Niche penetration of a market is often more effective than a frontal attack. The Japanese have used this approach in most new markets. Instead of launching massive frontal efforts, they address small, application-oriented niches. They offer cars with ceramic engine parts, four-valve engines, lightweight nonmetallic body panels, and other features. Few American cars offered these options in 1987. U.S. automakers wanted to "leapfrog" the Japanese with huge technological breakthroughs. Meanwhile, the Japanese incremental improvements kept widening the gap the Americans had to leap (Peters 1987).

Canon and Savin infiltrated the copier market in the 1970s. Xerox paid attention to its large rival, Kodak. Xerox ignored "little stings" from Savin and Canon in "pipsqueak market segments." Patton's skunks got under the front porch. The frog didn't notice the water heating around him. Machiavelli's physician didn't recognize the early symptoms. Suddenly, "these mice moved out of their corners and became lions; Xerox lost more than half its market share before it stemmed the tide" (Peters 1987, 281).

Attack Where No One Opposes You

> Use innovative distribution channels to bypass competitors' defenses.

During the 1950s, Bulova and Swiss watchmakers controlled the marketplace. Swiss watches had reputations for excellent quality. The Swiss sold their watches through jewelry stores. Rather than face the Swiss in the jewelry market, Timex began selling its watches in drugstores. The Swiss did not recognize Timex as a threat for some time. By the time they did, Timex had a good start toward market leadership. The Swiss could not easily follow Timex into this new distribution channel. Doing so would have alienated their traditional retailers, the jewelers (Porter 1985).

Peters cites, "oddball forays through distribution channels and from competitors you wouldn't expect (e.g., TV home shopping, and the explosion of catalogers in retailing)" (Peters 1987, 281). We can add home computer services that allow subscribers to buy products electronically. Be innovative in looking at distribution channels. New, short, and efficient channels can bypass a competitor's defenses.

Guerrilla Marketing

A company can be the big fish in a small pond.

Ries and Trout (1986) list several aspects of guerrilla marketing for small competitors. The tactics include many aspects of light troops and small business units. Ries and Trout prescribe them for small firms. We extend these prescriptions to the light troops (entrepreneurial small business units) of large firms.

Note that guerrilla marketing does not require guerrillas or partisans. The guerrilla company is similar to the guerrilla employee in its familiarity with a specific competitive environment. Its employees, however, are likely to be the light infantry/cavalry type. They will have a high level of training. Their orientation and organization will be entrepreneurial and flexible. The key aspect of guerrilla marketing is focus on a specialized competitive environment. This means focusing on a niche or market segment.

The segment or niche may be geographical, economic, or a specialized product. For example, Rolls-Royce occupies a luxury car niche. None of the big automakers think it is worthwhile to go after this relatively small segment. If they did, they would be at an enormous disadvantage because of Rolls-Royce's reputation.

American Motors Corporation's Jeep has been very successful. AMC sells about 100,000 Jeeps each year. It is not worth GM's while to attack this product niche. Ries and Trout think AMC is making a mistake by challenging Chevrolet with Alliances and Encores. AMC actually loses much of what it makes on the Jeep by competing with GM. Instead, AMC should produce only the Jeep and its relatives, like the AMC Eagle.

Inc. magazine is a demographic guerrilla. Instead of competing with *Business Week*, it addresses the needs of small business owners. *Business Week's* main orientation is big business. Its circulation is about 800,000. There are more than 5 million corporations in the United States. Most are small businesses. This is another example of the principle of attacking where no one opposes you.

Crain's Chicago Business is a geographic guerrilla. Again, it does not meet big publications like *Business Week* head-on. Addressing a local market garners a circulation of 40,000. In Chicago, *Business Week's* share has 36,000 subscribers. While *Business Week* is 20 times as big as *Crain's Chicago Business* nationally, *Crain's* is the local leader.

Triod Systems is an industry guerrilla. It specializes in a computerized inventory management system for automotive part wholesalers. The automotive part wholesaling industry is Triod's special market niche.

Ries and Trout emphasize the need to keep the organization lean and agile. We have already covered the idea of avoiding excessive hierarchy and staff. Bureaucracy is expensive, and it reduces the flexibility of the organization.

ATTACKING ESTABLISHED MARKET SHARES

> Do not attack established market shares without a special advantage.

What should a company do when it faces an opponent with an established market position? A simple frontal attack is a poor idea. We need a special advantage to win.

The Art of War lists four strategies for waging war. In descending order of preference, they are as follows: (Sun Tzu 1963)

1. Attack or thwart the enemy's strategy.
2. Disrupt the enemy's alliances.
3. Fight the enemy army.
4. Besiege the enemy's fortresses and cities.

Sun Tzu describes the progress of a siege. Attackers must prepare shielded wagons, arms, and equipment. Their engineers must build a ramp up the enemy walls. This takes time and uses supplies. If the general is impatient and attacks without these preparations, he will lose a third of his troops without succeeding. The same principle is true in the field. If the enemy occupies a high position, it is foolish to attack it there (Sun Tzu 1963).

This principle was true until about a century ago. In the seventeenth century, the military engineer Sebastian Vauban developed a formula for capturing fortresses. The procedure relied heavily on the pick and shovel. Vauban's formula guaranteed capture of the fort. It also guaranteed spending weeks or months on the siege. Defenders did not rely on fortresses to stop an enemy. They relied on them to cost the attacker precious time. If the attackers bypassed a fort, they had to leave troops behind to contain the garrison. If the attackers tried to cut corners with a frontal assault, the result was a massacre. (C. S. Forster's *The Gun* gives an example of a premature frontal attack on a fort.)

Reducing and Bypassing Strong Points

> To reduce an opposing strong point, we need a special advantage. Otherwise, we can bypass it.

At the start of the First World War, the Germans had to reduce several Belgian fortresses. They were in a hurry, since the Schlieffen Plan called for a rapid march through Belgium. An infantry assault on one of the positions was disastrous. Then the Germans used giant siege guns. These ranged from 21 cm (8.2 inch) to 42 cm (16.5 inch). Some of them were apparently loans from Austria-Hungary, whose Skoda Works made excellent artillery. These weapons made short work of the Belgian positions. At the start of World War II, the Maginot Line actually stopped those Germans who attacked it. Germany won by bypassing it.

These historical examples show that we have two viable choices against a strong position. If we have a special advantage, we can overcome it. A castle full of archers and spearmen was very formidable to a medieval army. It would offer little resistance to modern artillery. (A Data General commercial showed a scenario like this several years ago.) We also can bypass the position.

Special advantages include the following:

- A new product can make the existing one obsolete. This is like having a cannon against bows and catapults. Most mature, well-established products eventually succumb to new ones. An innovative company will make its *own* products obsolete. Remember that *passive* market barriers do not offer permanent security. Constant improvement and innovation provide an *active* defense.
- Strong advantages in product quality, cost, or service can win. This is how the Japanese displaced American automakers from their market share. Recall Tom Peters' advice to make manufacturing a marketing weapon. The manufacturing system dictates product costs and product quality. A superior manufacturing system is a decisive competitive weapon.
- A short distribution chain can win by reducing the customer's costs. For example, mail-order personal computers have overwhelmed computer retailers. A later section discusses the distribution chain.

Bypassing the position means capturing unprotected market segments and niches. We can always consider markets in complementary and substitute goods. A complementary product is something the customer uses with the product. For example, tires and oil are complementary goods for cars. A substitute is something the customer can use instead of the product.

AVOID MARKETING VIETNAMS

> Avoid price wars in mature and declining markets. The low-cost, high-quality producer has a decisive edge in these markets. Quality and productivity improvement techniques help achieve this.

A marketing Vietnam is a protracted conflict over a mature or declining market. We need to recognize and avoid these situations. The Vietnam War was an obvious example of a protracted conflict.

Sun Tzu and Clausewitz: "We Told You So."

Sun Tzu and Carl von Clausewitz told us exactly why we would lose the Vietnam War. LBJ didn't listen.

Why did the United States lose the Vietnam War? How could we win every round, but lose the fight? Our armed forces didn't lose even one major battle. We inflicted massive casualties among the enemy's troops. The U.S. Air Force swept enemy planes from the sky. We had total command of the sea. Nonetheless, the enemy won. Had Lyndon Johnson read the second chapter of *The Art of War,* this disaster would not have happened. Sun Tzu devotes most of the chapter to warnings against protracted wars.

The Art of War cites the following specific effects of a protracted war.

1. Your soldiers lose their morale.
2. You deplete your treasury and impoverish your country.
3. Your economy suffers inflation.

President Johnson also could have read Clausewitz's *On War.* "Wearing down the enemy in a conflict means using *the duration of the war to bring about a gradual exhaustion of his physical and moral resistance*" (Clausewitz 1976, Book 1, chap. 2). "All campaigns that are known for their so-called temporizing, like those of the famous Fabius Cunctator [The Delayer], were calculated primarily to destroy the enemy by making him exhaust himself" (Book 6, chap. 8). Retreat to the interior of the country (as the Russians did in the Second World War), is a form of indirect resistance. It "destroys the enemy not so much by the sword as by his own exertions" (Book 6, chap. 25).

The Thirty-Six Strategies include, "face the weary in a condition of ease." This means forcing the enemy to expend energy while conserving one's own (Cleary 1991, 87).

The United States suffered these effects during the Vietnam War. Many men of military age looked for ways to avoid fighting. Popular sentiment eventually forced the government to abandon its foreign policy goals. Vietnam was a gross blunder that even a novice student of the art of war would have avoided. It was the Fool's Mate of U.S. foreign policy. (The Fool's Mate is a checkmate in two moves. It requires almost deliberate self-destruction by the victim.)

The Soviets suffered the same fate in Afghanistan. Since Russia was North Vietnam's ally, this is especially surprising. We would have expected the Soviets to learn from our mistakes and their ally's success. The Soviets are supposedly ardent students of *The Art of War* (Clavell 1983).

Other Forms of Protracted War

A protracted campaign often helps the weaker side; however, this is not true in business.

In actual war, one side can benefit from a protracted campaign (Clausewitz 1976, Book 1, chap. 1). This side usually cannot defeat its enemy in the field. Commerce raiding, submarine warfare, and mines are the weapons of a weak navy. The stronger navy usually seeks a decisive engagement. The weaker side in a lawsuit also likes delays. Usually, the defense tries to delay the trial. It hopes the hostile witnesses' memories will fade. Time also affects the defense witnesses, however, the plaintiff or prosecutor has the burden of proof. They must win the case. The defense succeeds by not losing. *"The very lack of a decision constitutes a success for the defense"* (Clausewitz 1976, Book 6, chap. 8).

In business, we are not trying to wear down and destroy the competitor. We are trying to make money. Protracted market conflicts are not consistent with this goal.

Mature and Declining Markets

A mature market is no longer growing. The pie is not getting bigger. The only way to get a bigger piece of pie is to take someone else's. This means a zero-sum game or win-lose situation. If one organization wins, someone else must lose an equal amount. Clausewitz refers to this as polarity. A declining market is even worse. We have to take someone else's share to stay even.

Polarity and the Prisoners' Dilemma

A declining market looks like a no-win situation. There is no profit in contribution pricing.

Mature and declining markets can cause devastating *price wars*. If the industry has excess capacity, competitors will resort to contribution pricing. This means making as much as they can sell as long as they cover their direct costs. (Remember that we have fixed costs and overhead whether we run the plant or not.) This keeps their people and machinery working. It also keeps anyone from making a profit. It is, however, the most profitable course (excepting illegal agreements to restrain trade). It is the old prisoners' dilemma problem, without the cooperation option. Table 6.2 shows the prisoners' dilemma. The first number refers to side A and the second number to side B. A positive number is a benefit and a negative number is a cost. For example, let A cooperate and B compete. A loses two units and B gains two.

In the prisoners' dilemma, the prosecutor asks each prisoner (separately) to testify against the other. If both do so, the court will convict both of a minor crime. If just one does, he or she gets off and the other gets a long prison term. If neither does, both can plea bargain for probation. Refusing to testify (cooperating with each other) is the best joint action for the prisoners; however, neither knows what the other will do. Testifying (competing) is the safest action. An arms race is similar. If both sides spend on butter (cooperate), their people will prosper. Suppose one side buys guns while the other buys butter. Then the first side can take the other side's butter. The safest course for each is to buy guns. This drains each side's economy, but avoids total ruin. Cooperation is possible when the players can exchange information, however, cooperation by restraining trade is illegal. Even where antitrust laws don't exist, cartel members often cheat on quotas.

Options in a Declining Market

Don't fight price wars. Get out, or become the low-cost producer.

What choices do we have? We can divest by selling our assets and getting out. Per the discussion on exit barriers, this may not be easy. No one wants specialized equipment for making a mature or declining product. This is an argument against buying inflexible, special-purpose equipment in the first place. Suppose, however, this is our situation. The only hope for survival and prosperity is to be the low-cost, high-quality producer. This is, in fact, the preferred course in a mature or declining market. The organizational and human resource techniques discussed earlier can

Table 6.2

The prisoners' dilemma.

	Side B cooperates	Side B competes
Side A cooperates	+1/+1	–2/+2
Side A competes	+2/–2	–1/–1

help. A lean organization with minimal bureaucracy and highly skilled employees is in a good position. Techniques and tools like SPC and QITs are helpful in reducing costs. For example, multifunctional QITs can discover and implement ways to cut costs. Product quality is a selling point. If we can sell on quality, we don't have to sell on price. This helps avoid the casualties of an all-out price war.

Downsizing as a Last Resort

> Downsizing often fails to solve our problems.

Is downsizing an option? Suppose we close a plant and discharge the workers. This rarely solves our basic problems. The equipment will be worthless or have significant value. Specialized equipment for making a mature product is almost worthless. So is obsolete equipment. We won't get much for it. If it has value, someone can use it. They may use it against us. (Remember that a competitor can turn automation, or artillery, against its original owner.) For example, General Motors plans to close its Tarrytown, New York plant. Who will GM sell it to? Toyota, Honda, or Nissan might buy it. Then the Japanese automaker can make even more cars in the United States. Since American workers will make them, even "Buy American" sentiment won't help GM. The Japanese can even hire the experienced autoworkers GM discharges. This is like selling the enemies a battery of artillery and letting them hire the gun crews in the bargain. GM's alternative is to close the plant and get nothing for it. Toyota is actually considering buying a GM plant to make midsize pickup trucks.

Discharging workers is contrary to the Way of lord and retainer. It hurts commitment and morale. Companies like IBM and Matsushita avoided layoffs even during the Depression. It is a last resort, like gnawing off a leg to get out of a trap. While staying in the trap may mean death, losing a leg will probably just delay it a while. It means accepting a permanent loss of competitive capability. The company loses the experienced workers. If it wants to expand later, it must hire and train new workers. High turnover, whether from layoffs or resignations, is characteristic of noncompetitive organizations.

Flexible Automation Lets Us Get Out

> Flexible automation lets us "get out of Vietnam."

Ideally, the plant and equipment will have some flexibility. This gives us the option of switching to a more profitable product line. It also lets us fill specialized niches and satisfy individual market segments. A flexible plant lets us "get out of Vietnam." We don't have to stay in the jungle and waste our assets in a protracted price war. This is how Elgin Corrugated Box Company thrives in an industry with excess capacity.

SHORTEN THE DISTRIBUTION CHAIN

> Every link in the distribution chain must justify itself. A short distribution chain is a competitive advantage.

Sun Tzu (1963) pointed out the expense of transporting supplies to a distant front. The commentator Chang Yu added that transportation costs could exceed the value of the supplies. Sun Tzu later warns against fighting a distant enemy. The same lesson applies to business competition.

Distributors and Intermediaries

Each intermediary adds *economic distance* to a transaction. Each entity in the distribution chain has to make money on the transaction. The manufacturer's goal is to deliver value to the customer. Sun Tzu warned that transporting supplies to a distant army used most of the supplies. Transporting goods through several intermediaries can consume most of the goods' value. Here is the key question. What value does the intermediary add to the transaction? Is it more than it consumes?

Intermediaries as "Hidden Plant"

> Distributors, wholesalers, and retailers are hidden plants. When we use them, we pay for their capital investment and overhead.

The term *hidden plant* usually refers to the portion of a factory that fixes nonconforming products. The hidden plant concept helps show managers the real cost of poor quality. A manager might not care about a 5 percent scrap rate. He or she will care that 5 percent of the fixed capital and labor are there to replace bad parts. We can apply this concept to the distribution chain. *The manufacturer pays for the intermediaries' fixed assets and personnel.* What costs does the distribution chain add to each transaction?

1. Each intermediary must pay salaries, wages, and benefits for personnel.
2. The intermediary has fixed assets with their associated costs (overhead).
3. Each intermediary must earn a profit.
4. A long distribution chain delays and suppresses feedback from customers. This is an intangible cost. It affects the company's ability to adapt its products and services to customer needs.

Distribution costs hurt the Compaq and Apple computer companies. These companies sell personal computers through authorized retail dealers. The dealer adds a markup of 20 percent to 40 percent. Dozens of companies now sell computers by mail order. The *Computer Shopper* lists hundreds of ads for computers and complementary products. Shipping costs may be 2 percent to 3 percent of the item's price. The dealers' advantage of local service is disappearing. Some mail-order companies service their warranties by sending a service representative to your site. Others ship replacement parts, sometimes by overnight mail. It is easy to open a computer case and replace a part. (The dealers, however, do get business from people who are uncomfortable working on their own machines.) Even IBM is now selling some computers by mail order.

YKK, a Japanese zipper company, captured market share from Talon by shortening its distribution chain. YKK bypassed wholesalers and sold zippers directly to clothing manufacturers (Porter 1985).

DAK (Drew Alan Kaplan) Industries' catalog has an ad that shows how shortening the distribution chain saves the customer money (see Figure 6.1). The ad shows "fat-cat middlemen with their expensive warehouse overhead and commissions." The ad says the retail price for a push-button direct-access world-band radio ranges from $179 to $500. DAK can offer this product for $69.90 by buying directly from the manufacturer. Again, someone has to pay for the intermediaries' fixed costs, personnel, and inventory cost. DAK gains a competitive advantage by cutting out these distribution costs. The mail-order firm itself is an intermediary, however, it plays a useful role in getting the product from the manufacturer to the customer. It provides a marketplace for several manufacturers, and convenience for the buyer.

Innovative Distribution Strategy for Cars

> Detroit should stop discharging autoworkers. The automakers should sack their dealers.

Here is a venture for an innovative car manufacturer that likes the just-in-time (JIT) philosophy. The idea is to make cars to order instead of making inventories. The current practice is to make cars and put them on dealer lots. The manufacturer usually floor plans the cars. This means loaning the dealer money to carry the inventory. Interest on the loans adds to the customer's cost. The dealer also must earn a profit on each sale. Most of us know about some shady tactics car dealers use to do this.

General Motors' recent problems include plant closings and layoffs. We contend that GM is laying off the wrong people. It is trying to cut costs by severing productive assets like factories and autoworkers. It needs to ask the following questions. How much value does a car factory create for the customer? How much value does a car dealership create for the customer? Maybe GM should lay off its dealerships. The obvious objection is that dealers sell the cars. This is how traditional push marketing works. We make a product and pay someone to peddle it. If no one wants the product, we are out of luck. This is why there are so many incentives and rebates at the end of a car's model year.

Figure 6.1

Why so cheap?

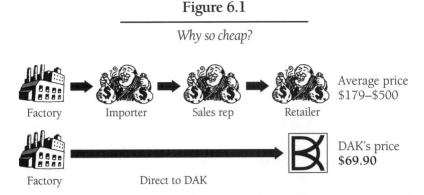

| | | | | Average price $179–$500 |
| Factory | Importer | Sales rep | Retailer | |

DAK's price **$69.90**

Factory   Direct to DAK

The only way to offer this receiver for an industry-rocking price was to go straight to the factory. By eliminating all the fat-cat middlemen (with their expensive warehouse overhead and commissions), DAK can offer the only push-button direct-access world-band radio for just $69.90.

Source: DAK catalog, summer 1992, chapter 6, p. 5. Used with permission of DAK Industries Incorporated, 8200 Remmet Ave., Canoga Park, CA 91304-4182.

Why do automakers need a showroom to sell cars? Any reputable service station can provide the warranty service. Consider the following arrangement. To keep the production line running, the manufacturer makes subassemblies like engines, bodies, and transmissions. Instead of showrooms, the manufacturer has retail outlets that take orders. Authorized service stations could perform this function. Customers could specify their cars on minicomputers. For example, a CD-ROM (compact disk, read-only memory) could contain every car and every option. The customer also could get descriptions of each option, and its price, from the computer. The computer also shows each body and upholstery color. A representative would be available to answer technical questions. When the customer finishes his or her selections, the computer generates an order. The customer signs a contract and makes a down payment.

Now the factory puts the subassemblies together to make the car. The customer gets exactly the options and colors he or she wants. The manufacturer does not have to store inventories of complete cars. (Ideally, a steady stream of orders will keep the subassembly stocks low.) Look at the competitive advantages the manufacturer gains.

1. It cuts out the salesperson's commission and salary. The only sales cost is the cost of processing the order.
2. It cuts out the expensive showroom (fixed asset). The service station can warehouse one of each model for test drives. Compare this to a parking lot full of inventory.
3. It avoids ending the model year with inventories of cars with colors and options no one wanted. Every car that leaves the factory has a buyer.
4. The customer gets exactly what he or she wants, not what the dealer wants to push off the lot.

Adopting this JIT strategy could give an automaker a decisive advantage over its competitors. By selling directly to the customer, the manufacturer can offer a lower price and earn a larger gross margin. This money doesn't come from nowhere. It was the retailer's share.

Utility of Distributors and Retailers

> Intermediaries can add value to marketing operations. We just need to be sure they justify their cost.

Do distributors and retailers have any redeeming features? Sometimes they can give value to the manufacturer and consumer.

1. Retailers and distributors are convenient. It is inconvenient to buy food directly from a farmer or a food company. The farmer gains an economy of scale by selling crops in large lots. Consumers gain convenience through one-stop shopping at a grocery. They do not have to go to a dairy, meat packer, and miller for their products. Retail clothing stores offer similar convenience; however, catalog companies like L. L. Bean and Land's End offer one-stop clothing shopping. These companies do not have to pay for floor space and sales personnel, the way Sears does. The Computer Shopper is a one-stop shopping resource for computer buyers. A mail-order catalog can provide much of the retailer's convenience without the costs.
2. The distribution system is a source of market intelligence. A company's own sales force often provides the best feedback. It

has no divided loyalties, but it can be expensive (Carr 1988).
The sales force also can get ideas from customers for new products and services.

3. Agents and distributors may have access to a widespread distribution system.

4. Distributors and retailers know their local environments. Small
retail businesses may have a regular clientele. The owners' personal contacts in the community are a valuable marketing asset.
This factor becomes even more critical in international marketing.

In summary, we must ask the following questions about each level of
the distribution chain. What value does it add to our marketing operations? Does its cost justify its existence? (Carr 1988).

Physical Distance and Transportation Costs

> The nature of the product affects its transportation costs. What is the
> ratio of the shipping cost to the product's value?

Transportation costs are the other part of distance from the marketplace.
For some goods, these costs are negligible. A $20–30 shipping charge for
a $1000 computer or plotter is minor. A delivery charge of $500 for a
$20,000 automobile is still not a big problem. *What is the transportation
cost versus the value of the item?*

We often call a soft drink or beer plant a bottler. Why is there always
a bottle-making or can-making plant at the drink-packaging site? The
same is true for liquid detergents and similar products. Why don't the
manufacturers buy their containers from somewhere else?

We can buy corrugated boxes for delivery to our factory. The box
maker folds the boxes almost flat. Many will fit in a truck or railcar. Once
we make a can or bottle, we can't fold it. If we put empty bottles in a truck,
it transports mostly air. Cans and bottles are worth very little by themselves. The transportation costs are very high in comparison to the value of
the containers. Putting the drink (or detergent) in the container adds value
to the product. It costs little more to ship full bottles than empty ones. We
don't have to make the liquid product at the bottling site. The liquid can
get there by tank car. It is the containers that shouldn't travel empty.

The same argument applies to "popcorn" packing material and bubble wrap. These packing materials are mostly air. It makes sense to make the packaging material at the point of use. The key point is to ship product, not air.

Price-to-Weight Ratio

> A product with a high price-to-weight ratio can compete anywhere in the world.

Menlo Tool Company cites price-to-weight ratio in its exporting successes. The company makes small carbide tools. No tool is more than 6 inches long, or 1 inch in diameter. The company, however, adds a lot of value to its products. The tools sell for about $100 per pound. Even overseas shipment costs don't add a big percentage to the cost. The company president says, "We can put 60 lb [sic] of product—worth $6000—into a 14 by 12 by 8 inch box, give it to any air-freight carrier, and ship it quickly and economically overseas overnight." A UPS shipment can leave Warren, Michigan on Friday, and arrive at a customer in England by Monday morning. "If we have it in inventory here and a competitor over there does not, we will beat them every time" (Kastelic 1993, 104).

In summary, distance is a critical factor in marketing. Distance includes distribution and transportation costs. Distribution and transportation do not add value to the product or service. We must cut them to an absolute minimum. A product with a high price-to-weight ratio can compete anywhere in the world.

EXTERNAL RELATIONSHIPS— CUSTOMERS AND SUPPLIERS

Customer relations are critical in marketing success. *To sell our product or service, we must satisfy customer needs and wants.*

The *product-oriented* marketing approach means making a product and turning it over to the sales force. It emphasizes the product and the needs of its manufacturer. The sales force must create a demand for the product (Holtje 1981). This is the "invent a better mousetrap and the world will beat a path to your door" approach.

The *customer-oriented* approach means developing products and services to meet customer needs and wants (Holtje 1981). This means finding out whether the customer has a rodent problem before working on mousetraps. A few years ago, IBM introduced the market-driven quality program. It means tailoring product quality and function to meet customer needs. The following story shows the difference between the product-oriented and customer-oriented approaches.

Long ago, the Greeks founded a city. Athena, the goddess of wisdom, wanted to be the patron deity of the city. Her uncle, the sea god Poseidon, also wanted this honor. They agreed to a contest where each would give the city a gift. The mortals would decide which gift was the most useful.

Poseidon struck a great rock with his trident. A stream of water gushed out to provide a spring. When the Greeks tasted the water, however, they found that it was salt water. Poseidon was the sea god, and salt water was his product. Everybody he knew—fish, dolphins, Nereids, and so on—lived in and breathed or drank salt water. He didn't know anything about fresh water.

Athena gave the city an olive tree. The tree provided fruit, oil, and wood. She won the contest, and Athens bears her name today.

Customer Relationships

> Happy customers provide a steady revenue stream. They also provide word-of-mouth advertising. Unhappy customers do the opposite. It costs a lot less to keep a customer happy than to find a new one.

It is vital to maintain good relationships with customers. It is far more expensive to get a new customer than to keep an existing one. To get a new customer, a company must spend time, money, and effort on advertising and promotion. Repeat business from existing customers does not require extensive advertising and promotion. Also, word of mouth is a form of advertising. It can be positive or negative. Each happy, satisfied customer provides free, unbiased publicity to several friends and associates. Each angry, dissatisfied customer provides negative publicity.

Tom Peters says the Federal Express courier should see $180,000 when he or she walks into Peters' consulting firm. His business spends $1500 a month on Federal Express. That's $180,000 over 10 years.

Grocer Stew Leonard says, "When I see a frown on a customer's face, I see $50,000 about to walk out the door" (Peters 1987, 120). Leonard is referring to the value of repeat business. If the customer spends $100 a week on groceries, that's about $50,000 over 10 years.

The following factors affect customer satisfaction.

1. Do customers perceive value in the product or service? Are customers getting their money's worth? Function, or what the product can do, affects the product's value.
2. Are product quality and reliability good? In industry, *continuity of operations* is important. Everyone notices downtime in a manufacturing operation. Downtime is friction, according to Clausewitz's (1976) definition. We don't want downtime with our machine's name on it.
3. Is the product economical to use? This is especially important in industrial applications.
4. Is the product safe?
5. Is the product easy to service?
6. Does the company service what it sells? Is service prompt, courteous, and effective?

Quality and Service Leave Lasting Impressions

> Customers don't exist to meet our needs. We have to meet theirs.

A couple of years ago, my auto insurance company hit me with a hefty rate increase. My driving record hadn't changed. The insurer explained that the state had approved a rate increase. This was the second premium increase in two years. I shopped around with several other companies and found one that offered a much lower rate. I learned of this company through a satisfied customer. After buying a policy from the company, I wrote to my old insurance company. "Congratulations on getting your rate increase approval. I no longer require your services." Later, I spoke with an associate who also received a rate increase from this company. I gave him the name of the new company. He changed companies too. "The repeat customer is also any firm's principal vehicle for powerful word-of-mouth advertising" (Peters 1987, 121). The unhappy customer is a good vehicle for losing business. When our competitor takes customers from us, those customers may take others.

The point here is that customers don't care about *our* needs or problems. We have to meet *their* needs. Do customers care whether the state approves our rate increase? The customers care about getting the lowest rate. Jacking up the premiums encourages customers to shop around. If they find a better deal, we lose the customers.

Detroit is learning this lesson slowly. There are bumper stickers urging Americans to buy American goods. One says, "Unhappy? Out of work? Then eat your rice burner!" One American auto company had a ceremony where it smashed a Japanese car with sledgehammers. It should have taken the car apart to examine its design and construction. Appealing to patriotism is not a substitute for building quality and value into products.

In 1987, this author bought a new, full-sized, American-made car. During the first year, the car had the following problems.

1. It came with a nonfunctional cruise control.
2. It came with a cracked engine block.
3. The windshield leaked. It took four visits to the dealer to fix this. Actually, it still leaks.
4. The windshield wiper motor burned out three times.
5. The power steering pulley came off and flew into the fan. It took several other belts with it, including the cooling pump's. One can drive without power steering, but not without the cooling pump.
6. The paint on a ridge on the hood came off. The 1992 *Consumer Reports* buying guide shows a "much worse than average" trouble index for this model year's paint.

The following problems occurred after the first year, but within 41,000 miles.

7. The radiator coolant leaked into the transmission and wrecked it. The transmission was under warranty, but the radiator wasn't. This cost more than $400.
8. The water pump's bearings went bad.
9. The ignition system failed. It cost more than $200 to tow the car home from an out-of-town engineering conference.

Customers have long memories. I have told these stories to friends and associates without concealing the company's name. The company did not lose just one customer. It may have lost several. How much will the company have to spend on advertising to replace these customers?

Recently, however, the company agreed to repaint the car. This is something I will remember in its favor.

In fairness to American automakers, an associate had problems with a Japanese-made car. Despite repeated visits to the dealer, the problems continued. She hung an empty plastic lemon from the rearview mirror to show her opinion of the vehicle. How does this affect her associates' decision to buy the company's products?

Another associate told me about a Honda he owned. He drove it for more than 100,000 miles without any major repairs. If I didn't prefer full-sized cars, I would have seriously considered Honda.

I once ordered a disk drive by mail order. It came without screws. When I called the seller, its representative was rude and insulting. He said, "We assume the buyer knows how to install the disk drive." (There were no instructions either, but I know how to install a drive. Attaching the electronic cable is simple. Securing the drive with two machine screws is easy too—if you have the screws.) The company promised to send screws, but never did. I finally got them from a hardware store. Will I buy anything from this vendor again? This is definitely a black mark against them.

Compare this behavior with Intel's. I ordered an 80287-10 (10 megahertz or MHz) coprocessor chip from a mail-order firm. It sent an 80287-XL. This was supposedly better than the 80287-10; however, some of my software didn't work with it. Intel tried to help by replacing the chip with an 80287-10. It turned out that the XL wasn't at fault. The software had the same problems with the 80287-10. Nonetheless, Intel had absorbed the cost of trying to fix a possible problem with its chip. What impression does this leave? "Intel stands behind its products." This is the impression we want our customers to have. Intel's service representatives were helpful and courteous too.

Quality information does not need to circulate through word of mouth. Before buying a car, I got a copy of the 1987 *Consumer Reports'* buying guide. I dropped one brand from consideration because of its poor repair record. Most Japanese cars had above-average or top ratings in every area. German cars had mixed ratings, as did American ones.

Day-Timers supplies planners, calendars, business stationary, and similar items. They are not cheap, but they are reasonable. The quality of the merchandise is high. The company is very responsive to its customers. I have used their products and recommended them to associates for several years.

In summary, customer satisfaction is vital. A company must do its best to maintain customer loyalty. L. L. Bean's Golden Rule sums up the proper attitude. "Sell good merchandise at a reasonable profit, treat your customers like human beings and they'll always come back for more." The founder, Leon Leonwood Bean, said, "A customer is the most important person ever in this office, in person, or by mail." This is the excellent company's attitude toward its customers.

Customers and Innovation

> Some of our best ideas can come from customers.

Customers are an excellent source of ideas for new products and services. Procter and Gamble has a toll-free telephone number for customer complaints and ideas. It gets many product improvement ideas through this avenue. Levi Strauss did not invent Levi's jeans. A buyer of Levi's denim suggested the idea. Bloomingdale's suggested that Levi's make faded jeans. Many of IBM's early inventions came from cooperation with its main customer, the Census Bureau (Peters and Waterman 1982). We have already seen how Milliken's customer action teams work closely with customers to develop new ideas.

Supplier Relationships

> Treat suppliers as partners, not adversaries.

Supplier relationships have often been adversarial. Traditionally, companies have looked to the low bidder as a supplier. The customer often has an incoming inspection to make sure the supplier is not sending junk. Companies often keep two or more suppliers to make sure there is no interruption in the flow of supplies.

Competitive operations require friendly partnerships with suppliers. JIT manufacturing requires close coordination with suppliers. The suppliers must be willing to send parts as necessary instead of in bulk shipments. JIT requires trust in the suppliers' quality control systems. Under JIT, the suppliers often ship directly to the customers' stockroom or manufacturing floor. Incoming inspection would be an interruption in the shipment process. Therefore, quality assurance must take place at the suppliers' facilities.

Tom Peters (1987) says companies should have partnership relations with a few suppliers. Suppliers can participate in product innovation and improvement. For example, the A.O. Smith company became a partner in the development and production of the Ford Taurus. Another company developed louvered interior lights that did not interfere with the driver's vision. The carpet supplier developed a carpet whose fibers all lay in one direction. This gave the carpet a uniform appearance. A plastics company developed a fold-out tray for tailgate parties.

Robert Hall of the Association for Manufacturing Excellence criticizes General Motors' supplier relationships. He says, "The company is now breaking contracts in the only place it can get away with it—with suppliers. GM is demanding 20 percent and 30 percent price reductions. . . . GM's actions give no reason to trust its commitment to 'partnership' in what should be mutual improvement processes. . . . Quality suppliers will reserve their best efforts for customers they can trust—and quit GM if they can" (Hall 1992, 65). We can compare this behavior to Ford's supplier relationships.

Milliken and Levi—Partners for Profit
Milliken & Co. has an excellent partnership with Levi Strauss. Levi trusts Milliken's quality and accepts shipments with no incoming inspection. The textiles go directly to Levi's factories. The Milliken truck is a "warehouse on wheels" that delivers the desired fabrics. The fabrics go straight from Levi's loading dock to the cutting and sewing machines. Levi thus avoids carrying inventory and spending money on incoming inspection. The setup also gives Levi enormous flexibility in responding to changing fashions.

This partnership requires close communication between Levi and Milliken. Good communications help Milliken meet Levi's standards for color. Milliken also puts the textiles on rolls of exactly the right size for Levi's machinery (Peters 1987).

Suppliers as Partners—Not Surrogates

> Don't surrender technological capability to suppliers.

Does this advice conflict with the previous discussion of mercenaries and auxiliaries? The danger with suppliers is in using them to do what we should be doing. Recall how Rome lost its virtù. It hired mercenaries to do what Roman citizens should have done. A company can lose its technological edge by hiring a vendor to supply leading-edge technology. Eventually, everyone in the company becomes a supplier interface. The company loses the ability to do high-technology work for itself.

Look at the Levi–Milliken partnership. Levi Strauss is not in the textile business. Its business is making clothing. Milliken is doing nothing for Levi that Levi should be doing itself. Levi Strauss is in no danger of losing its technology or skills in its area of business. Similarly, textiles are Milliken's business. Letting Levi Strauss make the clothing does not imperil Milliken's critical technology or skills.

We can have successful supplier relationships if we hire suppliers to work *with* us and not *for* us. Innovation is faster if we make our organization more porous to customers and suppliers. We do not surrender our own technological capabilities. We merely open our organization to advice and feedback from outsiders.

The Sole Supplier/Single Sourcing

> Even reliable sole suppliers are vulnerable to circumstances beyond their control.

Is the sole supplier a good idea? The traditional approach has been to defend against the risk of losing a critical supply. Companies keep two or more suppliers or massive inventory stocks. This is the decoupling concept, however, the trend is toward single suppliers. Tom Peters advocates this approach.

If the supplier is trustworthy and reliable, we can use it as a single source. There is a caveat, though. What if circumstances beyond the supplier's control keep it from delivering? Situations could include the following:

- A strike could idle the supplier. If the supplier is following the advice in chapter 3, this shouldn't happen; however, we must recognize the chance. In November 1992, 260 workers at General Motors' Lordstown metal stamping plant went on strike. Four hours later, GM's Saturn assembly plant in Tennessee ran out of parts. The plant was using a JIT system and had no inventory. The Lordstown walkout idled 40,000–50,000 workers for nine days. This cost about $50 million a day. (What opportunity costs were also lost?) (Courtney, Steven, "Modern Manufacturing in an Old-Fashioned Setting." *Hartford Courant,* 7 December 1992).

- The supplier's own suppliers could fail to deliver raw materials or subassemblies. Using sole sources places us atop a pyramid. Failure of *any* portion puts us out of business, unless there is redundancy in the system. (Consider series and parallel system reliability.)
- A natural disaster or accident could put the supplier out of action for weeks or months. ("Auntie Em! I don't think our subassemblies are in Kansas any more!") Consider a Roman CEO whose sole source was in Pompeii or Herculaneum in 79 C.E. We don't want a sole supplier on the slopes of Vesuvius—or on the San Andreas Fault.

Sumitomo owns one factory that makes 60 percent of the world's supply of an epoxy resin for semiconductor encapsulation. In mid-1993, a fire disabled the plant. Every semiconductor company that uses this resin (that is, almost everyone) is now afraid of running out. Fortunately, the damage was less extensive than originally thought. The Sumitomo plant may be operational sooner than originally expected ("Resin crisis averted" 1993).

Therefore, some decoupling or emergency provisions are still necessary. For example, an in-house job shop should be able to make most subassemblies if it has to. (Most of the time, it should do something else.) An in-house batch chemical plant could make specialty chemical intermediates if it had to. It is available in case something interrupts the external supply. Another option is to buy off-the-shelf products from other sources. These forms of contingency manufacturing or procurement will be more expensive than our supplier-partner's product. If the alternate source is not part of our JIT/ship-to-stock system, we will have to do incoming inspection. The purpose of these plans is to keep operations going if something disables the supplier. Total dependence on any one supplier is hazardous, no matter how trustworthy it is.

Another form of protection is redundancy in the supplier's facilities. If it has several factories in different places, we are safe. One could fall into the San Andreas Fault. A tornado could carry another off to Oz. A hurricane could disable the plant in Florida. Our supplier, however, would have to be astronomically unlucky to lose all three plants at once. The reliability engineering concept of a parallel system applies. All the parts have to fail to put us out of business.

In deciding whether we need decoupling from a single source, we must consider its reliability. Reliability means more than its willingness and ability to meet schedules and quality requirements. It includes reliability despite problems beyond its control. These include natural disasters and problems with the source's own suppliers.

CONCLUSION—THE WAY OF STRATEGY

War is a matter of vital importance to the State; the province of life or death; the road to survival or ruin. It is mandatory that it be thoroughly studied.

—Sun Tzu, *The Art of War*

Competition is vitally important to the Organization. It is the province of success or failure. The Way of strategy is the path to victory.

War involves far more than moving troops and using weapons. We can wage war without troops or destructive weapons. Economics, diplomacy, propaganda, and espionage can decide an issue as decisively as swords and arrows. Commitment, morale, communications, and organizational structure all influence victory or defeat. War is simply a contest between two or more organizations. Without its violent aspects, how does war differ from business, politics, or statecraft? Despite their peaceful aspects, business and economics can be weapons of war.

Much of the Cold War was an *economic* contest. The United States won a third world war by wearing down the Soviet economy in an arms race. We thwarted their strategy and disrupted their alliances, per Sun Tzu. We never had to meet their troops in the field. We may blame the Reagan and Bush administrations for our present economic problems. We may worry about the deficit. We no longer have to worry about T-80 tanks coming through the Fulda Gap, or SS-18 missiles coming over the North Pole. Reagan and Bush deserve some credit for this. Remember that the master of strategy wins without fighting. He or she often remains obscure and receives no thanks. Rambo and Conan the Barbarian get all the publicity when they win on the field. In an age of nuclear weapons, we prefer the former approach.

The success of an organization in a competitive environment depends on these factors.

1. Leadership
2. Management of human and physical resources
3. Responsiveness to competitors and the environment
4. Strategy and tactics

Leadership
1. Leaders follow *Bushidō* and *Kshatriya Dharma.*
2. Leaders see themselves as stewards of the organization. They foster the welfare and vitality of their subordinates and the organization.
3. Leaders practice virtù, lifelong learning, and personal detachment.

Management of human and physical resources
1. The organizational structure and culture promote teamwork, communication, and human performance. Intrinsic motivation supports productivity. An organic system promotes flexibility and responsiveness.
2. The structure, including the performance measurement system, is there to serve the organization. The people are not there to serve the system or structure.
3. The organization seeks human resource superiority through training and education. Like the individual warrior, the organization seeks continual self-improvement.
4. Management of physical resources is usually a technical matter. It is important, but physical resources cannot win by themselves. Physical resources must be flexible and appropriate for the job.

In summary, we can repeat Chang Yu's description of good human and physical resources. "Chariots strong, horses fast, troops valiant, weapons sharp—so that when they hear the drums beat the attack they are happy, and when they hear the gongs sound the retirement they are enraged. He who is like this is strong" (Sun Tzu 1963, 65–66).

Responsiveness to competitors and the environment
1. The organization seeks insight into opponents' cultures. It tries to perceive their psychological and social patterns. The organization seeks similar understanding of customers and market segments.

(In politics, replace *customers* with *electorate*. In war, consider the populations of neutrals and belligerents.)
2. The organization pays attention to other environmental factors. Much of the analysis is mechanical or technical; however, close cooperation with customers yields valuable information on their needs and wants.

Strategy and tactics

The remaining part of the Way of strategy is mechanical and technical. For example, the length of the distribution chain (supply line) is a technical question. Location strategy is a technical issue. Engineering economics, science, and technology are very important. The excellent organization pays attention to them, however, they provide little advantage without excellence in leadership, organizational structure, and human resources. Recall Clausewitz's warning against relying on analysis alone.

Leadership and dharma foster commitment and loyalty. Leaders act with virtù and evoke vitality in their followers. The organizational framework helps people achieve pride in workmanship and self-actualization. The organization knows the ground, weather, and enemy. Such an organization wins the present and inherits the future.

References

American Heritage Dictionary of the English Language. 1969. Appendix.

American National Standards Institute and the American Society for Quality Control. Q90-1987. *Quality management and quality assurance standards—Guidelines for selection and use.* Milwaukee: ASQC.

Anderson, R. A., I. Fox, and D. P. Twomey. 1988. *Business law.* Cincinnati: South-Western Publishing.

Anthony, R. N., and J. S. Reece. 1983. *Accounting—Text and cases.* 7th ed. Homewood, Ill.: Richard D. Irwin.

Aquarian Tarot Deck. 1975. Dobbs Ferry, N.Y.: Morgan Press.

Asprey, R. B. 1986. *Frederick the Great.* New York: Ticknor & Fields.

Aurelius, M. 1964. *Meditations.* Translated by M. Staniforth. New York: Penguin Classics.

Bilby, J. G. 1993. A better chance ter hit. *American Rifleman* (May): 48.

Blum, R. 1987. *The book of runes.* New York: Oracle Books.

Booth. 1992. President's column. *Manufacturing Engineering* (October): 4.

Brown, C. J. 1987. America's industrial competitiveness will necessitate change in status quo. *National Society of Professional Engineers/ Professional Engineers in Industry Industry Forum* (August-September): 2–3.

Buck, W., trans. 1973. *Mahabharata.* Berkeley: University of California Press.

———. 1991. *Ramayana.* Performed by Ram Dass. Berkeley: Audio Literature/Ten Speed Press. Audiocassette.

Buckley, J. 1988. We learned that them may be us. *U.S. News & World Report,* 9 May, 48.

Bulfinch, T. 1979. *Myths of Greece and Rome.* New York: Penguin Books.

Burroughs, E. R. 1967. *Synthetic men of Mars.* New York: Ballantine Books.

Capra, F. 1992. Interview by M. Keller. *Business Ethics* (January/ February): 28–30.

Carnegie, D. 1977. *How to win friends and influence people.* New York: Pocket Books.

Carr, L. 1988. Union College lectures with author.

Carrière, J. C. 1987. *Mahabharata.* Translated by P. Brook. New York: Harper & Row Publishers.

Carroll, P. 1993. *Big blues—The unmaking of IBM.* New York: Crown Publishers.

Cateora, P. R. 1987. *International marketing.* 6th ed. Homewood, Ill.: Richard D. Irwin.

Cavendish, R, ed. 1970. *Man, myth, and magic: An illustrated encyclopedia of the supernatural.* New York: Marshall Cavendish.

———. 1989. *Legends of the world.* New York: Crown Publishers.

Chappie, A. 1992. Recession leaves firm with hard-earned lessons. *Engineering Times* (January): 9.

Clausewitz, C. V. 1976. *On war.* Translated by M. Howard and P. Paret. 6 vols. Princeton, N.J.: Princeton University Press.

Clavell, J., trans. 1983. *The art of war,* by Sun Tzu. New York: Delacorte Press.

Cleary, T. 1991. *The Japanese art of war.* Boston: Shambhala Publications.

———, trans. 1989a. *The art of war,* by Sun Tzu. Boston: Shambhala Publications. Audiocassette.

———, trans. 1989b. *Mastering the art of war,* by Zhuge Liang and Liu Ji. Boston: Shambhala Publications.

Contino, A. V. 1987. Improve plant performance via statistical process control. *Chemical Engineering,* 20 July, 95–102.

Cooper, J. 1990. *To ride, shoot straight, and speak the truth.* Paulden, Ariz.: Gunsite Press.

Corey, E. R. 1983. *Industrial marketing, cases and concepts.* Englewood Cliffs, N.J.: Prentice Hall.

Courchaine, W., and K. Williams. 1992. Continuous quality improvement. Paper presented to the American Production and Inventory Control Society, Mid-Hudson Chapter, 11 March, at Newburgh, New York.

Covey, S. R. 1991. *Principle-centered leadership.* New York: Summit Books.

Crossley-Holland, D. 1980. *The Norse myths.* New York: Pantheon Books.

Cypress Semiconductor moving assembly offshore. 1992. *Semiconductor International* (August): 15–16.

Deal, T. E., and A. A. Kennedy. 1982. *Corporate cultures.* Reading, Mass.: Addison-Wesley.

Deshimaru, T. 1982. *The Zen way to the martial arts.* New York: E.P. Dutton.

Dooley, K., D. Bush, J. C. Anderson, and M. Rungtusanantham. 1990. The United States Baldrige Award and Japan's Deming Prize: Two guidelines for total quality control. *Engineering Management Journal* 2 (September): 9–16.

Fechter, W. F. 1993. The competitive myth. *Quality Progress* (May): 87–89.

Feigenbaum, A. V. 1991. *Total quality control.* New York: McGraw-Hill.

Gallant, R. 1987. So you want to be a manager? *Chemical Engineering,* 9 November, 55–79.

Garvin, D. A. 1988. *Managing quality.* New York: The Free Press.

Gies, J. 1991. Automating the worker. *American Heritage of Invention and Technology* (Winter): 56–63.

Graber, J. M., R. E. Breisch, and W. E. Breisch. 1992. Performance appraisals and Deming: A misunderstanding? *Quality Progress* (June): 59–62.

Gropper, R. S. 1992. Marketing professional services. Paper presented at the New York State Society of Professional Engineers, Dutchess-Ulster Chapter, 30 May, at Poughkeepsie, New York.

Hall, R. W. 1992. Shall we all hang separately? *Industry Week,* 9 September, 65.

Harbrecht, D. 1993. Animals in the ad game. *International Wildlife* (November-December): 38–43.

Harris video dedicated to Mountaintop. 1993. *Harriscope,* 5 March, 1, 4.

Hayes, R. H., S. C. Wheelwright, and K. B. Clark. 1988. *Dynamic manufacturing: Creating the learning organization.* New York: The Free Press.

Heizer, J., and B. Render. 1991. *Production and operations management.* Boston, Mass.: Allyn and Bacon.

Held, R. 1957. *The age of firearms.* New York: Bonanza Books.

Hogg, I. V. 1979. *Guns, and how they work.* Secaucus, N.J.: Chartwell Books.

Hollow victory. 1992. *U.S. News & World Report,* 20 January, 40–44.

Holtje, H. F. 1981. *Theory and problems of marketing.* New York: McGraw-Hill.

Hoover, C. W., Jr. 1991. Design for global competition. Paper presented to the Cornell Society of Engineers, 26 May, at Ithaca, New York.

Hope, A. 1967. *The prisoner of Zenda.* New York: Airmont Publishing.

Hradesky, J. 1988. *Productivity and quality improvement.* New York: McGraw-Hill.

Iscoff, R. 1992. Assembly automation: How much is too much? *Semiconductor International* (May): 86–90.

Jennings, W. D. 1968. *The ronin.* Rutland, Vt.: Charles E. Tuttle.

Kastelic, F. M. 1993. Exporting is easy. *Manufacturing Engineering* (August): 104.

Keynes, J. M. 1936. *The general theory of employment.* New York: Harcourt Brace.

Kipling, R. 1982. The rout of the white hussars. In *Rudyard Kipling, illustrated.* New York: Crown Publishers.

———. 1940. *Complete verse.* New York: Doubleday.

Klein, S. M., and R. R. Ritti. 1984. *Understanding organizational behavior.* Belmont, Calif.: Wadsworth.

Koch, H. W. 1982. *The rise of modern warfare.* Englewood Cliffs, N.J.: Prentice Hall.

Koren, L. 1990. *Success stories: How eleven of Japan's most interesting business came to be.* San Francisco: Chronicle Books.

LeGuin, U. 1968. *A wizard of Earthsea.* New York: Bantam Books.

Levinson, W. A. 1987. Business management—Samurai style. *Chemical Engineering,* 14 September, 109–113.

Lewis, C. S. 1952. *Mere Christianity.* Book 3. New York: Macmillan Publishing.

Lorenzen, J. 1992. Quality function deployment. Paper presented to the American Society for Quality Control, Mid-Hudson Chapter, 26 May, at Poughkeepsie, New York.

Machiavelli, N. 1965. *The prince.* New York: Airmont Publishing.

———. 1965. *The art of war.* New York: Da Capo Press.

Mahan, A. T. 1980. *The influence of sea power upon history, 1660–1805.* London: Bison Books.

Mandino, O. 1968. *The greatest salesman in the world.* New York: Bantam Books.

Mascaro, J., trans. 1962. *The bhagavad gita.* New York: Penguin Classics.

Melan, E. 1992. Total quality management. Presentation to the American Society for Quality Control, Mid-Hudson Chapter, 24 March, at Poughkeepse, New York.

Miller, R. B. 1985–1986. Union college lectures with author.

Musashi, M. 1974. *A book of five rings.* Translated by V. Harris. Woodstock, N.Y.: Overlook Press.

———. 1982. *The book of five rings.* New York: Bantam Books.

Newman, J. 1989. *Bushidō—The way of the warrior.* Greenwich, Conn.: Brompton Books.

Noble, S. 1991. *Three hundred one great management ideas from America's most innovative small companies.* Boston: Inc. Magazine.

O'Connell, R. 1988. The Roman killing machine. *The Quarterly Journal of Military History* 1, no. 1: 36–47.

Orff, C. Fortuna imperatrix mundi, from *Carmina Burana*. Minneapolis, Minn.: Pickwick International. Sound recording.

Page, R. 1991. Harley-Davidson's new quality hawgs. *Creativity* (December): 7–8.

Palmer, R. R., and J. Colton. 1971. *A history of the modern world.* 4th ed. New York: Alfred A. Knopf.

Paradigm pioneers: The business of paradigm. 1992. Produced by J. Barker. Charthouse International. Videocassette.

Parker, G. 1987. *The thirty years' war.* New York: Military Heritage Press.

Peters, T. 1987. *Thriving on chaos.* New York: Harper & Row.

―――. 1989. When surviving is not enough. Presentation to the Cornell Society of Engineers, 28 April, at Ithaca, New York.

Peters, T., and N. Austin. 1985. *A passion for excellence.* New York: Warner Books.

Peters, T., and R. Waterman. 1982. *In search of excellence.* New York: Harper & Row.

Porter, M. E. 1980. *Competitive strategy.* New York: The Free Press.

―――. 1985. *Competitive advantage.* New York: The Free Press.

Preston, A. 1981. *Battleships.* London: Bison Books.

Rapp, S., and T. Collins. 1990. *The great marketing turnaround.* Englewood Cliffs, N.J.: Prentice-Hall.

Regan G. 1987. *Great military disasters.* New York: M. Evans and Company.

Resin crisis averted. 1993. *Semiconductor International* (October): 26.

Ries, A., and J. Trout. 1986. *Marketing warfare.* New York: McGraw-Hill.

Rowe, A. J., R. O. Mason., and K. E. Dickel. 1985. *Strategic management and business policy.* 2d ed. Reading, Mass.: Addison-Wesley.

Rubin, R. 1993. Placebos' healing power. *U.S. News & World Report,* 22 November, 78.

Schermerhorn, J. R., J. G. Hunt, and R. N. Osborn. *Managing organizational behavior.* 2d. ed. New York: John Wiley & Sons.

Shaku, S. 1906. *Zen for Americans.* Peru, Ill.: Open Court Publishing.

Shreve, R. N., and J. A. Brink. 1977. *Chemical process industries.* New York: McGraw-Hill.

Sōhō, T. 1986. *The unfettered mind.* Translated by W. S. Wilson. New York: Kodansha International.

Spector, R. H. 1991. The first battle of the Falklands. *The Quarterly Journal of Military History* 3, no. 2: 76–85.

Sprow, E. E. 1993. Benchmarking—A tool for our time? *Manufacturing Engineering* (September): 56–59.

Storry, R. 1978. *The way of the samurai.* London: Orbis Publishing.

Strothman, J. E. 1990. The ancient history of system 360. *American Heritage of Invention and Technology* (Winter): 34–40.

Stuelpnagel, T. R. 1993. Déjà vu: TQM returns to Detroit and elsewhere. *Quality Progress* (September): 91–95.

Sun Tzu, 1963. *The art of war.* Translated by S. Griffith. Oxford, England: Oxford University Press.

Time-Life Library of Nations. 1985. *Japan.* Alexandria, Va.: Time-Life Books.

Toch, T. and Wagner, B. 1992. Schools for scandal. *U.S. News & World Report,* 27 April, 66–71.

Tribus, M. 1992. *Quality first.* Washington, D.C.: National Institute for Engineering Management and Systems.

Turnbull, S. 1987. *Battles of the samurai.* New York: Arms and Armour Press.

Twain, M. 1989. *A Connecticut Yankee in King Arthur's court.* New York: Harper & Row.

Untermeyer, L. 1957. *Story poems.* New York: Washington Square Press.

Wagner, R. 1972. *Siegfried,* translated by S. Robb. New York: ABC Records. Sound recording.

Wenschel, B. 1991. Engineering education for global competition. Paper presented to the Cornell Society of Engineers, 26 April, at Ithaca, New York.

Williamson, P. B. 1979. *Patton's principles.* New York: Simon & Schuster.

Wing, R. L., trans. 1988. *The art of war,* by Sun Tzu. New York: Doubleday.

Yagyu, M. 1986. *The sword and the mind.* Translated by H. Sato. Woodstock, N.Y.: Overlook Press.

Yamamoto, T. 1979. *Hagakure* (Hidden leaves). New York: Kodansha International.

Yoshikawa, E. 1961. *Musashi.* New York: Kodansha International.

Index